MOIRA HODGSON

IT SEEMED LIKE A
GOOD IDEA AT THE TIME

Moira Hodgson was the restaurant critic for
The New York Observer for two decades. She
has worked on the staff of *The New York
Times* and *Vanity Fair,* and is the author of
several cookbooks. She lives in New York
City and Connecticut.

IT SEEMED LIKE A GOOD IDEA AT THE TIME

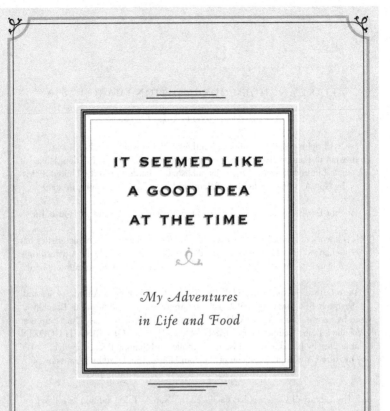

IT SEEMED LIKE
A GOOD IDEA
AT THE TIME

My Adventures
in Life and Food

MOIRA HODGSON

Anchor Books
A Division of Random House, Inc.
New York

FIRST ANCHOR BOOKS EDITION, MARCH 2010

Copyright © 2009 by Moira Hodgson

The Library of Congress has cataloged the Nan A. Talese edition as follows:
Hodgson, Moira.
It seemed like a good idea at the time : my adventures in life and food /
Moira Hodgson. —1st ed.
p. cm.
1. Hodgson, Moira. 2. Women food writers—Biography. 3. Cookery, International.
I. Title.
TX649.H63A3 2008
641.5092—dc22
[B] 2008002050

Anchor ISBN: 978-0-7679-1271-6

Book design by Pei Koay

www.anchorbooks.com

For Alexander

Memory is hunger.

ERNEST HEMINGWAY

IT SEEMED LIKE A GOOD IDEA AT THE TIME

INTRODUCTION

I HAVE A DISH OF MINT ICE CREAM in a fancy French restaurant, and all of a sudden I'm back at my French lycée in Stockholm, where this treat was a reward for finishing the dreaded boiled cod we had for lunch on Fridays (I used to stuff my fish into an envelope under the table). A club sandwich reminds me of a picnic at Long Hai in Vietnam, where we had our lunch in the shade of a bombed-out villa by the beach, unaware of the snake skins hanging from the rafters above. The smell of beef vindaloo takes me, of all places, to my English boarding school, where the cook's version was so hot it made you break out in a sweat. Wimps were allowed "mince" instead, a pallid stew of ground meat, but if you finished your curry, you were a person to be reckoned with.

As a child I traveled continuously, changing countries and continents every two years because my father was in the British Foreign Office. By the age of fifteen I had lived in Egypt, Beirut, Sweden, Vietnam, Berlin, London and Sherborne (in Dorset in the southwest of England, where I was born), and I had been to twelve different schools. After I left the final school, which was in England, instead of remaining in my native country, I went on to live in the United States.

I grew up at a time when England still bore a strong resemblance to the country it was in the late nineteenth century. Yet our life was anything but conventional. When I was a child, food was a symbol not just of comfort but of continuity, which our lives lacked. It was also a way of establishing a connection to a place. I spent my childhood trying to adapt to strange, new environments, foreign languages and foreign food. By the time I'd grown up, adaptation had become a habit. The stories, moreover, were ingrained in my memory.

PART ONE

THE WAITER STOOD OVER ME, pen at the ready. "Signorina?"

For lunch I ordered sardines on toast, pickled herring, a grilled mutton chop, buttered green beans, *pommes lyonnaise* and lemon sherbet.

I was twelve, sitting with my family in the dining room of Lloyd Triestino's MV *Victoria* as we sailed through the Strait of Malacca, en route from Singapore to Genoa. Once again, we had packed up and were moving on. Those were the days of the great ocean liners, and my first meals out were not in restaurants, but on ships.

A color reproduction of an eighteenth-century Italian Romantic painting decorated the cover of the menu. It told a story. A young woman with downcast eyes hastened across a balcony in Venice, a black veil artfully draped over her hair and shoulders to reveal her pale, comely face and low décolletage. She was holding a letter behind her as if it contained some news she couldn't bear to read. The title of the picture was *Vendetta*, which a translator had rendered, insipidly, "Requital."

The long menu was in Italian, with an English translation on the opposite page. The words had a dramatic poetry that made my imagination soar: "jellied goose liver froth . . . Moscovite canapé . . . glazed veal muscle à la Milanese . . . savage orange duck . . . golden suprême of swallow fish in butter . . ." And darkly: "slice of liver English-style." Because the ship docked in Bombay, Karachi and Colombo, there was also Indian food, a curry of the day described only by a town or region—Goa, Madras, Delhi—served with things I'd never heard of—pappadom, chapatti, paratha, dal and biriani.

For the next three weeks, the menu changed every lunch and dinner, with a different Italian Romantic painting on its cover (always a portrait of a beautiful woman; this was an Italian ship, after all).

I ticked off the dishes I ate and pasted the menus into a blue scrapbook. I am looking at it now. It opens with a display of black-and-white postcards of the long, elegant white ship, built in 1951, so different from the bloated shape of today's cruise liners. A Lloyd Triestino paper napkin signed with the names of the seven young members of the Seasick Sea Serpents Club, founded by yours truly, shares a page with a yellow matchbook stamped in red with the steamship company's far-flung continents of call: Asia, Africa and Australia. The passenger list erroneously records the family as em-barking in Karachi. A brochure of useful hints advises "easy dress" for lunch and "formal attire" for dinner. The programs for the day's activities, slipped under the cabin door each morning, are also pasted onto my book's faded, dog-eared pages, their covers printed with commedia dell'arte figures: Pierrot, Columbine, Harlequin and clowns, one of them with a red nose, holding out a tumbler of wine. There were concerts by the ship's orchestra (as many as four a day), fancy dress balls and bartender Carlo's special cocktails, such as gin with lemon and green Chartreuse. I also glued in brochures of the places we visited when the ship docked in a port of call: a "luxury" coach tour of Bombay (where I saw vultures cir-cling funeral pyres that burned behind high walls) and a sleepy Ital-ian fishing village called Portofino "for people seeking rest and quiet." Pink and orange tickets to horsey horsey and tombola make a collage with the ship's airmail envelopes and its itinerary, illus-trated with a red pagoda. But most of the pages of my scrapbook are taken up with menus.

Potatoes *pont neuf* were thick french fries. "Norcia pearls," served with Strasbourg sausage, were lentils. Rollmops were fillets of marinated herring wrapped around pickles. Hoppel poppel "in saucepan on toast" was a fry-up of onions, potatoes, pork and eggs. "Crusted pie Lucullus" turned out to be a pâté laced with chunks of foie gras; chicken quenelles were dumplings, flecked with black truffles; "golden reserve" pheasant *in volière* [*sic*] arrived in a sauce made with "fine" Champagne. Chicken cream soup "Agnés Sorel" was named for the mistress of the French king Charles XII, who died suddenly at the age of twenty-eight, thought to have been poisoned. A strange name for a soup.

I was allowed to order whatever I wanted as long as I had a "properly balanced meal." The food arrived under a silver dome that was whisked off by the waiter with an operatic flourish (and not without a touch of irony) to reveal my choice du jour with its two requisite vegetables: potatoes always (available in more than two dozen ways, from "Hungarian cream" to "Castle-style," roasted with rosemary), and often, curiously, stewed red cabbage. I was even permitted half a glass of wine.

"Hai una buona forchetta!" the waiter would say, setting down my lunch of châteaubriand with mashed potatoes and Parmesan cauliflower, or cannelloni with a side order of peas. "You have a good appetite." The translator of our menus would have said, "You have a good fork."

I was tall for my age and rail thin. But I ate for two.

What were those meals really like? Would they impress me now, after years of dining out in restaurants, most often as a critic?

Those three weeks on the *Victoria,* eating whatever exotic dish struck my fancy, left a lifelong imprint. They were the first step to loving good food. Meals were an occasion. We bathed and changed for dinner. My father wore a tropical-weight dinner jacket, my mother one of the copies of Paris fashions she'd had made by a dressmaker in Saigon.

I bounded up the stairs when the gong sounded for the first sitting, my little sister, Philippa, in hot pursuit, hoping she'd be allowed spaghetti and meatballs yet again. I wanted to try everything. I wished I could always eat like this, in the dining rooms of ocean liners, sailing between continents, with a ravenous appetite brought on by the sea air, wondering whether today I should order Stewed Veal "Stanley" or take a chance on the cold table's Blown Poularde "Rose of May."

MY PARENTS BELONGED TO a hierarchical and class-conscious generation. Keeping up appearances was a nerve-racking job, and nowhere was that more evident than in the British Army and the diplomatic corps.

"I feel wrong," my mother, Lyla, would often say as she stood in front of the mirror, putting on her long gloves and patting her hair in exasperation. It was a refrain I heard throughout her life. Her forehead was too high. Her curly auburn hair was too thin, her pale skin too fine and prone to wrinkles.

There was nothing wrong with her looks. My mother was a beauty. But behind the glamorous façade, she was often frightened, as if some catastrophe were about to take place and she was helpless to prevent it.

It wasn't the travel, the upheaval involved in changing countries every two years, that made my mother so often feel "wrong." It was lack of money, insecurity, the rigid British class system. She was acutely aware of rank, of who was a third secretary or a counselor in the embassy, who sat "below the salt," who was placed to the left and the right of the host and hostess of a dinner party. She pronounced the word *brassiere* to rhyme with *sassier,* and flinched at the lower-middle-class words *toilet, lounge* (unless in a hotel or an airport) and *pardon?* instead of *what?*

She had a high upper-middle-class English voice, but her parents were Scots Irish who'd left Ulster for England in 1922 to get away from the Troubles. It was lucky that her mother had found a job as a science teacher at Sherborne School for Girls in Dorset. My grandfather, an engineer, spent much of his life either working in Africa, unemployed (during the Slump) or on sick leave, so the family scraped by.

Salaries in the diplomatic corps, moreover, were based on the assumption of a supplementary private income. Wives were not allowed to work. They were supposed to support their husbands by throwing dinners and cocktail parties, attending teas and luncheons, and knowing just enough French for the refrain *"Et combien d'enfants avez-vous, madame?"*

Even food was about class distinction. The table betrayed everything. "Don't hold your knife like a pencil [lower middle class]. And don't spread your bread with butter all at once [working class]. Break off a small piece at a time [upper class]."

Working classes referred to lunch as "dinner" and dinner as "tea." Middle classes put the milk in first when they made a cup of tea. Working classes not only put the milk in first, they drank their tea at odd times of day.

Even the innocent question "What's for pudding?"—the first thing you'd ask when you sat down at the table—revealed what class you came from. The upper-class word for dessert was *pudding*. Lower-middle classes said *sweet*.

My father, Philip, didn't give a damn about any of it.

My parents were students at Cambridge when they met in 1939, the year Britain declared war on Germany. My mother read science, a subject forced upon her by my grandmother. She hated it ("I'd rather have read a book"), and went to too many parties. My father, who was on full scholarship, read modern and medieval languages. They were nothing more than friends.

After my father got his degree in 1943, he went to Sandhurst to train as an army officer. My mother tested bombs at the Royal Air Force base in Farnborough in Hampshire. She went up in a "harrier," a propeller-driven airplane with an open cockpit, and dropped dummy bombs, noting the angle of their fall.

In Farnborough, one of the officers took her out for a drink at a local pub and regaled her with tales of his dangerous flights. After lighting cigarettes for the two of them, he tossed the matchbox onto the floor.

"And there," he said, pointing down at the matchbox, "was the aircraft carrier . . ."

When she told this story, my mother would drop a matchbox on the floor and I'd gaze down at it, feeling quite vertiginous. We'd laugh, but most of those pilots hadn't come back.

My parents ran into each other again in a restaurant in London when my father was on a winter leave from Sandhurst. One evening several months later they sat in the dark in his parents' flat, which looked out over Buckingham Palace, as Hitler's bombs dropped around them. He proposed and she accepted. It all happened very fast. On July 29, 1944, when they were barely twenty-three years old, they were married in Sherborne Abbey, Lyla in a long white dress and a veil and Philip, a captain in the First Airborne Division, in a brand-new military uniform.

My mother was already pregnant with me when, just over six weeks after the wedding, on September 17, my father was dropped at Arnhem, a small town on the lower Rhine River in Holland. Operation Market Garden, as it was called, was the largest airborne campaign ever launched (the subject of the novel and film *A Bridge Too Far*). Its purpose was to secure the bridges that were under German occupation and advance into the Ruhr. But the British were outnumbered and suffered a crushing defeat, failing to capture the bridge at Arnhem. As they retreated from the Germans, my father gave up his place in one of the boats to a wounded friend and swam across the Rhine. Only a quarter of his unit made it back.

In May, the month I was born, my father was part of the liberation of Norway, where he received a medal from King Haakon VII.

The only thing he ever told me about that time was that in Oslo he'd met a twenty-four-year-old man who had been tortured so badly by the Gestapo his hair had gone completely white. My father then spent a year in Schleswig-Holstein, where there were camps for displaced persons, involved in "mopping up" operations, whatever that meant. Like all the men in our family who came back from the war, he maintained his silence. I knew terrible things had happened that he could not bring himself to tell, and I always wondered what they were.

My father was two months younger than my mother, six foot one and very good-looking, with dark brown eyes and straight brown hair. He was born in London, the youngest child of four by a decade. My mother said this had made him taciturn. "Nobody in that family talked except his mother, who never stopped."

His father worked at the Board of Trade and was knighted by the Queen for his services. Sir Edward, a wine connoisseur who played bowls in his spare time, died at the dinner table, age seventy-five, his arm raised in a toast. But Sir Edward had had no money. So my father was always short of it too.

On his eighth birthday, while on a family holiday in Keswick, he was given a bicycle. He rode it to a sweetshop, parked by the front door and went in to buy a chocolate bar. When he came out a few minutes later, the bicycle was gone.

"That's too bad," said his parents. "Sorry, but there we are."

They never bought him another one.

My mother thought my father was cold because, although he liked to play the clown, he rarely revealed his emotions. She came from an Irish family where books were brought down from the shelves during dinner to prove a point, exchanges were volatile and confrontational, and meals regularly wound up with the slamming of doors or fists banging down on the table, often followed by a great deal of laughter.

With Philip there was much laughter too, but few exchanges of confidences, glimmers of vulnerability or unexpected revelations about his inner life, even after a few drinks.

"He never asked what I was thinking about, either," she said. "I thought he simply didn't care."

So they had a perfectly dreadful honeymoon in Torquay, where it rained the whole time.

It was years before she realized that he was chronically shy.

Thanks to my father's job, we led a privileged life way beyond my parents' means. The government paid for private schools, servants, nannies and even chauffeurs. Cigarettes and liquor were duty-free and there was no dearth of drink: Pimm's No. 1, laced with slivers of cucumber and sprigs of mint, pink gins served straight up in martini glasses with a drop of Angostura bitters, whisky and water (no ice), a decent bottle of claret, brandy, Calvados, Madeira, Poire Williams, framboise, port and a digestif popular with the American wives, crème de menthe.

But wherever we were, in England or abroad, there was English food at home for the children (and often for the grown-ups too). It was familiar, stable and safe.

Things on toast: scrambled eggs, creamed mushrooms, sardines, baked beans and Heinz canned spaghetti in tomato sauce.

Things wrapped in pastry or batter: sausage rolls, Cornish pasties, toad in the hole.

Quivery things that slid easily down your throat: banana jelly, blancmange, Bird's custard.

Every day there was tea, with Digestive biscuits, Peek Freans's chocolate Bourbons, "squashed fly biscuits" (so called because they had bits of raisins pressed into them) and Cadbury's chocolate fingers. Whether I was in Beirut or Saigon or Berlin, there was always a jar of Marmite (yeast extract) on the table too, with its familiar round yellow label showing the soup pot from which it got its name, its unctuous contents thick, dark and shiny as tar. And when you poured the tea, you never put the milk in first.

MY PARENTS WERE ONLY TOO GLAD to leave behind them the gloom and deprivation of postwar Britain when our family stepped from the docks of Southampton onto a freighter bound for Egypt in 1949. My mother never got over the ship's lavatories. "They had an inverse reaction to the sea."

Of that journey I remember only the flying fish, the shuffleboard and agonizing times with my father, who was teaching me to read. "No! The cat is in the hall, not the 'hal.' With a ball!"

When we arrived at Port Said, gully-gully men in painted boats swarmed around the ship and climbed on board, peeping chicks hidden under the sleeves of their galabiyas. "Ai-ee gully gully, ai-ee gully gully!" they would call out, and lo and behold, there was a tiny yellow chick in their hands, bewildered and blinking.

"Don't touch it! It might have a disease."

We drove from Port Said on a long, dusty road to Ismailia, where the British had a military base. The town was on the Suez Canal by Lake Timsah, midway between the Mediterranean and the Red Sea. England had been quiet, well-mannered, gray and damp. Here, the air was like velvet, the colors bright, the streets in the center of town crowded and full of commotion. Men in white galabiyas shouted in loud guttural voices as they urged on donkeys and camels with sticks. Cars honked and veiled women, covered head to toe in black, scurried past, dragging the arms of their children. They stood with baskets on their heads on wooden barges moored in the canals. The barges, called feluccas, had tall patched sails attached to thin curved masts, a design unchanged since the time of the pharaohs. The sandy roads were lined with eucalyptus trees and palms that had fronds like feather dusters. I remember the nights were noisy with the clamor of insects, crickets going "heh heh heh" as if laughing at some private joke.

In Egypt my mother fell in love with The French.

The French had their toxic side (and they always took over the best houses and had the best beach clubs), but their language, their cuisine, their music, their conversation, everything about them, captivated her. She began studying French, reading Proust and learning French cooking. Over the years, it dawned on me that a great deal of the attraction of the French was French men. Like my grandmother, my mother preferred the company of men.

French officers were considerably more interesting than those in the British military, many of whom had faces that looked like pink balloons about to pop, and who thought that the only way to make yourself understood by foreigners was to shout. She was delighted by the way a Frenchman would kiss your hand when introduced instead of pumping your arm, or, if he was being very superior, simply brush the air over the back of your hand with his lips. The house was filled with the music of Maurice Chevalier, Yves Montand and Edith Piaf, along with strains of the Egyptian singer Oum Kalsoum, and wafting out from the kitchen came the fumes of garlic, olive oil and French wine.

Ahmed, a Sudanese who came from the north of Egypt, was our cook. He was lanky and handsome, with blue-black skin, and wore a white galabiya and the hard red fez called a tarboush. When the muezzins' call to prayer rang out from the minarets, Ahmed would stop in the middle of whatever he was doing and drop to his knees with his face pressed against the floor. When I saw him like this I was embarrassed and would tiptoe away.

"Mummy, why is Ahmed always smelling ants?"

Ahmed spoke English and his cooking was Anglo-French. He was a gentle soul and my mother was devoted to him. Every morning he would sit down with her and together they would do the shopping list.

On the list were many things she hadn't seen since before the war. For the past six years an orange or a lemon had been practically unobtainable in England. Then Jaffa oranges started coming in from Palestine, but they were expensive. In Ismailia, Ahmed returned from the bazaars with his string shopping bag filled with exotic fruits—pomegranates, apricots, small watermelons—and spices such as cumin, paprika and coriander wrapped in cones made of old newspaper. He also brought back live chickens, which he carried upside down, holding them by their feet. He said it wasn't cruel; when the blood rushed to their head it tranquilized them.

One time, at Christmas, two turkeys had to share a box in the kitchen. One was for us, the other for a friend of my parents. The turkeys didn't like each other, and for nearly a week we were deafened by "gobble gobble gobble" and shrieks, day and night. Then, on Christmas Eve, silence. One of the turkeys reappeared at lunchtime the next day, stuffed with chestnuts and sausage meat, surrounded by chipolata sausages, bacon rolls speared together by toothpicks, silver platters of roast potatoes and Brussels sprouts and silver bowls of gravy and bread sauce. An English Christmas.

Ahmed used an entire bottle of brandy for our Christmas pudding. Half of it went into the butter. The rest he poured over the pudding and set it alight at the table, where the flames leaped a foot high.

After lunch, one of the guests, a little girl with a halo of curls, came up to my mother and asked, "Are my peeks chink?"

One day my mother asked Ahmed to buy some sweetbreads. She wanted to serve them in a cream sauce with mushrooms, for vol-au-vents—à la financière. The French were coming to dinner.

"Do you know what sweetbreads are?"

Ahmed looked at her with a dreamy smile. "Me?"

He made a few Egyptian dishes too. He allowed me to help him stuff vine leaves, rolling them over a mixture of rice, ground lamb and pine nuts to form messy little packets that he redid later. He toasted eggplant over charcoal, scraped out the flesh and mixed it with lemon and olive oil. The broad beans we knew in England were sold dried in Egypt. Ahmed soaked them overnight in water and made them in a dish called *ful medames*. The beans were simmered on top of the stove, tossed with olive oil and lemon (wasn't everything?) and sprinkled with chopped hard-boiled eggs. We ate this with hot flat bread. And there was tabbouleh made with parsley, mint, onions and tomatoes. The secret of a good tabbouleh is to use lots and lots of parsley, much more parsley than grains of bulghur wheat.

But basically Ahmed's food was French. One of his specialties was soft-shell crabs with black butter and capers. My mother said she'd never eaten better soft-shell crabs. I didn't like the look of them at all: fried spiders.

I was looked after by Nadia, whom I adored. She felt soft; she had a soft, billowy bosom, long, soft black hair and humorous brown eyes. She was warm and easygoing. I was only four and a half, but I have vivid memories of her always lifting me up and cuddling me and egging me on to do things that were fun and messy. She taught me how to eat spaghetti (canned, of course, by Heinz in tomato sauce): you bent your head over the plate and sucked up the strands like a vacuum cleaner. When you were done with the spaghetti, you ate the buttered toast that was served underneath, soaked with tomato sauce so it was nice and mushy. She never made me eat the crust. As I vacuumed spaghetti she would break into peals of laughter, so I would do it some more. She used to take me to bed with her, wrapped in her fat, comfortable arms where I would fall asleep. Often there'd be a man in her bed too, and not always the same one.

The days were brilliant with sun or murky with dust, and at

times the heat was insufferable. In the street, children held out their hands, crying, *"Baksheesh! Baksheesh!"* as they trailed behind us in the street, and then Nadia would shout, *"Yalla!"* which meant go away, or *"Imshi!"* which meant the same thing. The children's noses ran and their faces were covered with flies.

I always held on to Nadia's hand, wary of being blinded when a sandstorm blew up from nowhere, without warning. It was terrifying. The sand would get into your eyes and ears, fill your mouth and pile up in the corners of a room if the window had been left open. It lay in heaps on the veranda, like dunes in the desert.

Once in a while after sunset, if the air was still warm, I was taken to watch cartoons screened on a sheet hung outside in a courtyard. We swam in the Red Sea and the Dead Sea, where I lay on my back, floating. There were so many minerals in the water, you couldn't sink. I went on donkey and camel rides by the Pyramids. The sand was searingly hot, so we kept our shoes on. My father, dressed in khaki army shorts, would hold one of my hands while I carried a walking stick in the other. I wore a long-sleeved jacket against the sun.

My parents had been lucky enough to get one of the beautiful white stone houses Ismailia was known for, even though the French had taken the best of the pick. The house was close to the British Officers' Club on the beach by the Suez Canal. My parents would play tennis while I swam there, went on the swings and down the slides, and built castles in the sandboxes under the eye of Nadia. Tankers and freighters passed slowly down the canal and we would stop to watch. When we were thirsty, we drank Kai Ora, an English orange squash, or Ribena, which was also English and made from black currants. My mother didn't approve of these drinks. They weren't anything more than water and sugar with fruit concentrate.

I spent hours and hours on that beach. Insufficiently coated with sunscreen, I swam in the Suez Canal. God knows what came up from the water, where ships dumped everything from garbage to raw sewage. It was brown. We swam in it and survived. The "Other Ranks" beach, next to the Sweet Water Canal, was said to be even more polluted.

The sun covered me with large, dark freckles that spread like blotches over my face, arms and back. "They're the sun's kisses," said Nadia. I looked like a leopard. The French more accurately call freckles *tâches de soleil*. *Tâche* was a word that would later be applied to my school notebooks: stained, spotted, marked up with inkblots; what a mess. It certainly applied to my face. "Don't you sometimes wonder what would happen if all your freckles joined together?" asked Nadia.

I was jumping rope in the living room one day when my mother came in and told me to stop. There was a vase on the mantelpiece, painted with figures running in a circle around it. It was unique, something my parents had discovered in a bazaar in Palestine: an Arab policeman chasing a Palestinian chasing an Israeli.

She left the room.

Just one more skip of the rope!

And a crash.

NOT LONG AFTER THIS EPISODE, I learned that my mother was pregnant. An English nanny was on her way to live with us, and Nadia was dismissed. It was not a good idea to have a nanny who had a different man in her bed each night. From the moment this new member of the household walked into our lives, it was clear that things were going to change.

On Nanny's first night, my parents went out for an official dinner. My father wore a white dress uniform with gold braiding and his Sam Brown. A Sam Brown is a combination of a pistol belt and shoulder strap that was invented by General Sir Samuel J. Brown, who lost an arm fighting in India in the mid-nineteenth century. The belt is intended to carry the weight of a heavy pistol. My father's

Sam Brown, which he'd worn at Arnhem when he swam across the Rhine, was made of chestnut-brown leather, with a square brass buckle and a matching strap that went diagonally across the chest and over the shoulder.

My mother wore long black gloves and a black feathered hat with a small veil that had black polka dots like beauty marks. She looked like a movie star.

But still, she was never satisfied with her appearance. "If only I'd been born with a thick skin," she would say, peering into her mirror, which had three folding sides so you could see yourself from all directions, into infinity. "Your father has a thick skin, and he hardly has any wrinkles at all. Plus he has a small head, which always makes one look younger. But he doesn't look good in hats. Hats make him look swamped."

She looked great in hats. Big, broad-brimmed hats, tiny cocktail hats with veils, a pink and white silk polka-dot pillbox hat, a green felt Borsalino. For she was certainly beautiful—long necked, with high cheekbones; a chiseled, straight nose; intelligent, lively blue eyes; and luminous Irish skin. She didn't look anything like the mothers back in England who wore tweed "coat and skirts" and sensible shoes, did their hair in tight perms and had brisk horsey voices. She was slender and glamorous. Her real name was Lilian, but when she was a girl she'd changed it to Lyla. The name means "night" in Arabic (spelled *Leila*). She used Fire and Ice lipstick, smoked Benson & Hedges cigarettes that came in red tins, and drank pink gins.

Tonight in Ismailia, my parents were the beautiful young couple; they were still in their twenties, just a year younger than fat King Farouk.

It was a hot night, and after they'd gone I couldn't sleep. I was thirsty. So I sat up in bed and, following Egyptian custom, I clapped.

No response.

But I could hear the click of Nanny's knitting needles. I clapped several more times, to no avail. What was wrong? Nadia would have come running. Finally, exasperated, I poked my head out through the mosquito netting and clambered out of bed. I went out to the door, which was half open because I was afraid of the dark. Nanny was ensconced in an armchair, knitting and smoking.

I stood in the doorway in my long white nightgown and stared at her.

"I clapped," I said with dignity.

There was a pause. She eyed me through her spectacles, picked up her cigarette, which was smoking in the ashtray, and took a drag.

"I don't come when people clap."

I was dumbfounded. When Egyptians sat at the table, they clapped for service. If they didn't want the food that the servant offered them, they would make a "tsk" sound and toss back their head or simply shrug their shoulders and turn away. But I never clapped for Nanny again. She told the story for years.

Nanny used to begin a sentence with what sounded to me like one word: "Fahweryoo."

"Fahweryoo I'd think twice before I did that. Fahweryoo I wouldn't play with my food! Fahweryoo I'd take my elbows off the table right now! Do you want me to tell your father?"

Nanny was from Bristol in Somerset, just an hour's drive from Sherborne, where I was born. She was fat like Nadia but not as motherly, though she had a good sense of humor and was kind. Soon after she arrived, my sister, Philippa, was born, and Nanny was often up during the night tending to her. A strong smell of stale tobacco always heralded her arrival, for she chain-smoked Player's cigarettes. Her spare time was spent poring over old issues of *Woman* or *Woman's Own* ("A Crisp White Blouse Goes with Everything") that were sent to her by slow post from England and listening to serials on the radio.

She had a florid West Country face, cornflower-blue eyes and thick, round National Health glasses with clear rims. Her glossy black hair was parted in the middle and held up like wings on each side with combs, and she always wore dark red lipstick. But she never used face powder. She didn't believe in it. She looked like a nurse, dressed in her starched white short-sleeved uniform.

Nanny's real name was Sheila Davis, but she was known as Nanny Hodgson. At the time it never occurred to me that replacing her name with ours was anything less than a way of embracing her as a member of our family.

Like all children in my situation, I spent more time with my nanny than with my mother, and I never thought twice about it. My sister, Philippa, knew her from birth. The English nannies would meet and smoke and gossip about their employers while we played on the British beach at the Officers' Club by the Suez Canal or at Lake Timsah.

Nanny was cheerful and certainly had a sense of humor, but she was not about to put up with a lot of "nonsense." "A joke is a joke and that is the end of it."

"Don't make horrible faces. The wind will change and then you'll be stuck looking like that forever."

At the dinner table: "Play with the salt and you wet the bed." "Take the one that's nearest to you, not the one you fancy most."

Children were, as the Victorians decreed, essentially to be seen and not heard. They had dinner with their nannies, after which they were produced with clean hands and faces, in their nightclothes, to say good night to their parents. My father most often would be putting on black tie or dress uniform, and my mother applying finishing touches of makeup. The bedroom would smell of scent and face powder. An evening dress would be laid out on the bed. Sometimes my father would be "zipping up" my mother. She would sit in front of the dressing table, filling a small satin or beaded evening handbag with a silver powder compact, lipstick and a white lace handkerchief. Then a kiss, and a promise from me to go straight to sleep, and they would be off for the evening.

For my sixth birthday party Ahmed made a chocolate cake,

which he covered with a thick layer of a rich dark chocolate icing. The children, wearing colored paper hats and stained party clothes, their chins barely level with the top of the dining room table, devoured the cake, along with glasses of Ahmed's homemade lemonade. Parents and nannies ate it too, and came back for more. But it had a strange aftertaste. When everyone had gone home, my mother went into the kitchen to compliment Ahmed on the cake.

"By the way, what did you put in the icing?"

"Little bottle from Papa Stratis," he replied proudly.

"What little bottle?" she asked apprehensively.

Ahmed rooted through the rubbish bin and pulled out the little bottle. It was a jar of bootblack.

Not long after my party my father was posted to Beirut. We had been in Egypt for two years. So now, no more mornings at the Jardin d'Enfants and afternoons at the beach. My mother found her beloved Ahmed a job working with another British couple who had just come out from England. A month later she wrote to them asking how he was.

"Ahmed was most peculiar," the wife wrote back. "He went mad. He thought people were chasing him. One day he ran away and we never saw him again."

Bukra bukra fil-mishmish
("Tomorrow tomorrow when the apricot flowers."
In other words, dream on.)

LEBANESE SAYING

കൂ

WE HAD BEEN LIVING IN BEIRUT for only a few months when my mother met an English woman at a cocktail party who said to her, do you know, there's a woman here who has had nine cooks!

That woman was my mother.

My father threw one of the cooks down the stairs when he discovered him lighting the boiler by turning on the gas, standing back and tossing matches at it. Another was shown the door after she produced her specialty, *bouchées à la Reine*—soggy puff pastries cut in different shapes and filled with unidentifiable things swimming in glutinous cream. Another served us raw macaroni and cheese. Instead of boiling the macaroni, he put the hard shells into a Pyrex dish, topped them up with milk and cheese and baked them for an hour. When yet another cook showed up for an interview, the housemaid Mona, who was a Copt (a Christian), came shrieking into the living room, *"C'est une musulmanne!"* It was indeed, a creature shrouded head to toe in black, who was every bit as horrified as Mona.

My mother missed Ahmed. Finally she gave up the search for a cook and handed the job to Mona. She turned out to be very good. Of course, her cooking was Anglo-French.

It was 1952, and we had left the Canal Zone none too soon. Soon after our departure, there were riots in Ismailia and the families of British servicemen were evacuated. But now we were in Beirut, the Paris of the Middle East, the city my parents loved above all others.

They could ski in the mountains in the morning, swim in the sea in the afternoon and in the evening relax on the veranda over "gin and French" (gin with a dash of Noilly Prat dry vermouth, served straight up), looking at a spectacular view of the city, with the snowcapped mountains in the distance. They went to military parades, where they sat under tents patterned with Cedars of Lebanon watching turbaned Lebanese soldiers in jodhpurs and capes riding by on white horses. The city was also a hotbed of spies and double agents. Surfacing among them some years later was Kim Philby, a member of the notorious Cambridge Five, who betrayed Allied secrets to the Russians. Guy Burgess and Donald Maclean defected in 1951; Philby escaped in 1963 on a Soviet freighter docked in Beirut.

Our family albums are filled with photographs of my parents at parties, many of them fancy dress: my father as a Victorian weight lifter with a handlebar mustache and a wig like a haystack, clad in a striped jumper and shorts, and holding up a set of cardboard weights. My mother as a music hall dancer wearing a mutton-sleeved blouse, a locket and a flounced skirt. At another party my father is disguised as a Spaniard, with spit curls, a fedora and a sinister little black mustache; my mother wears a black lace mantilla and peers out from behind a fan.

For all the complaints about having no money, her dresses, which were made on the cheap by local seamstresses, looked like the work of a Parisian designer. A dark blue chiffon, flecked with gold, had a band of gold stripes that stretched from shoulder to shoulder. A pearl-gray silk sported thin velvet shoulder straps and a flounced skirt cut on the bias that swung when she walked. Even more beautiful was a strapless gown made with yards of pale lavender netting over matching silk, sewn with circular patterns of tiny colored sequins. This was her first ball gown, bought for her by my grandmother when she was eighteen. These dresses later made their way into the "dressing-up box," castoffs worn by my sister and me for our plays, and eventually turned into rags.

In Beirut, we ate not just Anglo-French food, but Lebanese dishes too—many of them similar to ones we'd had in Egypt: tabbouleh, hummus, stuffed vine leaves, baba ghanoush, kebabs and grilled chicken, foods that children like. The peaches and apricots served with custard for "pudding" were fresh instead of out of a can. But I remember only one dish clearly: Mona's artichokes.

She brought them back from the market and laid them on the kitchen table: strange prickly things with violet-colored leaves. Mona used to stuff the artichokes with bread crumbs, garlic and parsley and serve them on blue and green Mouski glass plates. The glass was handblown, made by melting down wine and beer bottles. Each plate was a slightly different shade and had bubbles inside that caught the sunlight. Mouski glass was cheap, and my parents had bought boxes of it in Ismailia. To eat Mona's artichokes, you took off the leaves one by one and dipped them into a lemony mixture of melted butter and olive oil that ran down your chin.

اؘ

IN BEIRUT MY FATHER'S KHAKI UNIFORM was decorated for official receptions with his medals, pips and gold braids that hung down across one shoulder. Sometimes he wore an even more glamorous white dress uniform, and on certain occasions, a black dress uniform with a high collar that made him look like a hussar. He looked extraordinarily handsome in all of these uniforms, so it was hardly surprising that he spent money and time on them.

After his death my mother told me that his passion for uniforms got him into serious trouble. Without asking permission beforehand, he had taken some money from petty cash in order to buy some new ones.

"It was considered a serious offense," she said. "I had warned him beforehand to keep the receipts, but he didn't listen."

It was a strange story. My father was deeply afraid of disapproval. He was punctual, anxious and obsessive with details. Every month he would write down all expenses, from the money paid for a newspaper to a new trowel he'd bought for the garden at Woolworth. But in the case of the uniforms, he hadn't realized he should have kept copies of the receipts. Perhaps that's why when I knew him, he kept such meticulous records of everything.

Not long after the incident, a man came down from Egypt to visit my father. My mother described him as a strange and rather louche character: "He was most peculiar and dressed very oddly. But he was quite nice."

The louche character offered my father a job in the Foreign Office.

So, because of a misunderstanding over an armful of uniforms, my father, who was then a major, decided to leave the military to become a diplomat.

Our life in Beirut was cut short. We were sent back to England right away. Mona hugged us for the last time, and we got into the car. I was crying and so was Philippa, who was now two. Mona was holding on to the handle of the car to stop us from driving off, then letting go and running after us for as long as she could until we turned the corner and she was gone.

And then we were on board another freighter. Somewhere in the middle of the Mediterranean Sea, it was announced over the ship's radio that King George VI had died.

FOR THE NEXT YEAR, we lived in Sherborne. This market town, dating back to the Middle Ages, lies between the peat moors of Somerset and the green rolling hills that lead to the chalk cliffs and pebbly beaches of the Dorset coastline. Its ancient buildings, made from sandstone dug from the nearby quarries of Ham Hill, have a soft golden hue. The fifteenth-century abbey and its Saxon doorways are built of this stone, as are the stern, mullioned classrooms of Sherborne School.

Until I was three, my mother and I had spent a great deal of time at Kenelm, one of the boarding houses at Sherborne School for Girls, which my Irish grandmother had run since 1932. The war was over but my father was still in the army, away first in Norway and then in Germany.

When my grandmother wasn't in her science lab with her pupils, pouring things into test tubes and creating noxious fumes over Bunsen burners, she loved to cook. She clipped recipes out of magazines and newspapers, collected them from friends and copied them into a notebook. When she tasted something that really pleased her, she would say, "You could give it to *anyone!*"

After her classes she would take me for walks along the green fields around Sherborne and identify the grazing cows. "That one's Blossom, that's Daisy, that's Buttercup . . ."

I believed, as Granny recited their names, that she really knew each cow personally.

"If you hold a buttercup under your chin and it makes your skin glow yellow, it means you like butter," she told me.

She knelt down and I held one under her chin. She liked butter. So did I. Butter was central to the perennial task of "feeding me up." Granny eked out her supply of butter, a tiny amount she got after standing in line with her rationing book, giving me most—but not all—of her share. I remember standing over a mixing bowl with a wooden spoon, helping her stir a packet of orange powder into white lard to make it look like butter.

But when rationing was finally over, sometime in the mid-fifties, there was no end to the butter, slathered thickly on bread and toast or cut in chunks that melted over boiled potatoes, which she cooked in their skins because that was where the vitamins were.

In 1918, at the end of the First World War, my grandmother started writing down her favorite recipes in a neat, flowery hand. The book she created has lost its cover and the lined pages are brown with age. It is three hundred pages long, ending in 1962 when it runs out of paper.

Half the recipes in her book are for puddings. My grandmother served them almost every day. But she wasn't the only one to exult in the sight of a glorious pudding, turned out of its bowl onto a platter, served with a bowl of custard sauce or treacle. Everyone else loved a good pudding too. Up until the 1960s, puddings were as integral a part of a meal in Britain and Ireland as cheese was for a Frenchman or pasta for an Italian. Even though most middle- and upper-class households no longer employed cooks because they could no longer afford them, a pudding was still expected at the table.

My grandmother's puddings, sweet and savory, were steamed in a deep, round china bowl with a thick rim covered with greaseproof paper tied around with string and placed in water that came three-quarters up the side. "Boiled" puddings were wrapped in cloth and submerged. Some were a light sponge; others were made with suet and dried fruit.

Canary pudding, one of my favorites, was a yellow sponge as light as a soufflé, doused with Lyle's Golden Syrup, which is made from sugar cane and comes in a tin decorated with green and gold lettering. It was spooned out in a dense, sticky stream.

Canary Pudding ("Good")

2 eggs
Their weight in butter, sugar and flour
$^1/_4$ teaspoon baking powder

Grease pudding mould. Cream butter and sugar. Add eggs one by one and a little flour if necessary to keep from curdling. Sift the rest of the flour and baking powder. Beat in lightly with a spoon.

Fill mould $^1/_2$–$^3/_4$ full. Steam for 1–$1^1/_4$ hours or until firm to the touch.

Besides canary pudding, my grandmother's book includes recipes for bread and butter pudding, milk pudding, tapioca pudding, syrup pudding, baked rice pudding, marmalade pudding with marmalade sauce, ginger pudding with ginger sauce and ginger snaps, cheese pudding, date pudding, sea foam pudding (egg whites and lemon), hot chocolate pudding, Mayflower pudding (filled with bread crumbs, syrup and ginger), baroness pudding, Swiss apple pudding, West Riding pudding (made with pastry), baked coconut pudding, spotted dick (white suet pudding laced with raisins and currants), sponge pudding, steamed ground rice pudding, plain plum pudding, and for Christmas, the pièce de résistance, a rich plum pudding, doused with brandy, set alight and brought to the table wreathed in flames.

The first recipe in my grandmother's cookbook was for mince pudding. Was this what her cook served to my grandfather when he came back on leave from the war in Mesopotamia? It bears no relation to the glazed hot mince pies she made us for Christmas, which were stuffed with nuts and chopped dried fruit soaked in brandy. This pudding is filled with another sort of "mince": ground beef.

The instructions call for a "fine dough" made with flour, baking powder and shredded suet, which is then mixed with cold water and rolled out. (Suet is the solid white fat around beef, veal and sheep kidneys.) The cooked "mince" is thinned with more cold water and spread over the dough. Then it's sprinkled with salt and pepper, chopped raw onion and a teaspoon of Yorkshire relish "if desired." The whole thing is rolled up in a cloth, secured with string, plunged into water and cooked for two hours. "The water must be boiling," my grandmother adds in a note at the end.

She approached cooking as a science and wrote out advice with her recipes. "Vegetables must be thoroughly cooked. Cellulose cannot be digested by our gastric systems and therefore must be cooked."

"When making fruit suspended in jellies use fresh and tinned. The tinned fruit will sink to the bottom and the fresh fruit will rise to the top. When the jelly is turned out the tinned will then be on top and the fresh at the bottom of the mould."

As housemistress, my grandmother was responsible not only for looking after the welfare of the boarders in her care, but for their meals as well. The house motto was, appropriately, *Res parvae concordia crescunt* ("From small things big ones grow"). The girls had huge appetites. She organized the menus with Marjorie, the head cook. Many of the recipes in Granny's book give a grim picture of what confronted her charges at the dinner table during the war.

Wartime Sponge Cakes

1 gill (about 1 cup) flour
1/2 level teaspoon cream of tartar

¹/₄ level teaspoon bicarbonate of soda
4 level teaspoons dried egg
1 gill (about 1 cup) sugar
6 tablespoonfuls water

Sieve flour and raising agents three times. Beat sugar, egg and water until stiff. Fold in flour etc. and mix to dropping consistency. Bake in greased and floured tins. Moderate oven (325–375°F). Eat them the day they are made.

Wartime Cream
("Very good over cornflour puddings")

Blend ³/₄ ounce cornflour with a little cold milk; stir it into ¹/₂ pint of boiling milk and cook for 3–4 minutes, stirring continuously. Leave until nearly cold. Cream together until quite light 1 ounce butter or margarine and a dessertspoonful sugar. Add it to the cornflour and whip with a wire whisk.

Dried eggs went into everything—into the cakes and puddings, mock mayonnaise, salad dressings and pancakes. They were mixed with anchovy sauce, rolled into balls and boiled for ten minutes. These "dried egg balls" were then cooled and put into salads.

On a Saturday, to give the girls strength before they went out to play a hockey or lacrosse match in the afternoon, there were "liver pigs" for lunch, the liver sliced into small pieces and fried in batter. Wrote Granny: "Liver cooked this way is as tender as spring chicken."

To make meat and vegetables go farther, they were served in batter or hidden inside layers of potato or suet. Fish was cut into fillets and baked in custard. Steak and kidney pie had a wartime substitute, Ox Kidney Mould, made with chopped kidneys mixed with bacon, onion, parsley and bread crumbs, and steamed. A pudding. It was served with a good thick brown sauce made from kidney gravy spooned over and around it.

Kidney toast was made with sheeps' kidneys and sieved yolk of egg. Tongue was pickled in saltpeter for two weeks, pressed and boiled and served with a glaze. ("Too much rough skin indicates age.") She shaped meat "cutlets" out of a dried egg mixture. ("Stick in a piece of macaroni to represent bone," she wrote in her recipe book.)

So Marjorie made sixty-two of these, rolled them in bread crumbs and fried them in fat. The girls pretended they were eating lamb chops.

But rationing did not diminish the variety of cakes and puddings served at Kenelm during the war. My grandmother gives three variations in her book for what she calls "War Cake," subtitled "The Dug Out," spiced fruitcake made with sultanas and dried eggs. You weren't supposed to eat the cakes until they had "ripened" for at least a week in the tin.

Her cooking reflected her personality: she threw herself into it unconditionally and with passion. As much as anything she enjoyed the chemistry. What made the soufflé that you placed in the oven with trembling hands rise up to new heights over the sides of its dish? And why did it sink down if, God forbid, you should open the oven door too soon?

By the time my grandmother's recipe book ends, the soufflé and the mousse hold sway instead of traditional puddings. For during the fifties, British food had begun to change. People began to travel abroad again and brought back new ideas. My grandmother's meals became more elaborate too. Whom did she entertain for lunch with such dishes as smoked salmon quiche and *poussin polonaise?*

"With the quiche drink a white Laville Haut-Brion 1953 Bordeaux," she suggests. With the poussin, "stuffed with the best possible stuffing, including the liver," she advises a 1954 red Haut-Brion. "Plainly cooked flageolet beans are enough for its accompaniment. Buttered apple slices to follow. The Men will like this."

My grandmother liked cooking for The Men. "The Men always like a good stew." She would get in whisky for The Men too, and for the women, Yugoslav Riesling.

The last recipe in her cookbook, dated 1962, is for Carnation Chocolate Soufflé, made with evaporated milk. "Note by H.O.H." (Harriet Oldfield Hamilton), she has written at the end of this recipe, "Try fresh cream instead."

During the war, my father came on leave from the army for a weekend at Kenelm. He caught the train at Waterloo and settled down in the compartment with his newspaper. A recipe caught his eye: Mock Roes on Toast. It was made with tapioca and tinned pilchards.

He knew my grandmother was always on the trail of inventive new dishes, so he clipped the recipe out of the paper and handed it to her.

"You could give this to anyone," he said.

*

BY THE TIME the family came home from Beirut, my grandmother had retired from being a housemistress. She was still teaching science, so she and my grandfather had moved into Penrhyn, a small house provided by the school. My father worked in London and came home on weekends. I went to Newell House primary school and for a while my parents rented the Wye, a bungalow that had walls made out of pebbles and seashells. Then, for a few months, we moved into my grandparents' house.

My grandfather, whom we called Ganga, would lean toward Philippa and me over the breakfast table. "Chew each mouthful thirty-two times."

Ganga's bristly black mustache, streaked with gray, bobbed up and down like a small craft on a choppy sea. Although he was an Irishman from County Antrim, he shared with Henry James a firm belief in Fletcherizing his food—chewing each mouthful thirty-two times, until it was reduced to liquid. Ganga's penetrating blue eyes watched me masticate spoonful after spoonful of the porridge he had made that morning.

It was over fifty years since Dr. Horace Fletcher, the Victorian health guru from Massachusetts, had convinced a large part of the English-speaking population on both sides of the Atlantic that for optimum digestion, each mouthful of food must be chewed thirty-two times. By the time my grandfather joined the ranks of "the Salivation Army" (as a weekend guest at Henry James's house in Rye once called it), the venerable writer was long dead. But apart from the joys of munching, the two men had little in common, either in looks or interests. James was massive, bulky and bald, with a pale, round, fleshy face; Ganga was lean and spare, with a head of thick white wavy hair cut short at the back and sides, black eyebrows, a firm jaw, slightly protruding ears and an unusually high forehead. He held himself ramrod straight like the army captain he had been. Good posture was another of his pet causes, and he often had me walk around with books balanced on my head.

Ganga always made the porridge. He spooned it out into pale green bowls that were passed around the table and sprinkled with the soft, treacly crystals of the sugar known as "Old Brown" (named by my father after the owl in Beatrix Potter's *The Tale of Squirrel Nutkin*). I'd pour thick, yellow "top of the milk" into my bowl before beginning the exhausting task of Fletcherizing each mouthful of the porridge Ganga had made that morning.

My grandparents' dining table was set with beige wooden chairs that had matching padded plastic seats, and was spread with a green-and-white-striped seersucker cloth, a drip-dry fabric. Each person had a seersucker napkin striped with his or her color. My parents' colors weren't hard to remember: red for my father because he sometimes made my mother angry, blue for my mother because she was often depressed. Philippa's was yellow. Mine was green.

Each of us would sit before a laminated yellow place mat embossed with an eighteenth-century engraving of a landmark London building. My sister and I would fight long and loud over whose turn it was for the mat with the picture of Buckingham Palace. To settle the argument, Nanny would take it for herself.

Every morning there would be a jar of James Keiller & Son's Dundee marmalade, thick-cut, which my grandmother would spread generously on her toast. My grandparents didn't have an orange for four years during the war. And one day—it was October 1944—an American soldier came into town and brought one to the house. It tasted like nectar.

Our eggs came from the snaggle-toothed Burkhardt sisters, who taught biology at the school and lived in a place straight out of *Cold Comfort Farm,* with pigs lolling about the kitchen and hens pecking under the dining room table for crumbs. The eggs were as filthy as the Burkhardts themselves usually were, with mud and bits of straw sticking to them. The yolks were a brilliant orange, sometimes flecked with blood. (Ganga said that when he was an amateur lightweight boxer in Ireland, he ate his eggs with their shells on.) With our eggs we ate sausages made by Wall's as unnaturally pink as they still are today, with a generous amount of bread mixed with the pork. I loved them.

Of course, I not only obeyed my grandfather in Fletcherizing but in other things as well. With his jet-black eyebrows and blue eyes he struck terror, not just in children but in the toughest of the old buzzards who lived in Sherborne.

During the football season he took immense pleasure in confiscating the rugger balls that used to sail over the goalposts on the playing field next door, high above the ten-foot chicken-wire fence the boys' prep school had erected along the hedge at his behest. Whenever one of the boys knocked on the front door and asked for the ball back, my grandfather would stand for a minute on the threshold in his tweed plus-fours, checked Austin Reed shirt, sleeveless V-neck Fair Isle sweater and Argyll socks, arms folded behind his back, his shoes a gleaming reproach to the mud-covered reprobate from Sherborne Preparatory School. Then he'd close the door and make the boy wait outside in the cold while he pretended to look for the ball. What he was doing was letting the air out of it.

I would hide in the sitting room, mortified.

At last Ganga would throw open the front door. "Here's your ball!"

There it was indeed. Flat as a pricked balloon.

And I had to walk past the boys' playing field every afternoon and hear the remarks.

My grandmother didn't Fletcherize her food because she had false teeth. One day she had paid a visit to the dentist and he'd taken out the whole lot in one go, just like that.

Her name was Harriet, but Ganga called her George. When I once asked her why, she just shrugged. "He didn't like the name Harriet."

Perhaps he called her George because not only had she worked all her life, much of the time she'd been the main wage earner in the family. She also played the piano and sang, and she knew long tracts of Tennyson by heart. "Now sleeps the crimson petal, now the white . . ." was one of her favorite poems.

During the twenties my grandfather was in the army in Mesopotamia, fighting the Turks in Baku and Waziristan. Then he was hired as an engineer in West Africa, a job that took him abroad for months at a time. He returned home under a cloud, after slamming down a window on a thief's hands. It was a bad time to be out of work. He developed a duodenal ulcer, which was operated upon ("Ganga's only got half a stomach, don't you know?"); he was often in pain and he didn't climb stairs. His province was the breakfast room, with its pale green walls, worn beige linoleum floor and view of a patch of lawn, a beech tree and my grandmother's rosebushes. It was used for all our other meals too, because my grandparents slept in the dining room.

The breakfast room was the warmest place in their house—the only warm place in fact. Ganga's easy chair sat next to the coal-burning stove, which he kept going day and night, opening the iron lid with a clang and shoveling in more coal. The stovetop was hot enough to boil the teakettle. Sometimes he came after us children with the shovel and tongs, chasing us around the room and into the garden, roaring and bellowing, "I'll get you yet!" Philippa adored him.

On our last morning in Sherborne, there were just six of us at breakfast: Granny, Ganga, my mother, Nanny, Philippa and me. My father had a post with the British Embassy in Stockholm and he had left earlier in the summer to find a house.

I didn't want to go abroad again. I liked Newell House school, and I didn't want to leave my grandparents.

But two good things happened in the late spring of 1953, just before we left for Sweden, that restored my spirits as well as everyone else's in drab postwar England. On May 29 Edmund Hillary, with his Sherpa guide, Tenzing Norgay, at his side, placed a Union Jack on the top of Mount Everest. Even though he was a New Zealander, Hillary's response to the momentous occasion was that of an Englishman. "I stretched out my arm for a handshake," he said, "but this was not enough for Tenzing, who threw his arms around my shoulders in a mighty hug."

Four days later, on June 3, Queen Elizabeth was crowned at Westminster Abbey. To commemorate the glorious day of the coronation, Granny gave me a model of the gold royal carriage drawn by white horses, with a tiny figure of the Queen inside. And she made Queen's pudding, adding another recipe to her precious book.

Queen's pudding dated back to Queen Victoria's reign. My grandmother baked it in a Pyrex dish so you could see the layers: the white of the bread, the scarlet stripe of jam and the high puff of lightly browned meringue. The pudding was served with the rich "top of the milk," from the bottle with the gold label, if those "dirty devils," the starlings, hadn't gotten there first.

Queen's Pudding for the Family 1953

Put 3^1/2 ounces bread crumbs with 1 dessertspoon sugar (keep a vanilla pod in the sugar) into pie dish. Boil up ^{3}/4 pint milk, 1 ounce butter. Add to crumbs. Let sit for half an hour. Add yolks of 4 eggs and put in the oven for half an hour at 380°F. Add raspberry jam on top. Add beaten whites of eggs with a little sugar to put on top. Brown in a cool oven.

When my father had landed in Stockholm earlier in the year he'd sent us a postcard from the SS *Patricia,* the ship he had taken across the North Sea. The card was hand colored, and showed a cheerful assembly of people with pink, flushed faces and unnaturally red lips lined up alongside a buffet table decorated with Swedish flags and Union Jacks. They were helping themselves to a feast: sides of salmon, fillets of raw herring, meatballs in cream sauce, pickled onions, beets, sliced smoked reindeer, roast chickens, raw egg yolks in nests made of ground raw meat, heaps of scarlet prawns and glasses of schnapps. Before you even arrived in that permissive country it was making a point: even the food was a free-for-all. This feast, which has made its appearance in bastardized versions on hotel buffet tables all over the world, is of course known as smörgåsbord.

"Will they have ice cream for pudding?" I asked my mother as we packed.

"Yes, I'm sure they will," she answered.

"If there are tomatoes in the smörgåsbord will I have to eat them?" I loathed tomatoes.

"No, you can choose what you like."

"Anything?"

"Within reason."

"Will they have blancmange?" I asked.

"Perhaps," she answered, as she put plastic bottles filled with lotions into the square mirrored carry-case she called her "face."

"If it's shaped like a rabbit can I have the head?"

Nanny made blancmange from the powdered contents of a packet emptied into boiled milk, stirred until smooth and poured into an aluminum mold. When it had set, the blancmange was turned out onto a serving dish: a pink, quivering, strawberry-flavored rabbit. The head was the best part. My sister and I fought over it every time.

"I very much doubt they'll have a rabbit. Anyway, get on with sorting out your toys. Which ones do you want to leave behind?"

None.

For the two nights on board ship, I was allowed to take a small suitcase, which I packed with my overnight things, along with the souvenirs of the coronation (a pop-up book and a lead replica of the Queen's coach), a five-year diary and my collection of marbles. Great Aunt Grace had sent a box of Kendal mint cake, and that went into the suitcase as well.

Kendal mint cake had seen unprecedented sales that summer, when the world learned it was Sir Edmund Hillary's and Tenzing Norgay's favorite snack on Mount Everest. To think that they had stood all the way at the top of the mountain, looking over the vast expanse of snowy mountain range they'd just conquered, eating the very same Kendal mint cake I had packed in my bag! And Tenzing had even left a few packets there, not as litter, but as an offering to "his gods."

Swedish food is nothing but sill [herring], dill and swill.

A DIPLOMAT AT THE BRITISH EMBASSY, STOCKHOLM, 1953

IT WAS LATE AFTERNOON when we arrived at the harbor in Tilbury. The SS *Patricia* was one of Swedish Lloyd's fleet of passenger ferries, a white ship with a funnel decorated with a black stripe above a yellow star inside a blue circle, the colors of the Swedish flag. Trunks and wooden crates wrapped in thick ropes were stacked on the quay and loaded by workmen in blue uniforms onto hooks that hung on the end of cranes. The luggage swung precariously in the air as it was lowered into the hold. At last the gangways were lifted and the *Patricia* sounded her siren as she prepared to pull out of the harbor, followed by a flock of screeching gulls.

Clutching the packet of Great Aunt Grace's Kendal mint cake, I leaned over the wooden railings and waved at the figures on the quayside as they grew smaller. The sea was gray as slate.

Hardly had the coastline of England disappeared from sight than the ship began to roll. By now I'd finished the whole bag of Kendal mint cake and was beginning to regret it. I made my way queasily down to the lounge for tea. The first hint of what was in store came when I tried to draw my chair closer to the table and discovered that it was nailed to the floor. Nanny's tea swilled out of her cup and over her lap.

My mother distributed Dramamine tablets and we went to the cabin we shared to lie down. I was allowed the top bunk. By dinnertime, the pills seemed to be working because I began to feel a little better. I took my marbles out of the suitcase, emptied them from their velvet bag and spread them out over the blanket. My champion marble was like a cat's eye, iridescent green and yellow, flecked with black and brown.

The ship gave a shudder, and the marbles went spinning down the side of my bunk.

My mother groaned from below. "What on earth are you doing?"

The marbles rattled back and forth the length of the bunk between the mattress and the wooden paneling on the wall, like a hand running up and down the keys of a piano. I was buffeted from one side to the other, but I managed at last to get all of them back in the bag, except one.

"I've dropped a marble inside my bunk and I can't get it out."

"For heaven's sake!"

She rang for the steward and drew the curtain over her bunk; I threw up.

The steward, in a spotless white uniform, climbed the ladder to change my sheets. He tried in vain to locate the marble.

My mother poked her head through the curtains. "Isn't there anyone on the boat who can get it out?"

"No, Madam. We'll have to remove the paneling. We can't do that in this weather."

The next morning there was a knock on our door and the steward came in with cups of tea. My mother couldn't drink any; she lay in the bottom bunk of the adjacent cabin with her face to the wall. The marble kept on rolling.

On Sunday, the day of the smörgåsbord, there had been no letting up in the stormy weather and we were all still in bed, except Nanny, who was one of those blessed people who never suffered from seasickness. She went up to the dining room for lunch. When she came back she reported that one of the few passengers who'd shown up had been thrown to the floor so violently he'd broken his arm.

During the next couple of years we made the crossing over the North Sea four times, back and forth to England, on the Swedish Lloyd ferries *Saga, Patricia* and *Britannia.* The sea was always so rough that we were all ill, except Nanny. Whenever she ventured upstairs to the smörgåsbord, she found the dining room deserted. Yet the same spread was always waiting there, laid out on the long tables set with white cloths, Swedish and British flags, and piles of white plates, untouched, like a meal for which the hostess has forgotten to send out invitations.

When the *Patricia* docked in Gothenburg, I was still feeling sick. With an enormous sense of relief, I settled into my seat on a brand-new train to Stockholm. It was much faster than English ones. But as the train gathered speed, I felt a rolling sensation that was unpleasantly familiar. The train listed back and forth just like the boat.

We were all looking much the worse for wear when my father met us at the railway station in a new car, a powder-blue Hillman that sported the letters CD (Corps Diplomatique) above the number plate.

"What do they do with all that food?" I asked my father.

"Nothing," he replied. "It's made from plaster of Paris."

After an hour's drive from the center of Stockholm, we arrived at our new house. It was already dark and my sister and I were put to bed.

My parents went out to dinner. My father had booked a table at the Operakällaren, one of Stockholm's best restaurants. Its vast, opulent dining rooms, catering to patrons of the Opera House as well as the general public, are (to this day) decorated in the Beaux-Arts style, with high, suspended panel ceilings, gilded oak-paneled walls and crystal chandeliers, although the plush red velvet chairs are now blue. The restaurant was rebuilt at the end of the nineteenth century and decorated with gigantic murals of cavorting nudes. When the murals were unveiled the public was outraged, and Parliament condemned them as pornographic. The playwright August Strindberg (already facing blasphemy charges for one of his books) took up the gauntlet on their behalf. But the matter was settled by the king himself, Oscar II, who asked the painter if he would "allow the reeds to grow a little."

So as the nudes on the wall above gamboled their way through long and carefully placed reeds, my parents, seated side by side on a red velvet banquette below, were served the first artichokes they'd eaten since Beirut. They were filled with peas.

"The peas rolled around the plate like marbles," said my mother. "I couldn't eat a thing."

FOR A CHILD with the slightest modicum of imagination, our house in Sweden was the answer to a prayer. It looked like a castle. It was painted pale yellow and had a tower, covered balconies, gables and a sloping green turreted roof topped with a weather vane carved in the shape of a rooster. The house stood back from the street on the side of a hill in Djursholm, a leafy suburb of nineteenth-century mansions about forty minutes from Stockholm, and a three-minute walk up from Osterviken, one of the region's many lakes.

You entered a large front hall that had high, mullioned windows and was hung with a cast-iron chandelier. A baronial cupboard flanked by two heavy chairs with carved wooden arms and worn leather seats stood next to the door of the dining room, which was heated by a massive nineteenth-century stove made with ceramic tiles painted with birds and flowers. A wide front staircase led to the second floor, where every room had a veranda or balcony. The attic was accessible by a steep, narrow staircase with a polished wooden banister that ended abruptly on the landing outside my bedroom, where I would slide off with a crash.

If there was a prolonged silence in the house, my father would suddenly yell at the top of his voice, "Whatever you're doing, stop it at once!"

His voice would ring out of the blue when I was down in the cellar painting my nails with clear varnish, or upstairs investigating my mother's makeup, or when my sister was in his dressing room going through the chest of drawers, where she found a condom and blew it up like a balloon.

Our large, tangled garden had a sloping lawn and a long drive-way, lined with laburnum and silver birch trees, that wound its way behind the house to a double garage carved out of the side of the hill. One afternoon Philippa, left to her own devices, found two gallons of gold and red paint in the cellar. She found a thick brush too, and brought everything up the stairs. She covered the garage doors with generous daubs of the paint before knocking over both cans, spilling them over the driveway. When we left Sweden two years later, the tarmac still glinted.

My father had rented the house from Mrs. Seyberg, who was married to a general and lived in Gothenburg. She was particularly proud of the bamboo furniture, upholstered with cushions violently patterned with tropical flowers, that dominated the L-shaped drawing room where the yellow-green carpet matched the heavy velvet curtains. On her infrequent visits to the house, with a teacup poised in her hand, she would refer admiringly to her "bambew," sounding like a refined Australian.

Mrs. Seyberg had fallen in love with the "bambew" in Singapore: "We had the cushions made there for nothing! Nothing!"

I would lie on the "bambew" with a book and my father would play Sibelius very loud. On the other side of the Sibelius record was the Danish composer Carl Nielsen's Third Symphony. The end of the second movement, marked by the faraway voices of two singers breaking into the swell, like mermaids, filled me with strange new feelings of unfocused yearning and melancholy.

My parents found Swedish social conventions stultifying. When you went to a dinner party, guests would linger outside the front door beforehand, looking at their watches. They would ring the bell punctually on the stroke of the appointed hour, clutching a large bouquet of flowers for the hostess. Convention dictated that the flowers be odd in number and the wrapping paper removed in advance. When you sat down to dine, you couldn't drink until the host had said *skål*. Then, according to my mother, there was a lot of intertwining of arms and looking deep into your dinner partner's eyes and saying *skål,* a toast that was repeated endlessly throughout the meal.

She figured out that in Stockholm you said "thank you" for an invitation seven times.

You said thanks when you received the invitation, thanks again when you next saw your future hostess, and thanks yet again when you handed her flowers upon your arrival at dinner. After the meal the hostess would stand up in the middle of the room and the guests would line up to thank her once more. You thanked her as you took your leave, then you wrote a thank-you letter, and next time you saw your hosts, you thanked them all over again.

My parents weren't the only ones who found the Swedes solemn and humorless. When my father went on a business trip to Denmark, he discovered at the border that he had forgotten his passport. The immigration officer glared at him. "No papers! Where are you from?"

My father explained to the immigration officer that he had been stationed for two years with the British Embassy in Stockholm.

"Two years!" exclaimed the officer. "You poor man! You don't need a passport here. Welcome to Denmark! Stay as long as you like!"

و

IN SWEDEN, come December, it was dark by three o'clock. Our neighbors hid in their rooms behind windows lit like an aquarium and filled with leafy houseplants that survived day and night under grow lights. People brought out bottles of schnapps, which came in many flavors—caraway, coriander, cinnamon, anise and fennel. There were aquavits that tasted faintly of bourbon after being aged in sherry casks, and delicate ones made with cloudberries or gooseberries. This was the "swill" my parents and their friends referred to, and it came in handy on the ski slopes and in the long winter evenings.

Our house stood out like a magic castle among the fir trees, dazzling in the sunlight. Snow was piled on the roof and icicles glinted from under the eaves and the windowsills. Unlike the English drizzle that had passed for the season in my short experience, winter here was properly defined. The air was clear and cold, the skies sunny and blue. Around the house, the pine forests hinted at the presence of the small, hairy trolls I read about in my children's books.

When Lake Osterviken froze over, my father took us on a shortcut, driving across the ice in the powder-blue Hillman. Philippa and I sat in the back in enthralled and terrified silence, waiting for a wheeze and a crack. But people raced cars and flat-bottomed yachts across the lake, and in the evening bonfires were lit on the ice and skaters spun around in the glow. We lived near the golf course where we went to ski most weekends before it got dark. I remember Philippa, who never stopped clowning, dressed in layers of clothes under red waterproof overalls that were like a suit of armor, as wide as she was tall. If she fell, she could not get up unaided, but lay on the ground like a felled warrior, laughing.

After a morning's skiing, my parents would bring friends to our house for a late lunch. So that first winter in Djursholm my mother inaugurated the "elephant's foot."

The elephant's foot was a giant vol-au-vent that was stuffed with mushrooms and kidneys in a cream sauce, a popular Swedish dish. The flaky pastry shell was baked ahead of time, then warmed in the oven at the last minute, the heated filling poured in and topped with a pastry lid. Sometimes the elephant's foot was made with chicken, fish or beef stroganoff, but whatever it contained, it made a dramatic impression. Swedish guests would thank my mother for it many times over.

After lunch, my friends and I would take turns on the spark—a wooden chair on runners that worked like a sled. It had not been bought as a toy, but for the practical purpose of grocery shopping when the roads and sidewalks were covered with snow. Children and packages were put on the seat, and the driver walked behind, holding on to the chair and pushing the spark, one foot on a runner and the other pushing off the ground. We would put both feet on the runners, one of us steering, the other on the chair (feet up on the crossbar in front), flying down the hill until we landed in a ditch. One afternoon as we turned the spark around at the top of the hill in preparation for its descent we heard a munching sound. There on the neighbor's lawn, eating a rhododendron bush, was a moose.

This moose boasted a pair of antlers that seemed even bigger than those we'd seen in the Lapland dioramas at the natural history museum. Standing in front of us, it looked formal and bewildered, like an elderly woman in the wrong sort of hat. Then it went back to eating the rhododendron, chomping its jaws steadily in a manner that made it clear that our presence mattered not one whit.

"Ya! Boo!" we yelled. The moose went on eating.

The Elephant's Foot

A baked puff pastry shell, with a lid, about 11-12 inches in diameter	2 tablespoons lemon juice
	1 tablespoon Dijon mustard
5 shallots, chopped	1 cup chicken or veal stock (or more as needed)
6 tablespoons unsalted butter	
3 tablespoons olive oil	$^1/_2$ cup dry white wine
3 pounds mushrooms, sliced	$^1/_4$ cup Madeira or sherry
1 tablespoon thyme	$1^1/_2$ cups heavy cream
Salt and freshly ground pepper	5 veal kidneys, fat removed, sliced

Using a large skillet, soften the shallots in 4 tablespoons butter and 2 tablespoons olive oil. Add the mushrooms in stages so as not to overfill the pan, and saute, stirring, until they are lightly browned. Sprinkle with thyme and season with salt and pepper.

Add the lemon juice, mustard, stock, wine and Madeira. Bring to a boil and cook over low heat for about 20 minutes. If it gets too dry, moisten with water. Add the cream gradually, stirring constantly until the sauce has thickened.

Heat the remaining butter and tablespoon of olive oil in another large skillet and quickly brown the kidneys. Do not overcook them or they will be tough. Season them with salt and pepper and add them to the mushrooms. Discard the fat from the pan and de-glaze the kidney cooking juices with water. Add them to the mushrooms and stir well. Correct seasoning.

Re-heat the cooked pastry shell and the lid in a low oven for about 10 minutes. Fill the shell with the kidney mixture and top with the pastry lid.

SERVES 8–10

On Christmas Day, Mr. Hawsley gave me a toy stove on which I could cook food over a real flame. He also gave me a small chocolate beetle that I didn't eat but put away in a box to sleep. I kept it in the drawer next to my bed.

Mr. Hawsley was a second secretary in the British Embassy. He was tall and lanky, with dark brown hair parted in a clean line on one side, his bony face decorated with a small, neat mustache. When he wished to drive a point home, he would jump to his feet, stabbing the air with his cigarette. He was a bachelor, so he didn't have any children. If he had, he might have entertained second thoughts about the present he had given me. The stove came with a packet of squat, white candles that were lit under each of the four "burners" and beneath a rack in the oven. Tiny, thin aluminum pots and pans were provided for cooking the food.

After the roast turkey and the plum pudding had been dispatched, Mr. Hawsley pulled out a cigarette from a packet of

Player's, which was printed with the familiar picture of a bearded sailor's face framed by a ship's white life preserver. He held out the packet to me. "Would you like to try one?"

I most certainly would.

I sat down on the "bambew," crossing my legs and lounging back the way I had seen my mother do.

"Your first cigarette!"

I sucked at it like a stick of candy, bits of tobacco on my tongue. That brand of Player's wasn't filtered.

"Don't do that, you'll get it all wet!"

He lit the cigarette for me and I took one puff.

"Her first cigarette, Lyla!"

"I like it very much," I said, coughing and spluttering. My mother removed it from my hand and put it in her cigarette holder.

As far as I was concerned, Mr. Hawsley could do no wrong.

On my new stove, I scrambled eggs and heated up beans. I baked canned chipolatas in butter that turned grainy and brown in the oven. I burned chocolates in the saucepans, causing them to shrivel up and scorch. Soon the pans were buckled beyond repair and wax clogged the burners. I lost interest. The stove was consigned to the toy box. When we left Sweden, it didn't come with us.

"Wakey, wakey, rise and shine
The morning's fine
The sun will burn your eyes out!"

On the morning of my tenth birthday, my father's voice broke through my sleep.

I hated to be woken up, so the task usually fell to my father, who used techniques he'd learned from his drill sergeant.

"C'mon, gerrup! Quicker than the wind from a duck's arse. Hup, two, tree, faw . . ."

He would take hold of my feet and shake them until he got a response (he had a theory that this was the safest way to wake people up; grabbed elsewhere they might have a heart attack).

"Go 'way!" I snarled from under the bedclothes, trying to escape his grasp on my toes.

"Get up! There's something for you in the garage."

I pulled on my clothes and ran to the garage. My mother, seeing my excited face as I raced downstairs, realized I thought I was getting a bicycle. I'd been asking for one ever since we left England.

But my parents couldn't afford to buy me a bicycle. So they went for the next best thing. Propped up against the wall inside the door of the garage, decorated with a red silk bow, was a pair of wooden stilts.

The reactions of children can never be predicted. I wonder if my father, when his parents failed to replace his stolen bicycle, had felt as bad at the time as I did for him when I heard the story. But while my mother was upstairs grieving over my disappointment, all I remember is feeling that I was a giant. I held on to the sides of the stilts and stepped out ten feet tall.

That afternoon, my parents gave a birthday party for me. The children were invited to come dressed as grown-ups. How anachronistic that seems now, when middle-aged men and women routinely dress like their own teenagers, and preteen models dress like sultry movie stars.

I wore my mother's recent castoff, the long dark blue voile threaded with gold. Philippa, who was five, wore a gray silk cocktail dress gathered around the hips that came with a matching bolero jacket. Our hair was set in rollers and our faces made up with red lipstick and darkened eyebrows. My mother said Philippa looked like Roxie Hart, an allusion to the Rita Hayworth movie that escaped us children at the time. My mother was a maid in a black dress with white cap and apron, and my father wore a striped waistcoat, like a butler.

The guests arrived promptly at four o'clock, some of them even bearing flowers for the hostess. There were exclamations and gusts of chatter as Nanny this and Nanny that removed fur stoles from the shoulders of nine- and ten-year-olds, and hats that sank down like giant upturned pudding bowls over the ears of small boys were placed on the hat rack in the hall. The girls wore their mothers' cast-off evening dresses, trailing them on the floor. The boys had burnt-cork mustaches and bow ties. It looked like a convention of dwarfs.

My parents brought around trays of chipolata sausages on sticks and potato chips, and served martini glasses filled with bright "cocktails" made from fruit juice mixed with food coloring. They offered us chocolate cigarettes from silver cigarette boxes, which we smoked while drinking our cocktails to the sound of my parents' party records on the gramophone: "A Bunch of Bananas and a Bottle of Gin" (Rosemary Clooney and José Ferrer), Edmundo Ross, Eartha Kitt, Henri Salvador and "Surprise Partie à Cuba" (sambas and mambos). My favorite songs were "All the Boys Love Mary Ann" and "How D'Ye Do and Shake Hands," the latter sung by a rare teaming up of Danny Kaye and Groucho Marx. The other side was a song called "Blackstrap Molasses and Wheat Germ Bread," the second line of which ran: "Make you live so long you wish you were dead."

When our party games had run their course, we sat down to watch silent projections of black-and-white Mickey Mouse cartoons (in one of them he flew an airplane wearing goggles that had their own windshield wipers, a detail that I remember finding hilarious).

As for the stilts, alas, all too soon, I became a giant myself. I towered over the heads of boys my age. They refused to dance with me at parties. Once, when all the other partners were taken, a small fat boy was literally pushed in front of me by his mother, stamping his foot and crying, "I won't dance with her, Mummy! I won't! I won't! And you can't make me!"

In the spring, my mother took me to see the Royal Ballet dance

The Sleeping Beauty with Margot Fonteyn and Michael Soames. From the high vantage point of the very top seats of the opera house, we saw her lie on a giant bed in the center of the stage, waiting for the kiss that would awaken her from her hundred-year sleep. What is it about ballet that so enthralls young girls? Alas, Moira Hodgsonova was not to be (in those days ballet dancers still took Russian names). Whatever hopes my teachers held out for me were dashed later in 1955, when for two years that were crucial to my training, my father was posted to Vietnam, where ballet was not on anyone's mind at all.

WHEN I FIRST WALKED INTO Le Colonial, a Vietnamese restaurant on the Upper East Side of Manhattan, I felt right at home. It looked uncannily like the dining room of our house in Saigon, where we lived from 1955 to 1957. It had the same tobacco-yellow walls, the same green wooden shutters, the same ceiling fans, rattan chairs and large rectangular mirrors. Even the potted palms were similar, and the tiles on the floor, patterned in pastel green, pink and gray, were an exact copy of the ones in all the rooms of our house. It had been built in the 1920s, a vestige of French colonial architecture as seen in the films *The Lover* and *Indochine*. The only difference was that there were no trails of ants running across the restaurant's floors carrying broken leaves and crumbs. Nor were geckos making their guttural cries outside the shutters or lizards clinging motionless to the walls until their jaws opened up to snap a fly. (I once caught one and it ran away, leaving its tail in my hand.)

Our waitress, dressed in a black silk cheongsam, served us Vietnamese summer rolls made with rice paper wrapped around a stuffing made of shrimp and pork mixed with mushrooms and bean sprouts. We also had steamed ravioli filled with chicken, served in bamboo steamers, and skewers of grilled minced shrimp on sugar cane, a popular street snack called *chao tom*. You take the shrimp off the sugar cane, wrap it in leaves of lettuce with mint and cilantro, and dip it into a mixture of nuoc mam (fish sauce), vinegar and lime or a peanut sauce. When you're done you can chew on the sugar cane, which has a delicate, sweet taste.

Shrimp Mousse Wrapped on Sugar Cane
(Chao Tom) Le Colonial

1 pound medium shrimp	1 teaspoon salt
1¹/2 teaspoons sugar	Dash of black pepper
1 egg white	¹/2 cup vegetable oil
1 clove garlic, chopped fine	Twenty 3¹/2-inch sugar canes
¹/4 cup chopped scallions	(see note below)

Shell and devein the shrimp. Put them in a food processor and puree into a paste. Transfer to a mixing bowl.

Bring water to a boil in a steamer or preheat the oven to 300°F, depending on cooking method.

Stir in the sugar, egg white, garlic and scallions, and mix thoroughly. Season with salt and pepper. Rub some oil on your hands. (You may wish to wear latex gloves.) Pick up about 2 tablespoons of the shrimp paste. Mold it into an oval and start covering the sugar cane, but leave half of the cane exposed to use as a handle. Re-oil your hands as needed to keep the mousse from sticking. Place the sugar canes in a steamer for 15 minutes or set on a greased baking sheet and bake for about 15 minutes (until they turn pink). They are also very good grilled.

To prepare ahead of time, cook the wrapped sugar canes, let them come to room temperature and then refrigerate for a maximum of 24 hours. Five minutes before your guests arrive, put the sugar cane sticks on the grill and reheat, turning once. Serve with the peanut dipping sauce on the side.

NOTE: *Sugar canes packed in syrup are available in Asian markets. They should be drained and cut into lengthwise sticks with a sharp knife. Sugar cane swizzle sticks are also sold in the fruit departments of many large supermarkets and online.*

Peanut Sauce

1 tablespoon peanut butter
¹/₄ cup hoisin sauce
1¹/₂ teaspoons white vinegar
Roasted peanuts (optional)

Mix the peanut butter, hoisin sauce, vinegar and 2 tablespoons of
water in a bowl until smooth. Sprinkle peanuts on top of the sauce
if you wish and serve.

This was hardly the way I ate when I lived in Vietnam in the late
fifties.

My indelible first memory is of a lunch we had within days of
our arrival. My mother was trying out a cook (even the lowest-
ranking diplomatic household in Saigon would include a cook,
house servant, gardener and chauffeur, all paid the pittance that
constituted good wages by local standards). She'd asked the cook to
make a meal of her choice to display her best talents.

Our first house was on the road to the airport, so military vehicles and trucks kept up a continuous rumbling outside: the last of
the French were on their way home, and the Americans were coming in. A knot of beggars maintained a vigil at the gate, as they did
in front of every foreign house. We were never allowed to give them
anything, because if we did there would be "twice as many in the
morning." And indeed, on the occasions when I could bear it no
longer, and slipped them food or loose change, the word went round
in minutes and a small crowd of cripples, children with runny noses
and blind old men would gather outside with outstretched palms.

The family was seated on a muggy, hot day around a formal mahogany dinner table, its bareness punctuated by green place mats

(decorated with Vale of Aylesbury fox-hunting scenes), lacquer bowls of sticky rice and a few pieces of highly polished English silver that included a dish of melting butter. The Victorian candelabra, the little containers for cigarettes, the ashtrays, the salt and pepper shakers and napkin rings, engraved with initials, were solid reminders of England, which seemed far away indeed.

An old friend from Sweden was our guest for lunch. Wilfred Hawsley was now "our man in Haiphong." He was staying with us, having also just arrived in the Far East for the first time. He had retained his debonair Ronald Coleman mustache and wore crumpled white tropical suits and a Panama hat. I still kept his little chocolate beetle in a box.

Mr. Hawsley was one of my mother's coterie of admirers. He was a wine connoisseur and something of a health nut, claiming that one of his winter hobbies was skiing naked down the Swiss Alps. He came from a grand family where the Rolls was the "second car" and was used for carrying hay around the estate.

The previous day Mr. Hawsley and my parents had been to an elephant race in the presence of President Diem. As Diem drank rice wine from a long straw dipped in an immense earthenware jug, the elephants were made to bow down to him.

My father filmed the occasion. Two hundred elephants, with long white tusks, had been brought in from all over the country. You could see that they were sad old creatures. As the race began, the men who were perched on top, two to an elephant, began to yell and jump up and down, furiously jabbing the animals' flanks and necks with sticks, hatchets and spears. Many of the elephants kept sinking to their knees as if they were begging for mercy. By the time they had lumbered a couple of times around the track, they were as bloody as gored bulls. There was even a baby elephant in the race, with big, hairy ears, but it had only one rider.

"Well!" said Nanny after we watched the film. "Whatever will they think of next?"

Ah-Koo, our Chinese house servant, came through the door

from the kitchen bearing a tray. She wore black silk pajamas and flip-flops, and shuffled around the table, as she always did, with her legs bent as though she had just relieved herself in the seat of her pants. She wore her hair in a shiny black braid that extended almost to the backs of her knees, and when she smiled, she revealed two gold front teeth and an expanse of gum darkened by betel nut.

In front of each person she set down a green Wedgwood plate with a white rim. In the center, spare of garnish or decoration, lay what looked like an old misshapen tennis ball, wrinkled and brownish gray in color. It was much the same size as those wonderful spongy buns stuffed with sweet and slightly spicy minced pork that are served in metal steamers from a dim sum cart. But this thing looked as though it was waiting not to be eaten but dissected, like a specimen in a biology lab. Small white rubbery hoses poked through the skin, which was punctured with dark, sinister holes.

It was a whole pig's heart, boiled. At last, I had been served something I would not be made to spend the afternoon gagging over until my plate was cleaned of the last congealed scrap. I plunged my knife into it, lancing it like a boil so that it sent up a spurt of clear liquid. The heart split in half. Inside was a catacomb of crevices and caves.

My mother, ever the lady of the house, carefully spooned some rice onto her plate and picked up her knife and fork.

"Why Lyla, this is terribly recherché!" said Mr. Hawsley, taking out his glasses and polishing them. He looked around the dining room. It was so hot the overhead fan did little more than blow humid air over our heads, so that it felt as though we were dining underneath an engine. A lizard ran across the floor to the veranda, where the shutters had been closed against the midday sun.

"Is this a local delicacy?" Nanny persisted. Red-faced from the heat, she mopped her brow with a large white handkerchief she kept hidden somewhere in her ample bosom, pulling it out from time to time like a conjurer with a white rabbit.

"Can I have a boiled egg?" asked my sister. She was only five and still ate little else.

"I can eat anything—as long as I don't recognize what it was before it reached my plate and as long as it's well done," said Mr. Hawsley.

"Well, at least it's not brains," said my father. He had been unable to eat brains since the war.

"The other day I was served a dish called Pig Brain in Happy Sauce," said Mr. Hawsley. "It was accompanied by black wedges of preserved duck eggs that looked as though they had been through a nuclear war."

"Our neighbors eat monkey's brains," I said.

The people next door, a Frenchman married to a Vietnamese woman, kept animals in their garden tethered to posts by long chains. They included parrots, a couple of misanthropic Alsatians who barked day and night (my father used to bark back at them), a pig and several hysterical monkeys.

"They drill holes in the monkeys' heads while they're still alive and pick their brains out with chopsticks at the table," I added, hoping to impress Mr. Hawsley.

Ah-Koo shuffled off to the kitchen with the uneaten pigs' hearts. For pudding, we were served an entire tin of prized Bird's custard powder brought all the way from England. It was mixed with water instead of milk, in equal parts, and, like the pigs' hearts, boiled. When you put your spoon into it, it made greedy sucking sounds and held on to the spoon like quicksand.

After lunch my mother went into the kitchen to complain.

The cook was indignant. "Madame!" she said furiously, "C'est evident que vous n'aimez pas la cuisine française."

Ah-Koo brought in the coffee and Mr. Hawsley, bypassing the cigarettes in the silver holder by his plate, pulled out a yellow tin of Senior Service and drew one out, tapping it on the lid before he lit up. "A good cook, as cooks go," he said, quoting Saki. "And as cooks go, she went."

AH-KOO STAYED WITH US for the two years we lived in Vietnam. She spoke French with an extraordinary accent, using infinitives and a strong personal pronoun. *"Moi revenir à quatre heures,"* she would say as she disappeared into the back quarters for an hour off. Every morning she'd appear before breakfast in the doorway of my parents' bedroom with cups of tea and greet my father with *"Bong swa, M'sieu!"* It made no difference that he always replied *"Bon JOUR, Ah-Koo!"*

My mother she referred to as Malain. *"Bong swa, Malain!"*

The new cook, Yan, who was hired a couple of weeks later, was a success. She was Chinese but my mother taught her to make English food.

Americans are usually thought of as the ones who inflict their taste on the rest of the world. But we English, like dogs with fleas, also brought with us what we could not leave behind. And when our supplies ran out, more shipments came from England: not just Marmite and Bird's custard powder but also Bovril, Ribena, Keiller's thick-cut Dundee marmalade, lemon curd, Gentleman's Relish, Cadbury's chocolates, Bath Olivers, Digestive biscuits, Ovaltine and Christmas puddings from Fortnum & Mason (the latter soused with brandy and set aflame on a day when the temperature was inevitably somewhere in the nineties).

Yan made well-done roast leg of lamb, shepherd's pie with the leftovers, bubble and squeak (leftover mashed potatoes with cabbage), baked beans on toast and Queen's pudding. She made fresh lemonade every day, since Philippa and I were not allowed soft drinks. Her chocolate cake wasn't made from a mix but from a slab of dark chocolate melted over a double boiler and whipped by hand into a batter with eggs and flour. Sometimes she baked the cake just before teatime, and we ate it while it was still warm. She also made Marmite toast and brandy snaps, the latter a sort of caramel tuile folded into a tube and filled with whipped cream.

For the servants and her family, Yan made Chinese food. Their rooms were in the back of the house by the garage and the kitchens, where our meals were cooked in blackened pots over charcoal. The smell of charcoal drifted over the back quarters and its taste permeated everything, including the water, which was always boiled.

Our household consisted of the five of us plus four Chinese servants: Yan and her two small children, Ah-vwai and Ah-fong; Ah-Koo; Yune, the smooth-faced young chauffeur, with whom I used to trade 45s; and the gardener, who was known simply as Coolie.

Our house on Rue Legrand de la Liraye (or Phan-Thanh-Gian, as it is now called) was out of a cartoon by Charles Addams—three stories high, narrow and gabled, painted white, with a green roof and shutters. The ground floor was divided into four large rooms with a wide hallway and French doors that were kept open so that the air, such as it was, would circulate. But there was nothing to be done about the humidity. (Our books, many of which were paperbacks that my parents had leather bound for a pittance, were soon spotted with mildew.) There were four bedrooms upstairs, quite barely furnished, with tiled floors, and beds hung with mosquito nets. The third floor was the guest room, which had its own bathroom and balcony. "Monsieur en Haut" was the name Ah-Koo gave each visitor who stayed there, usually a man from the Foreign Office.

At night, the lights in the house would dim crazily and come on again for no discernible reason. Geckos and crickets kept up a steady chorus, like the engine of some old-fashioned airplane, punctuated by sinister animal noises and barking from the Alsatians next door. I washed from a huge Ali Baba urn and observed (as I had been instructed) that south of the equator water went down the drain the opposite way. Giant waterbugs climbed out of the drains, like workmen emerging from a manhole.

When we moved into the house, the garden was a flat wasteland without a blade of grass. Coolie, who was said to be a fugitive general from Chiang Kai-shek's army, sowed it with grass seed and, since the rainy season had just begun, we had a lawn within weeks. He lived in the garage, where he built himself a virtual house from the wooden packing cases that had brought the "heavy luggage." He had scars on his ankles that my mother told me, years later, were from leg irons.

My mother tried briefly to augment my father's meager income by teaching English to Vietnamese soldiers. But word soon came down from the Foreign Office that she was not allowed to work. Instead, with a view to improving Vietnamese-British relations under the shaky regime of President Diem, she was to entertain the wives of Vietnamese officials by inviting them at regular intervals to tea, along with some British and American embassy wives. The guest list even included, on at least one occasion, the notorious Madame Nhu (who was married to Diem's brother, chief of the secret police). These events would drag on with the inevitable *"Et combien d'enfants avez-vous, Madame?"* Polite conversation without the spur of liquor was not one of my mother's favorite recreations. She hated these teas and complained bitterly about them. So one afternoon I thought I'd liven things up with a practical joke.

When I was last in Sherborne, I had spent some of my pocket money on a nail I had bought at Chaffin's, a joke shop where I was a regular customer. The nail had been cut into two pieces and was joined in the middle by a U-shaped piece of wire. If you placed the wire over your finger or even the palm of your hand, from the front you could see only the top of the nail and the bottom, giving the illusion that the entire thing had been driven through.

So after my mother's guests had arrived and settled down to tea, I went into the kitchen and took a bottle of ketchup out of the refrigerator. Ah-Koo was horrified as she watched me place the nail over my thumb and cover it with ketchup. *"Toi méchante!"*

But I ignored her and, holding my bloody, impaled thumb out in front of me, I threw open the French doors of the living room and staggered in like Charles Laughton making his entrance as the Dauphin. The women looked up.

"Mummy! Mummy!" I cried.

My mother let out a scream and leaped to her feet. The blood had drained from her face, which had turned green, and she swayed as though about to faint.

"It's all right!" I yelled, terrified now at what I'd done, and pushed her away as I ripped the nail from my thumb.

No one laughed.

Ah-Koo, who had followed me into the drawing room, gave me a withering look. But a sudden downpour conveniently brought the incident to an abrupt finale. She closed the shutters against the rain and shuffled off with the trays. "*Moi revenir plus tard,* Malain."

༄

IN THE CLASS PICTURES that were taken at Le Couvent des Oiseaux I don't look like a troublemaker. I look like the teacher. I'm head and shoulders above the Vietnamese girls. I stand at the end of the row awkwardly, wearing a starched green striped sleeveless blouse and green skirt my mother had the dressmaker make for me, squinting at the sun, my arms folded primly behind my back. I have short blond hair and a pale face covered with freckles. I am only eleven, but compared with the others I look twenty.

I was used to dealing with new schools (I'd already been to six), as well as new people and new languages. Like any child, all I wanted was to fit in, and I made friends quickly. Now, however, for the first time in my life, disapproval met me every morning at 7 a.m. when I ran through the iron gates of Couvent des Oiseaux (which was known at home as "Wozzoh," thanks to Philippa, who attended its kindergarten). It was a Roman Catholic convent run by Belgian nuns, and most of the current pupils, now that the French had pulled out, were Vietnamese girls; boys were accepted only to the age of seven. I don't know what it was about me that provoked the nuns, so, for I surely can't have behaved as badly as they made out—at least not in the beginning. I didn't even have enough French to understand my first school report. I took it to the only other English-speaking girl there, a shy, intelligent, bespectacled American from Pasadena named Francie Moore, who became my best friend. If John Wayne had spoken French, it would have been with an accent like Francie's. She pronounced *Desirée,* a film we once saw with Marlon Brando as Napoleon, "Daisy Ray."

When she read my report she gasped. "You've got *pas d'étoile,*" she said solemnly, handing back the little pale blue book that contained the entries.

"What's *par day twal?*" I asked.

"No stars. That's really bad."

Each report consisted of a graph, with comments underneath. My graph line ran straight across the bottom, and for such things as *bonne tenue et ordre,* the answer was always the same, written in neat, spidery, purple handwriting: *insufficient.*

I was stunned.

The person responsible for this injustice was Mère Gertrude. She probably wasn't much more than forty, but to me she seemed as old as a witch from *Grimm's Fairy Tales.* Tall, stooped and mustachioed, crucifix clattering and beads perpetually running through her fingers as she sidled around the convent, keeping close to the wall, she had disliked me from the start because she'd been told I wasn't a Catholic.

But like anyone who is given a reputation, deserved or undeserved, I soon learned to live up to it.

I was *capable de tout.* And an object of curiosity for the other girls in my class. They were friendly but rather in awe of me, partly because of the strange way I looked—blond hair and freckles, tall as a grown-up—and partly because of the steady run of biweekly *"pas d'étoile"* reports I received. I missed my Swedish school, where I'd been a good student. At Couvent des Oiseaux I was shocked to find myself the object of unrelenting disapprobation. So in order to prove myself among my classmates, I embarked on a series of practical jokes. I made fake scars by squeezing my skin together, putting a piece of Scotch tape over the top and holding it under the hot water tap. When the wet tape was removed, the skin underneath remained stuck together. I squirted the ceiling with my water pistol and reported a leak. One day I turned my attention to Agnès, a pious shrimp of a French girl who made a big show of saying her prayers in a very loud voice to impress the nuns. Every fortnight on her report card she received a gold star.

I decided to make Agnès a valentine. I took a thick piece of paper and folded it in half. On the front I drew a big red bleeding heart like the ones on Catholic leaflets. Inside the fold I placed a metal ring I attached to the paper by rubber bands I threaded through two holes. Then I turned the ring around and around until the rubber bands were thoroughly tight and knotted. I put the card in an envelope.

On Valentine's Day we assembled for prayers first thing in the morning. When the nuns came in I silently passed Agnès the envelope. As I'd hoped, she was overcome by curiosity, and opened it in the middle of our Hail Marys. The ring, released by the rubber bands, flipped around like a motor out of control, and Agnès was too startled to stop it.

Within minutes Mère Gertrude had hauled me in front of the class and launched into a report on my sins. Finally, carried away by the heat of the moment, Mère Gertrude revealed to the class that I was a Protestant: a heretic.

After an earnest prayer session I was surrounded by excited girls pelting me with questions. One of them touched my arm cautiously. "Do all heretics have freckles?" she asked.

My mother marched in to the Mother Superior the following morning.

"I'm Irish, you know," she announced with cold dignity. "From the north. I sent my daughter here because I didn't want her to grow up an anti-Catholic. But now you're turning her into one."

The following week—and only that week—I received a gold star.

MR. HAWSLEY ARRIVED from Haiphong to be our Monsieur en Haut just in time for the celebrations for the Chinese New Year. Our household was very much involved in this holiday because the people who worked here were Chinese. In the days beforehand, the house was transformed, cleaned from top to bottom and decked with orange trees and red and gold banners symbolizing long life and good luck. On the day, a lion was to dance in front of the house and clear it of evil spirits.

I had my own special demon that had followed me from Sherborne and Sweden all the way to Saigon, where it lived underneath my bed. Each night I had to leap from the carpet onto the mattress without stepping on the floor, so the monster wouldn't catch me by the leg and pull me into a black hole below. A couple of times I brought down the mosquito net.

Even the rats behind the house, which were the size of cats and ran loose in and out of the garage, the servants' quarters and the kitchens, respected the New Year's cleanup. One of them, as though to enter into the spirit of things, sped down the garden path and out the front gate. Coolie, whose bearing was similar to that of a proper English butler, walked forward and politely shut the wrought-iron gate after it.

On the day, a small group of men, led by a lion in a lumbering dance, marched through the front gate. Joss sticks and images of Chinese deities in rice paper were burned. The noise was considerable enough to frighten away even the most recalcitrant of evil spirits: clashing cymbals, banging drums and exploding firecrackers that set off angry howling from the Alsatians next door, my father barking loudly in response.

The lion's head was red and gold, with flared nostrils, livid bulging eyes and ferocious teeth. Inside lurked a man whose job was to climb up a pole to the top balcony, which was in front of the guest room on the third floor. Philippa and I stood there holding out sticks tied with leaves of lettuce, and red and gold packets filled with paper money. Wearing silver medallions that read "good luck" in Chinese characters around our necks, we waited for him.

The climb, particularly under the heavy weight of the lion's head, was precarious. The pole wavered dangerously. At last, to much applause, the beast lowered its head and manipulated its mouth around the money, giving a hurried final pluck to the lettuce leaves. Our job done, Philippa and I ran downstairs. The lion also made its descent, and the man inside took off the head and placed it on the ground. Philippa, who was wearing a yellow pinafore and a big yellow bow in her hair, rushed forward and patted the head, as though it were a dog that had just done a good trick.

The house was now clear for the New Year. Or was it?

That evening, after the ceremony, Mr. Hawsley and my parents went out to attend a New Year's banquet. Philippa and I, meanwhile, were allowed to taste the traditional dishes the cook had made for her friends and family: pork dumplings, roast suckling pig with crackling (just as it was done in England!) and red-cooked carp. We were asleep by the time my parents returned after an equally abundant and delicious meal, during which much wine had been consumed. After a brandy nightcap, Monsieur en Haut repaired to his room, undressed and climbed into the large bed, which was covered with a mosquito net above which whirred a ceiling fan. He fell asleep within minutes. The next morning he came down to breakfast looking white and shaken. He seemed to have lost the power of speech.

It was not the dinner or the brandy. Mr. Hawsley had been awakened in the middle of the night feeling something sticky on his face. He turned on the light and discovered to his horror that he was covered in blood. He leaped up with a shriek. Blood was spattered all over the mosquito net and the walls. A bat had been caught in the fan.

We didn't know it at the time, said my mother later, but he was deathly afraid of bats.

THE VIETNAM I SAW was just an exotic background to the introspective life of a child around whom the world revolved. My father was often away when we were in Saigon, spending a great deal of time on mysterious field trips in the mountains. Upon his return we would be subjected to hours of 8 mm films of his visits to the Montagnard tribes in North Vietnam (human sacrifice had still been practiced there as recently as 1954). Junks with sails made of sacking and plaited straw, and dugouts and sampans poled by women in black journeyed along a scummy brown river against a background of bright blue hills. Bleary, red-eyed alligators snapped their jaws on the bank. Barefoot Katou men with bows and arrows, smoking hand-rolled cigars and dressed in loincloths, rakish red-embroidered black capes, rows of necklaces and shiny hoop earrings, lined up for the camera in villages of thatched huts. At every stop, my father was treated to elaborate ceremonies where he drank rice wine from bamboo straws dipped in clay jars. In one film a cow had been sacrificed and its head lay in front of one of the jars. Bare-breasted Montagnard women dressed in long black skirts, brass bracelets climbing up their arms, performed a line dance, a slow two-step, to a rapt audience of men, accompanied by music from bamboo pipes.

At odds with these idyllic scenes were the South Vietnamese officials, interlopers in white linen suits who handed out safety pins as gifts for the Katou, and soldiers carrying machine guns, clad in white undershirts and shorts, wearing cowboy hats made of camouflage material with rolled brims.

I knew that there were Viet Cong who came out of holes at night, terrorizing villagers and the Montagnards, and who by day posed as peasants, working in the fields. I knew that a war was going on in the jungles, the mountains and paddy fields and that the countryside had not been safe at night for decades, but I never had any sense of real danger. At this time, the Americans were replacing the French, coming into Vietnam in full force, increasing their presence by the day.

I began to spend most of my time with some American girls whom I found much more thrilling than anyone at Wozzoh. They had their own engraved visiting cards and were allowed to paint their toenails and wear vivid shades of lipstick, which they bought at the commissary. One afternoon my father came home to find me in red pedal pushers and matching toenails.

"You look like a child tart," he said. "And your room looks like a barracks."

He particularly objected to a photograph of Elizabeth Taylor I'd hung on the wall. "Her face always looks dirty," he said. "And so, at the moment, does yours."

My American friends were from army families and I developed something of a split personality now that I had entered into this sophisticated circle. In front of my parents I was careful to avoid the use of words such as *can't,* which I had been taught to pronounce "cahn't." I began to talk in a halting, foreign way, using *cannot* and *shall not* instead. But alone with my new friends I said "Aw heck!" and "See ya later alligator." I was passionate about everything American, most of all the movies. Even though the Americans had only been in Saigon a short time, they had already established their own schools (which were very bad, according to my mother, who would not let me leave Wozzoh). They also had a PX so that a day need not go by without access to Oreo cookies, Ritz and graham crackers, peanut butter, popcorn, root beer, Revlon makeup, 45s, movie magazines and Chesterfield cigarettes. They had a military movie theater known as the Alhambra, where I saw an average of three movies a week. I used to keep the ticket stubs from these films and stick them in my scrapbook with the name of the movie and the number of stars I awarded it written underneath.

I couldn't wait to be a teenager.

"We didn't have teenagers when I was growing up," said my father. "They're an entirely American invention."

One morning, with my American friend Reni, I watched a film crew shooting a scene for a movie called *The Quiet American,* directed by Joseph L. Mankiewicz. The novel by Graham Greene had been published in 1954, and was an indictment of Americans' involvement in Vietnam, depicting them as meddlers, ignorant of its history, customs and politics, who caused innocent people to get killed. The choice of Audie Murphy, a Texas cowboy actor, as the American (a New England Harvard boy in the book, full of intellectual idealism), was a piece of casting my father (along with everyone else) found preposterous. "All he can say is 'Yup!' Terrible fellow."

Terrible fellow or not, I hoped to get Murphy's autograph. But the square where we waited became white-hot by midday, and the actors were no more than shimmering figures in the distance. With our sweaty, unsigned autograph books in hand, we ducked into a clean, white snack bar called La Bodega. It had opened that very week on a corner near the Rue Catinat, Saigon's main shopping street. La Bodega sold only hot dogs—wrapped in paper napkins imprinted with its name—along with root beer, Coca-Cola and a fizzy Day-Glo orange drink, none of which were allowed in my house. The counter was manned by a young Vietnamese man in a paper hat, and each of the half dozen white Formica tables was set with two large squeeze bottles, one red and the other yellow-brown. Out-of-date Elvis Presley and Pat Boone records were played on the sound system.

The only sausages I'd had before were Wall's, which were made with pork and bread crumbs and fried in bacon fat that was kept in a can at the back of the stove. These hot dog sausages were different. They weren't browned, but boiled, and when you bit down the skin gave way with a slight pop. Underneath, the sausage meat was almost sweet and pleasantly bland, a taste echoed by the comforting softness of the roll. I ordered another and covered it with red and yellow squiggles. Even when it came to sausages, you couldn't beat the Americans.

IN OCTOBER 1957 we began a month-long journey from Vietnam back to England by air, ship and train. My mother was so ill just before we left that my father almost had to postpone the trip home.

"You've gone all yellow," I said one morning, looking at her as she lay upstairs in bed. She had indeed: a strange, luminous yellow. It was jaundice.

To give my mother more time to recover, we flew to Singapore instead of boarding the *Victoria* in Saigon. It was my first time in an airplane. When you were buckled into your seat the stewardesses handed out leaflets that looked like theater programs. Meet your Clipper Captain, with black-and-white photographs and short biographies of Pan Am captains around the world.

Apart from the marvelous meals we ate three times a day on the *Victoria*, there wasn't much to do on board the ship, which headed up to Colombo, Bombay and Karachi via the Suez Canal, continuing on to Naples, and finally docking in Genoa. There was the Seasick Sea Serpents Club, to which a small group of children formed allegiance (including Philippa, who was now seven). I befriended Belinda, a sexually precocious fifteen-year-old English girl who staked out available men. I had developed a crush on the Italian petty officer, who wore a white uniform and had an engagingly flirtatious manner with the ladies. But he was shorter than I was, barely five feet tall. When we docked at Aden, Belinda and I stood on deck and watched the petty officer go down the gangplank. He turned and waved to us when he reached the ground.

"Petit officer!" said Belinda. "Never mind. They're all the same size in bed."

I nodded sagely, wondering what she meant.

On deck, passengers whiled away the time with horse races, quoits, Ping-Pong, deck tennis, tombola (a form of raffle in which tickets were picked out of a revolving drum) and clay pigeon shooting.

How did I feel about leaving Vietnam? I was miserable. The girls at Wozzoh had made a book for me illustrated with their drawings and photographs, addressing me as "Chère Moira Dean," because they knew of my passion for James Dean. I kept looking at the book for months afterward and missing them.

I'd had no school since the end of the summer term, but my parents hoped I'd get into Sherborne School for Girls. So every day I sat in a deck chair and crammed for my Common Entrance exam.

When we reached the Suez Canal, all the passengers came up on deck to take a look. The ship took half a day to sail very slowly up the canal at around eight miles an hour. It was almost a year since the Suez Crisis, when "that bloody-minded oaf" Gamal Abdel Nasser had nationalized the canal and in response the British and French had bombed Egypt. Prime Minister Anthony Eden had resigned, and the canal had reopened to shipping in April. Now, six months later, it was littered with bits of wreckage and half-sunk ships. In the waters of Lake Timsah, where I had learned to swim, I could see the burned-out shell of a bombed oil tanker. But the beach in Ismailia, the children's paradise where I had played five years before, looked exactly the same, as if nothing had happened since then.

As we drew near to Italy, clouds began to thicken and the sky turned gray. Capri was shrouded in fog. We got off the boat at Naples in a downpour and trudged through the rain in Pompeii, which was all the more impressive for being virtually deserted and awash in water. From Genoa we took a train to London and another train from Waterloo to Sherborne, arriving at Penrhyn in November, after two and a half years away.

Everything was smaller. The house was cold and cramped. It rained, not in torrents as it had in Vietnam, but on and off all day, and you couldn't run outside in your bathing suit. And while I may have had a tapeworm in Saigon, at least we didn't have rationing. Rationing in Britain had ended officially in 1954, yet three years later, there were still shortages. Oranges were a luxury.

But once again I was among familiar things: Brueghel's *The Haymakers* still hung at the top of the stairs; van Gogh's *Wheatfield with Cypresses* was above the bed in my room, which itself looked out over a cornfield. Beyond it, across the green playing fields, loomed the sandstone classrooms and the clock tower of Sherborne School for Girls.

৻৻

JUST BEFORE CHRISTMAS, I learned I'd been accepted at the school. At the same time, my father was told his next post: political advisor to the British Army in Berlin. I was greatly relieved because Berlin was close enough that I could go there for all three school holidays, not just in the summer.

A few days after my acceptance, a lengthy document known as The Clothes List arrived in the mail. I already had most of the required clothes; they had been my mother's. In 1939, when she went up to Cambridge, Granny had packed them away in a trunk. Now, I was ready to inherit them. The style of the brown tweed "coat and skirt," the dress for "formal occasions," the green tweed cloak with its hood lined in silk house colors, and the shapeless green tunic known as a djibbah had remained unchanged since my mother's time.

The name *djibbah* was a legacy of British occupation of Arab lands. Egyptian Mohammedans wore djibbahs (or *jubahs*)—long, loose garments. Female Fabians wore djibbahs—and ropes of amber beads—when they accompanied George Bernard Shaw on his strolls around Hampstead. And English schoolgirls wore them too. In my mother's day at Sherborne they were worn with thick black stockings, white shirts and green ties striped with the house color. By the time I went there, black stockings were frowned upon because they were favored by beatniks and women who believed in "free love." They'd been replaced with long brown socks.

School shoes—brown lace-ups and brown loafers—were bought at Kitzerow's shoe shop on Cheap Street. At the back of Kitzerow's there was a brown machine the size of a small refrigerator. This congenial machine made a shoe-shopping expedition like a trip to a fun fair. Two steps led up to openings at the bottom into which customers placed their feet once they had been fitted with a new pair of shoes. At the top was a large funnel bordered with a strip of black rubber onto which the child, shop assistant and parent in turn could rest their faces, looking down through the hole. When a penny was inserted in the slot at the side, an eerie green light would go on inside the machine: an X-ray picture of the occupant's feet. The skeleton was surrounded by a pale and misty aura: the shoes.

I often went into Kitzerow's without any intention of buying shoes, but just for the pleasure of X-raying my feet. I especially liked to see what my toes looked like wriggling around in high heels my mother considered unsuitable. In fact, I seldom walked past Kitzerow's without going in for an X-ray. Unfortunately, I told my grandmother about it. She said nothing, but the next time I went to X-ray my feet, the machine had disappeared.

A pair of shoes with reasonably chunky high heels went into my trunk, to be worn on special occasions. As we finished packing, my mother seemed even more nervous than I was. Of course, she'd been only ten when she went to Sherborne School for Girls, brought over from Northern Ireland after living all her life on a farm with her mother's parents, whom she adored. And it can't have been easy having her firebrand mother on the staff either.

"Don't ever let anyone tell you that your school days are the best days of your life," she said. "It's a lie. They are not. Just remember that."

Dunholme, the house where I was to board, was a large red brick building dating from the 1920s; it had a slate roof and brown stucco covered the top two floors. It looked like a giant version of the semi-detached houses on the road from London to Heathrow Airport.

The Junior Sitting Room had that distinctive smell of wood and furniture polish that only exists in a school. Desks were backed onto each other and lined up along the walls under rows of small wooden lockers. In the center of the room were two long tables.

"Shall I put my stuff in one of those desks?" I asked a girl whose red hair was cut short like a boy's.

"Heavens no!" she replied. "Babies don't get desks. You don't get a desk until the Middle Fifth."

I was in Upper Fourth. A "baby." Two years to wait for a desk.

The three floors upstairs were divided into cubicles by wooden partitions along hallways paved with black linoleum. The "head of passage" was at one end, the "babies" at the other.

My cubicle was on the top floor facing the house garden. The narrow space was furnished with a chair, a chest of drawers and an iron-frame bed covered with a paisley cotton spread. Next to the bed was a marble washstand set with an enameled tin basin and a white china jug. Underneath, the cabinet where a chamber pot would have resided was empty. I used it to store my sweets: Cadbury's whole nut, Crunchie bars, Mars bars, Bounty, KitKat and Maltesers.

The next morning, at 6:50 a.m., we stripped our beds in silence. As we filled our white porcelain jugs with water in the bathroom, a prefect sauntered down the corridor and checked that each mattress had been stripped and flopped over the springs like a giant jam roll. We had to make the bed again from scratch for another inspection. On Friday, we moved the white cotton top sheet to the bottom and received a clean top sheet from the matron.

I spent my first few days bewildered, thinking all the girls in my form seemed so very young. I wished they were American. We were sent to bed at eight o'clock! I lay in the dark and, after finishing a Mars bar, cried myself to sleep, hardly the first new girl to do so.

Sherborne, like all British public schools, was run on a feudal system. As in the Foreign Office, hierarchy ruled the day. The head-mistress had Absolute Power. The teachers were the overlords who appointed the prefects and the heads of form, who punished offenses committed by the rest of the population and kept it under control. Offenders were summoned by two dreaded words: "You're wanted!"

I was "wanted" on my second day. I was wearing my mother's djibbah with a green striped cotton shirt and a pale-blue and green striped silk house tie. Yet only three months ago, in Saigon, I had been the "child tart" in pedal pushers and red lipstick. So that morning, I had been unable to resist putting on my gold plastic headband.

The weather was starkly different from the hot temperatures and humidity that I had become used to in Saigon. It was January; the classrooms were freezing. Long brown socks didn't keep my legs warm enough. So I solved the problem by putting on a pair of nylon stockings as well, worn in those days with a garter belt.

After lunch, before "silence," we were required to stand in a circle around the Junior Sitting Room and listen to "notices" read out by the head of house, Penny Allen. After notices, one of the "babies" came up to me.

"You're wanted," she said. I was thunderstruck.

She gave me a look of schadenfreude. "By Penny Allen!"

Minutes later, I knocked on Penny's door. She made it painfully clear. Gold headbands were "common." Stockings were most emphatically not allowed with the djibbah. This was the height of vulgarity.

"Kneel," she directed.

I knelt down in front of her.

"The hem of your skirt should not brush the floor when you kneel down. You must take your djibbah up."

The next day, with a nice wavy hem, I joined the dozens of others with mottled purple knees covered with red goose pimples. But there was worse to come.

In the evenings after "games"—hockey and lacrosse on muddy fields in a light drizzle—we were allowed to change into our own clothes for dinner. My first night I put on a blue wool dress that was a hand-me-down from my mother. A friend of hers had said it made me "sparkle." I wore it with stockings and beige shoes that had the faintest suggestion of a high heel.

The girls were appalled. Most of them wore Fair Isle sweaters, kilts and, of course, long brown socks. The kilts were a family tartan.

Like my mother, who said she always felt wrong, I felt very wrong indeed. Now I wasn't being stared at because of my freckles. I was stared at because of my peculiar clothes.

I was baffled by the rules. Our mail was scrutinized. Magazines were "held for the holidays." Envelopes with a Sherborne postmark were suspect and subject to confiscation. Their authors might be pupils at the boys' school. We were forbidden, upon pain of expulsion, to talk to boys.

No boys! But there were five hundred of them just across the games field!

The headmistress, Diana Reader Harris, had set forth her creed. The years between twelve and eighteen were the time, as she put it, for a "normal withdrawal from the opposite sex."

At boys' boarding schools, it was customary for older boys to develop crushes on younger ones (and often crawl into their beds after lights out). At girls' schools it was the other way around. I had been at school for only a couple of weeks when I was asked who my "pash" was. A "pash" was an older girl. You did not crawl into bed with her. You worshipped her from afar and became her willing slave. You left presents in her cubicle, cleaned her shoes while she was out on the games field, put flowers on her dressing table and turned down her bed each night.

I chose a prefect whose bulbous blue eyes were framed with long curly lashes that made her look like a cartoon fish. The night of her birthday I placed the chocolate beetle Mr. Hawsley had given to me in Sweden on her pillow. It was a treasured possession and I'd carried it about with me for two years. Underneath, it was white with age.

It never occurred to me that she would eat it.

Next to my cubicle was a room shared by three girls, Cox, Liz and Wonky. Liz, an American who lived in Geneva, became my best friend. She was tiny, with an angelic face that belied the fact that she was an even worse troublemaker than I was. Together we established the Cordon Bleu Supper Club. Loose floorboards provided a convenient storage place for midnight feasts. The menus for our Cordon Bleu suppers included canned peaches and pineapple, chocolate spread, puffed wheat, Digestive biscuits, canned cold soup and Farex, a baby food cereal of which I was extremely fond, mixed with milk. We also tried, unsuccessfully, to get drunk on hard cider, and we took snuff.

These suppers were accompanied by turns on the ouija board. We created our own board on the floor, using a waterglass that was placed upside down inside a circle of paper squares inscribed with the letters of the alphabet. We all put a finger on the glass, pressed down tightly and closed our eyes. Someone asked it a question. The glass seemed to glide over the floorboards as if by magic, speeding up faster and faster to deliver its messages. We became addicted to the ouija board, playing it in the afternoon in the attic after "games" and again at night by flashlight.

The room was directly above Miss Downing's, and one night the persistent grating of the glass on the floorboards above brought her upstairs to investigate. She crept along the passage without a sound and suddenly threw open the door, switching on the light at the same time. Our punishment was detention on two successive Saturday afternoons, when we were made to write out words from the *St. Matthew Passion*. My father wrote me an admonishing letter that began uncharacteristically by quoting the Bible: "It is hard for you to kick against the pricks."

Miss Downing had a black-and-white television set that we were allowed to watch in her drawing room when there was a program deemed "educational." Richard Dimbleby's *Panorama* on Tuesday nights passed muster because it was about current affairs. The other program concerned a subject second only to the Royal Family in popularity in Britain: real-life surgery, filmed in an operating theater.

I watched just one of these medical programs. After dinner, Miss Downing and twenty of the forty girls in the house sat spellbound as the camera panned from surgeon's mask to patient's groin. We groaned aloud as the knife sliced through the skin as though it were a piece of pie. The triumphant removal of the appendix underneath, which was pulled out and held aloft like a large piece of gristle, earned a round of applause.

After lights out that night, I got out of bed and emptied my water jug into the basin in loud spurts, pretending at the same time to vomit. My retching combined with the sudden, revoltingly realistic gushes into the basin provoked more groans, this time from the surrounding cubicles. I never had to watch an operation again.

MY GRANDPARENTS made school life bearable. On weekends I was allowed to take friends out to lunch or tea at Penrhyn. When we arrived, the smell of cooking would greet us at the front door. My grandmother would be in the kitchen, putting together another enormous meal. She had a passion for gadgets, and at this time, her kitchen was ruled by the pressure cooker. She had three. One for ham and stews, one for potatoes and one for other vegetables. The potatoes that she steamed in the pressure cooker were the size of tennis balls. Dug up in the garden by Ganga, they were light and floury and slathered with butter and more butter.

"Have another!" Ganga would insist. He scared the daylights out of my friends.

Ladling out more potatoes and ignoring protests, he wouldn't take no for an answer. "They're 90 percent water! You girls are big enough and ugly enough to have one or two more!"

Of course we were. And big enough and ugly enough for more butter too, since ours at school, eked out for the week, was usually rancid by the time Saturday came around. You stored it in your personal dish, kept in a cupboard in the dining room.

Of course, Ganga made everyone Fletcherize their food.

My grandmother also scared the daylights out of my friends. And she terrified the sixth formers to whom she taught science. "They don't know how to think for themselves. Bah!"

But even the dimmest student couldn't fail to be moved by her passion for science. Over boiled potatoes and "a good stew," she'd launch into what she thought was a highly simplified explanation of refractions of light, of magnetic and electric fields, of how Rutherford split the atom, of her meetings with scientists at the Royal Institution in London. How, when she was just seven years old in 1898, Marconi put up the radio tower in Ballycastle and beamed his signals to Rathlin Island. And how ten years later, at the age of seventeen, she'd made her own wireless set and heard Beethoven's Fifth for the first time. I'd listen to her, confused and enthralled. She always seemed to be at the forefront of the latest invention. (In 1969, when she was seventy-eight, not to be left behind, she took a course in computers.)

She may have been tough on her students, but when it came to me, despite the fact that I was hopeless at science and math, she was all-forgiving. I wasn't even any use at biology (the science for those who hadn't the brains for physics). But cooking, even though my grandmother called it a science, I could understand. I liked the mechanical acts of cutting and chopping, the frying and the mashing and the instant gratification when you produced something that people liked.

She taught me how to make potato pancakes, colcannon (potatoes mashed with cabbage), champ (potatoes with scallions) and boxty (potatoes with butter and flour). Potato bread was made from hot mashed potatoes and flour, kneaded and rolled out and browned on a griddle. It was nice baked with thin slices of apple on top, sprinkled with a little sugar. For tea, she made soda bread, a spongy, crisscrossed loaf with a floury brown crust.

Potato croquettes were made with leftover mashed, rolled in beaten egg and bread crumbs and deep-fried. Leftover cabbage was cooked in a frying pan with bacon and leftover mashed for "bubble and squeak." And after a "good stew" or a boiled ham with parsley sauce, there would always be a pudding.

Granny's apple pies were made with the delicious wormy apples from the garden. Sometimes she added blackberries my friends and I had picked along the hedgerows of Horsecastles' Lane, arriving at

Penrhyn with scratched and stained fingers, our berries wrapped in a handkerchief. In the spring, she used rhubarb from the garden to make a pie served with vanilla custard. Come summer, she made gooseberry fool with topped-and-tailed berries, stewed and sieved, and mixed with whipped cream. Best of all was summer pudding, a ruby-red molded dome made with slices of bread soaked in the juices of red currants, blackberries and raspberries and served with thick, yellow Devonshire cream.

Summer Pudding

12 ounces raspberries, plus more for garnish
6 ounces red currants (if not available, use more raspberries)
6 tablespoons sugar, plus more to taste
8 ounces blackberries and/or black currants, plus more for garnish
1 loaf white bread (homemade-style sandwich loaf, not packaged sliced bread)
Mint sprigs (optional)

Make the pudding the day before serving.

Place the raspberries and red currants in a stainless steel saucepan and add 3 tablespoons sugar. Bring to a boil, taste for sweetness and add more sugar if necessary. Cook for 3 to 4 minutes, or until the berries begin to burst and yield their juice.

In a separate saucepan, cook the blackberries or black currants with 3 tablespoons sugar, bringing the mixture briefly to a boil. Taste for sweetness and if necessary add more sugar.

Cut the bread in thick slices and remove the crusts. Cut one piece of bread in a circle, using an inverted cup as a template. Place it at the bottom of a 5- or 6-cup pudding mold. Line the sides with slices of bread, cutting some pieces in half so you leave no gaps for fruit to run out. Using about half of the fruit for each layer, put in a layer of the raspberry mixture, then a layer of the black currant mixture. Repeat the two layers, reserving half a cup of juice. Fill the bowl almost to the rim.

Cover the top with more bread and press it down so that it absorbs the juices. Put a saucer or small plate on top that just fits inside the bowl. Cover with weights such as a can of soup or another heavy object that fits tightly into the space between the refrigerator rack and the top of the saucer. Refrigerate overnight.

On the day of serving, remove the weights and use a palette knife to loosen the bread around the edges of the bowl. Put a plate on top and, holding it in place, turn the pudding upside down. The pudding should have turned a deep ruby red. If there are any light patches, pour the reserved juice over them.

Decorate with fresh berries or a sprig of mint if you like and serve with Devonshire cream, whipped cream or crème fraîche.

MAKES 6 SERVINGS

I LOVED COOKING with my grandmother, but I loathed cooking at school. It was, however, a required course. Under Miss Downing's supervision, the girls made inedible toad in the hole; the sausages were burned to a crisp and the batter was as dry as an old tennis shoe. When Miss Downing left the room, we hurled pancakes around like Frisbees. Our cheese straws weren't feathery; they snapped like dry twigs. Our jam tarts were misshapen and full of holes through which the jam seeped and burned on the tin pan underneath, where it stuck forever. Only a caveman would have appreciated the bits of raw, grisly meat that floated in our watery stews.

One day, Miss Downing ran out of patience.

"In future, you're going to have to take everything you've made back to the house for lunch. What you don't eat yourself, you must serve to the others, and they will have to eat it too."

Game, set and match to Miss Downing.

But my nemesis at school was not Miss Downing or even Penny Allen (who soon moved on). It was the headmistress, Diana Reader Harris. She was a bully, a hypocrite and a ruthless manipulator. My grandmother disliked her (though of course she could never admit it while I was still at school). My parents loathed her every bit as much as I did and said so.

DRH, as she was nicknamed by the girls, had great charm. She punctuated her sentences with smiles to draw you in, and frequently said, "Bless you!" She referred to us as "gels," pronounced with a hard *g*. *Surely* was pronounced "Shirley," as in "Shirley you can sing more in tune. If not, then in future don't attempt the descant, bless you!"

The phony charm worked better on fathers than on mothers. The fathers who fell for it were probably unaware that no man, apart from Jesus, had ever been known to elicit a twinge of desire from DRH. My mother said she was frigid. Power was her main pleasure, and with four hundred girls under her command, she enjoyed it to the fullest.

From the neck up DRH was a beautiful woman. She had a face like the actress Eleonora Duse, with a strong, straight nose, high, sculpted cheekbones and flawless ivory skin. She wore her mass of thick black hair, which was lightly streaked with gray, piled on top of her head in a loose chignon. Her dark green eyes were pools of compassion and sincerity. From the neck down, misfortune had struck. She was tall and narrow but her bosom stood out like a shelf, and from the back, she looked like the rear end of a cow, with knotty hips and spindly legs. She dressed extremely well, however, in timeless classics: well-cut silk dresses, Harris tweeds of sunny heather mixtures and pastel cashmere twinsets with a row of good pearls.

Her only idiosyncrasy was her disapproval of seamless stockings. Hers were silky textured with dark seams, and in another context they might have sent a different message. During the war women used to paint lines on the backs of their bare legs when they couldn't get silk or nylon. I longed to ask her if she had ever done that too, just to see the look on her face.

She had a lightbulb outside her office, which was at the foot of the stairs in the front hall of the main school building. When the red light was on, it meant she was inside. It was like seeing the flag over Buckingham Palace and knowing the Queen was at home. Or the Wicked Witch in her castle. For it was a familiar sight as you passed by to see some child quaking by the door, waiting for the light to turn from red to green, which would give her permission to enter.

Some time later, DRH's latest victim would emerge from the office, a handkerchief clutched damply to her bosom, its corner not boasting her own name woven by Cash's haberdashery in embroidered letters but the initials, white on white, DRH.

DRH knew what worked.

My hatred for her crystallized within weeks of my first year, when I became aware of the cold steel behind the phony charm. I don't know how our particular war got started, because at first I wanted desperately to please her. So I was surprised when early on I began to see through her, and I realized eventually that she hated me too, beyond normal bounds. I'm sure she disliked my outspoken grandmother, and that had a great deal to do with it. Soon the battleground was drawn, and our positions became so firmly entrenched that there was no going back. We remained deadlocked for the next six years. Moreover, I'd learned at Wozzoh that once you're given a bad reputation, you might as well live up to it.

But for all the problems I'd had with being "wrong" when I first came to the school, I'd made many friends. Not for nothing was I the child of a diplomat. And anyway, I liked people. My lack of team spirit did not prevent me from being elected to positions that were not under the control of DRH, and I was, at various times, head of half a dozen school societies. Meanwhile, I pored over books in order to glean quotations with which to goad her in scripture class. I would sit at the back with my hand raised politely until she was forced to acknowledge me.

"Yes, Moira, my dear, bless you!"

"What do you think George Moore means when he refers to Jesus Christ as the 'pale Socialist of Galilee'?"

Miss Reader Harris was a staunch supporter of the Conservative Party.

"Where do you think Jesus would stand politically today? Do you think we would worship him if he had been black?"

I would infuriate her with quotes from Bertrand Russell. "If the Bible says we are not to work on Saturdays, then why do Christians take this to mean we can't play on Sundays?"

There would be titters in the classroom, and Miss Reader Harris would redden at the neck.

"That is all so interesting, Moira, my dear, bless you!" Charming smile. "But *shirley* you don't want to take up the *gels'* valuable time? So do feel free to drop down to my study after the lesson and we can talk about it further."

Of course I never went. I plotted the next round.

One afternoon in my second year at school I was in the school sanitarium with the flu when suddenly, DRH appeared at the foot of my bed. "Bless you!"

I was listening to *Worker's Playtime* on the radio, which had large, old-fashioned earphones on wires attached to the head of the bed frame. I wanted to shout "Go away!" but said nothing. Sometimes she made visits to the San, sort of like the Queen doing her rounds.

She sat down on the bed and, horror of horrors, took hold of my hand.

"I'm very sorry to have to tell you that your grandfather died last night. Bless you, my dear!"

Go away. How dare you be the one to give me this news.

But I said nothing at all.

She remained holding my hand. I wasn't going to cry in front of her. I just lay there in silence until at last she blessed me again and left me to cry by myself, which I did for a long time without the use of a white handkerchief embroidered with the initials DRH.

Nevertheless, she dealt the first serious blow at the end of the Christmas term. Because of my curly red-blond hair, and because I was so tall, everyone assumed that I was the natural choice for the coveted role of Angel Gabriel in the Christmas pageant. I would get to wear a halo and wings.

When the day came for us to try out for the roles in the presence of the headmistress, I didn't feel well. An hour before we were due on stage, I developed the worst headache I had ever experienced, what I imagined a migraine must feel like times a hundred. I also seemed to have lost the hearing in my right ear. But I was determined not to miss the tryout.

I climbed up on the stage and looked angelic for what seemed, fittingly, an eternity. The pain in my head was so intense that it was all I could do not to scream. At last, when all the other parts had been filled, DRH asked me to stand down.

"I'm so sorry, Moira, my dear, but it's been worrying me all afternoon," she said, smiling. "Bless you! You look too feminine for the Angel Gabriel."

Upon my return to the house, Miss Downing noticed my chalk-white face and sent me immediately to the school sanitarium. An hour later I was taken by ambulance to a hospital in Weymouth, where I was diagnosed as having meningitis, a mastoid and a blood clot on the brain. They thought the meningitis might have been caused by the freezing rooms in which we slept and worked.

I nearly died. I went deaf in one ear. My mother came over from Berlin and sat every day at the foot of my bed where she knitted me a rust-colored sweater, her tears dripping on the wool as she worked. The operation removed part of the bone behind my ear and my hearing came back. The penicillin injections I had every day in my legs for two weeks saved my life.

My parents were advised by the doctors that I should take the next term off and stay with them in Berlin. My mother would take me home with her. I was thrilled. I was even more thrilled when my mother used my illness as an excuse for me never to have to play cricket again, in case I got hit on the head by a flying ball.

Next time I was in scripture class I was able to come up with some annoying questions on the sex of angels. And when Miss Cole, the drama teacher, offered me the role of Archbishop of Canterbury in the school production of *Richard of Bordeaux,* Miss Reader Harris never said anything about my being too feminine for it.

WHENEVER MY MOTHER WAS UPSET, she developed a stomachache. She had one now, as we sat over a lunch of sausages and chips with my father in the Naafi canteen in Hanover. He had just met us on the train from London. To get to Berlin, we had to drive through Communist East Germany, and the prospect was making her nervous. The Russians had been "bloody-minded" on my father's journey out, and had made him wait at the border for over an hour.

The Autobahn from Helmstedt, a stretch of road 110 miles long built by Hitler for his tanks, was the only way for the Allies to get to Berlin by car. Access to it was tightly controlled by the Russian and East German governments. At this time, the situation was extremely tense. Berlin was at the center of the Cold War.

There were two checkpoints at each end of the Autobahn. First we went to the British part of the Allied checkpoint, where the welcome was cordial, then to the Russian checkpoint, where it was not.

The Russian checkpoint was a wooden shack with a small shuttered window. Up came the shutter with a bang, and out came a hand for your papers. My father, who was now working as an advisor to the British military government in Berlin, handed our passports and identity cards to a stony-faced Russian guard who gave him a sheaf of documents in return. (In Berlin at all times we had to carry an orange identity card, written in four languages, stamped with a Union Jack.) The shutter was slammed down.

In a waiting room set with wooden chairs and hung with pictures of Marx and Lenin, my father looked over the rules for travel on the Autobahn. Do not take photographs, have picnics, leave the Autobahn for any reason, stop or pick anyone up. Have a full tank of gas, windshield wipers in order, everything checked on the car and ready to go. Our car was not in good shape. It had broken down twice over the past month in Berlin. The engine had boiled over when my father was driving to his office.

I shared my mother's nervousness. I had heard the lurid stories of atrocities committed by the Russian soldiers when they entered Berlin in 1945. They had raped every woman they could lay their hands on and killed unarmed, starving civilians, throwing the bodies in the Havel and looting their houses. The checkpoint soldiers certainly looked capable of anything, with their blank, sullen faces, their hammer-and-sickle badges and their jackboots. The East German soldiers, who had dark green uniforms, wore jackboots too, and were, of course, not recognized by the Allies. We had no obligation to show them our passports.

There was widespread harassment of travelers on the Autobahn by both Russian and East German soldiers. My parents had been warned to watch out for traps. Some Westerners traveling on the Autobahn had seen an old woman standing by the wayside, shrieking and waving a stick in the air. They took pity on her and stopped to pick her up. When she was safely in the car she removed her hood and the occupants found themselves confronted by a Russian soldier.

At last, in the checkpoint where we waited, up went the shutter again with a bang. Our documents, presumably photographed, were handed back, and the shutter was slammed down once more.

A Russian soldier escorted us to our car. But before we got in, my mother and I posed for a picture in front of a sign that said in English, "Do *Not* Cross the Autobahn." Above it was a skull and crossbones. We weren't smiling.

"Let's hope the engine doesn't boil over," my father said as we set off.

There was usually little traffic but the road was in bad shape, riddled with potholes, which made driving difficult. Not much to see either: it was flat, with beet fields in the distance. There was a speed limit, and you weren't meant to reach the other side in less than two hours. If you did, questions were asked and there would be further delays. If you hadn't reached it within four hours, patrol cars were sent out to look for you. There were often soldiers keeping a lookout from behind the hedges and trees along the road.

I kept my eyes peeled for soldiers in disguise and prayed that we wouldn't have a breakdown.

When we reached the checkpoints at the Berlin end, we had to go through the same tedious routine all over again, but this time the Russians were, as my father put it, "very civil."

I made several of these trips during the years my parents were in Germany, and they always gave my mother a stomachache.

When we first arrived in Berlin in 1958, about three-quarters of the rubble from the terrible bombing of the last days of the war had been cleared and disposed of by *Trümmerfrauen* ("rubble women") who picked up the bricks. It was used for making concrete and artificial hills where trees and shrubs were planted. The biggest hill, 120 meters high, was called Teufelsberg (Devil's Mountain) and was in the Grunewald where we lived. The Americans had put a radar tower on top.

The Kurfürstendamm, dominated by the ruins of the Kaiser Wilhelm Gedächtniskirche (Memorial Church), was the center of West Berlin, with its restaurants, cafés and the famous department store KaDeWe (Kaufhaus des Westerns). The ruined Gedächtniskirche has never been rebuilt, but left as a reminder of the horrors of war. My father said he suspected it was left in ruins more to show people what horrors the Allies had perpetrated. But then he had reasons for being cynical. He'd seen what the Gestapo had done in Norway.

And he'd seen many other horrors, not to be talked about, when he was "mopping up" in Schleswig-Holstein.

The British sector included the Olympic Stadium, built by Albert Speer for the 1936 Olympic Games, the Charlottenburg Palace and the Tiergarten, a park where nearly all the trees had been cut down for firewood in the winter of 1945–1946. The Soviets had built a huge war memorial here in November 1945, using the marble from Hitler's Chancellery, flanked by the first two tanks that arrived in Berlin. It ended up in the Western sector of Berlin, where it was guarded by goose-stepping Russian soldiers.

The eastern part of the city was sinister and frightening. It smelled of brown coal, which was used to heat the houses. In my memory it remains like those murky black-and-white photographs of ruined cities at the end of the war, and it was dominated by gray, desolate spaces and pockmarked walls.

The Reichstag, just on our side of the Brandenburg Gate, was still in ruins. On the other side of the Gate, further down, Marx-Engels-Platz was a wide, flat nothingness. On Wilhelmstrasse, the ruins of Hitler's Chancellery, a stone colossus with giant pillars built by Albert Speer in 1938, had been demolished. On the left-hand side of the road was Hitler's bunker: a nondescript mound, sprouting threadbare grass, in the middle of a chilly wasteland. A few Soviet-built apartment blocks had recently been erected nearby for party officials.

I had read with grim fascination about the last days in the bunker, the suicide of Hitler and Eva Braun, and how Joseph Goebbels's wife had killed her six children with cyanide pills.

No chance to look inside the bunker now. The Russians had tried and failed to blow up the concrete roof, so they had filled the bunker with water.

On Unter den Linden, the wide avenue that led to the Brandenburg Gate, part of the famous Hotel Adlon that had not been bombed to bits was still functioning. On the right, a vast Stalinist wedding cake, the Soviet Embassy, had been put up just after the war.

The Russians had rebuilt the Deutsche Staatsoper, a magnificent neoclassical building, in 1955. This had become a showcase for the East, with first-rate operas and ballets. Tickets cost only around a dollar (the value of the Deutsche mark in the East to the Western mark was four to one).

We went there one night in March 1959, just a few months after Khrushchev had issued an ultimatum for the Western powers saying they must evacuate Berlin or face "expulsion." With these threats of war hanging in the air, my parents took me to the opera house to see *Gayane,* a folk ballet with music by Khachaturian.

The British military were required to wear uniforms when they visited the East, and that night we were accompanied by officers of the Royal Scots and King's Own Scottish Borderers in kilts, their white jackets decked with medals. These bright dress uniforms drew stares, and I felt patriotic and proud to be associated with them. There was champagne from the Crimea at intermission.

The dancers in the ballet wore elaborate folk costumes. The women had long braids, Russian peasant headdresses and embroidered tunics; men decked out in Cossack boots and black jackets performed the sabre dance in a blaze of glory. I was moved to tears by the heroine, who wore a simple white dress and had the most beautiful arched feet in shiny white toe shoes that stabbed the floor like curved knife blades.

That night, while others in Berlin were lying awake worrying about the chances of a nuclear war with Russia, I lay awake dreaming about toe shoes and wondering how I could ever persuade my mother to buy me a pair.

❧

THE GRUNEWALD IS A FORMER FOREST that was once the Kaiser's hunting preserve. It was and still is the most luxurious residential part of town, inhabited by rich industrialists and businessmen, politicians, artists and academics. Many of its turn-of-the-century villas had been reduced to rubble by Allied bombing on February 3, 1945, but it didn't suffer anything like the damage to the rest of the city. When the Americans arrived, however, they took over 150 houses there, displacing over a thousand people and evicting the owners without compensation.

Our house, which was on Griegstrasse, had been requisitioned by the British Army. Its history was mysterious. The owner was said to have built the house after he had made a fortune from aphrodisiacs. I remember wondering what aphrodisiacs were exactly and why you could make a fortune from them. Whatever the circumstances, our house had been built by someone who had suddenly come into a lot of money and didn't know what to do with it.

It was not a turn-of-the-century villa, but modern, dating from the 1920s and influenced by Bauhaus architecture. The building was a long, gray, L-shaped structure two stories high, with a square chimney at either end and a shallow slate roof. Large rectangular windows were framed with false shutters made of decorative iron grilles crisscrossed like latticework. There was an imposing double front door, covered by similar iron bars over a background of dark green wood.

The house had been designed for a rich playboy. It had a vast beige and white drawing room; the master bedroom upstairs had a king-size bed under a canopy and the bathroom had mirrors on all four walls. The other bedrooms seemed like afterthoughts.

The army made a careful list of everything in our house, taking inventory down to the last knife and fork. Members of the catering corps came by periodically to check up. The things they thought of no interest were listed as "keepable objects," meaning my parents could take them if they liked.

One of the keepable objects was a two-foot-high wooden statue of the Virgin Mary and infant Jesus, which stood in a niche on the front stairs. It dated from the fifteenth century and was attributed to a pupil of Dürer.

The drawing room was the size of the entire ground floor of Penrhyn, with a grand piano and a glass-enclosed "winter garden," complete with trees and flower beds. The piano was a scene of bitter struggles with my teacher, an elderly German who had bad breath and wore crumpled gray suits. To encourage me, he told me that I had a piano player's fingers. But our lessons echoed with his cries of "*Ach! Gott im Himmel!* Do not hit the piano! It is your friend!"

The armchairs and sofa were covered with white slipcovers, the floor with Persian carpets; glass sconces shaped like urns hung on the walls, along with a round, built-in clock that had silver Roman numerals. And joy of joys, not only was there one of these clocks in every room, there was a built-in radio too, which picked up RIAS (Radio in the American Sector) so we could hear the Hit Parade on Friday and listen to Groucho Marx in *You Bet Your Life*.

The dining room had a recessed ceiling shaped like a dome and was intended for intimate dinners; no more than ten could fit at the round mahogany table, even when its extra leaves had been put in. For dinner parties a riot of candlelight was reflected in the mirrored walls, where two silver candelabra extended three long branches that looked like six. The table was set with my mother's Victorian silver. Light gleamed off the silver serving dishes and trays, the silver jugs and coffee pots; it danced on the silver cigarette containers and boxes that were arranged on the sideboard against the mirror.

The round table was tailor-made for the Elephant's Foot, the giant flaky pastry vol-au-vent that my mother had created in Sweden. It dominated the center of the table like a medieval castle on a plain. As its pastry ramparts were gradually demolished by serving spoons and forks, the walls caved in and the creamed kidneys and mushrooms ran amok, until the whole structure began to look unnervingly like the ruins we saw every day in Berlin.

Both dining and drawing rooms had French doors that opened

onto an L-shaped flagstone terrace where a stone pool built in the shape of a cross spouted arcs of water four and five feet high into the air. If you flipped a switch in the wall, the water was illuminated from underneath by colored lights. On warm nights my father would put on some music and pour a round of drinks; then we'd sit outside on white wooden rocking chairs under the vine-covered trellis, watching the sprays of water as they turned from pink to blue, green, yellow, orange and red.

Steps led down from the terrace onto a wide expanse of lawn, flanked by flower beds and clipped hedges, that came to a sudden end in a copse of silver birch and fir trees. One winter my father placed a single plastic daffodil in the snow under one of the trees. It was visible from the house and guests marveled at the freak of nature.

In their inventory the army corps had noted the fountain lights, but ignored the Etruscan mural on the other side of the terrace. It was a copy, of course, twenty feet long and eight feet high, exquisitely painted on hard stucco and sheltered from the elements under a roof. Two hunters on horseback brandishing spears chased a prancing tiger, aided by a man on foot with a bow and arrow.

On the other side of the mural was the gardener's flat. It was used as a guesthouse. One day my mother cleared it up for visitors. There was a Chinese lacquered cabinet brought back from Vietnam on the dresser, and after dusting it, she looked into one of its eight little drawers. It was full of cigarette butts. So were the rest. The culprit was Philippa. When she came back from school, she'd take a cigarette from one of the silver holders that were set out on the sideboard in the dining room and repair to the gardener's flat for a relaxing afternoon smoke.

Because we had an indoor "winter garden," Philippa and I were allowed pets for the first time. We had two small tortoises: Terry and Freddy. They didn't make a noise, and they didn't smell like dogs. They didn't scratch the furniture or shed fur all over the place. They didn't jump up and slobber all over you when you arrived home. They sat silently in the flower bed and ate pieces of lettuce, withdrawing into their shells whenever anyone came close. From December to March they hibernated. The first time this happened, I thought they were dead.

Hannah, who came from East Berlin every day to clean, felt that the tortoises were a waste of time. *"Sie sind zu nichts gut,"* she would say, wiping the leaves of the trees in the winter garden with a duster and staring down at the two immobile creatures whose heads were firmly inside their shells.

She had a point. They didn't do much of anything. I wouldn't have been surprised if she had polished them as well as the silver.

Hannah was in her fifties, gray-haired and large-bosomed, with a soft, open face; she wore faded flowered overalls with ruffled shoulders and wide, flat black lace-up crepe-soled shoes. The East German government frowned upon East Berliners crossing over to work, but there was nothing they could do about it (at that time around three hundred people a day were leaving the East for good). She had lost everything during the war, including her husband, and worked to support disabled relatives in East Berlin. She welcomed us as liberators, and she hated the Russians. They had knocked down every house that was on a corner. But she liked where she lived, and she had neither the money nor the inclination to move to the West. Besides, there could be reprisals against her family.

She wound up the day at the kitchen table, polishing the silver candlesticks and looking at Nanny's magazines, *Woman's Own* and *Woman*. When Nanny offered her the magazines to take home, Hannah was shocked. *Das ist mir zu gefährlich.* It was too dangerous. East Berliners were not meant to bring home things from the West, and certainly not magazines or newspapers.

A woman Hannah knew had nearly landed in jail just because she bought a West German fashion magazine. Someone reported seeing the magazine to the Stasi, the dreaded secret police, and she was fined two hundred marks for the possession of "Western propaganda."

The summer after we left the city for good, on August 13, 1961, the Berlin Wall went up, sealing Hannah behind it. She'd had a job with my father's successor but she failed to appear after that day. Her telephone was cut off and we never heard from her again. Like so many of the people who worked for us, after we left she vanished from our lives forever.

Apart from Hannah and my piano teacher, I didn't have much contact with Germans. I viewed them with a mixture of pity and suspicion. Nanny was unequivocal in her point of view: "They all say they were never Nazis, but they were." Except Hannah, of course.

I frequently had nightmares about Nazis, twigs snapping under their jackboots as they ran through the woods at the bottom of our garden, the sound of their harsh voices outside as they rattled the doors on the terrace. Where could I hide? They were coming up the stairs. Quick! Hide in the cupboard! We all hide there, holding our breath. Then I cough. In all the nightmares I am the one in the cupboard who coughs.

I read William Shirer's *Berlin Diary* and copied out a passage: "The war came and the Nazi blight and the hatred and the fraud and the political gangsterism and the murder and the massacre and the incredible intolerance and all the suffering and the starving and the cold and the thud of a bomb blowing the people in the house to pieces, the thud of all the bombs blasting man's hope and decency."

I was reminded of it every time I walked out the front door and saw the pile of rubble where people had been blown to bits in the house across the street.

In Berlin there was always an undercurrent of danger. The city was, of course, full of spies and provided a convenient line to the Soviets. In 1954–1955 the Americans, with British help, built a tunnel between the American and Soviet sectors equipped with listening devices. Little did they know that there was a KGB mole working for the British government in Berlin at the time. His name was George Blake.

Blake was a frequent visitor at our house. He was witty and urbane. He's even better-looking than Marlon Brando, I wrote in my diary. But Blake, it turned out, was a double agent. He had lived in Berlin for four years, during which time he'd informed the Soviets about the tunnel, among other things. Of course, nothing was known about this yet, and when my parents gave a farewell party for him and his wife, I was sad to see them go. Months after we left Berlin, in 1961, George Blake was caught. My father was tight-lipped and gray in the face when he heard the news. He was so angry that I could almost have thought it was he personally who had been among the betrayed.

Blake was convicted of spying and sentenced to forty-two years' imprisonment. The judge said each year was for a British agent he had betrayed to the Russians who had been tortured and shot.

All through the time I lived in Berlin the feeling of being in an embattled outpost was real. And yet we went on with our lives as if nothing was amiss. While Khrushchev was threatening a war over possession of the city, I went to a great tennis game at the Officers' Club where I saw the champions Pancho Segura, Mike Trabert, Ken Rosewall and Lou Hoad, and afterward got their autographs.

All day long at our house a steady stream of what I called "eligible bachelors" used to call upon my mother. She had acquired an admirer, a French army captain who drove a Citroën *hydro-pneumatique*. At the sound of his car turning into the drive, Philippa and I would start to giggle. We knew what was going on. Sometimes he took us out in his Citroën. When he pressed a button, the car gave an enormous sigh and slowly raised itself up off the ground. More giggles.

I thought the whole thing was harmless and funny. It never occurred to me that it was anything more than a flirtation, and my mother flirted a great deal, and not just with Capitaine Charlot.

The *capitaine* was debonair and good-looking, with thinning hair and brown eyes like a spaniel. When I arrived home in the afternoon his presence was indicated by his dark blue kepi, sitting on the table in the front hall like a visiting card, next to the statue of the Virgin Mary.

Capitaine Charlot would come to tea so my mother could practice speaking French. He spoke very little English. The two of them would sit on the white sofa in front of the marble fireplace, deep in conversation. He addressed my mother formally as *vous*, not *tu*, and called her *ma chère*.

When I entered the drawing room, I would find my mother radiant and animated, her hair slightly dishevelled. Capitaine Charlot, or Bernard ("Bear-nahr"), as my mother called him, flushed from the encounter, would jump up at once and kiss my hand and call me *ma chère*, just as he did my mother.

Later, when my father came home, they would switch to whisky and water or pink gins. My father never seemed to mind about the *capitaine*. He had had affairs too, my mother said years later when I asked her. "Only they were with bimbos and he never talked about them."

French music filled the house once more. There were strains of Edith Piaf singing "La Vie en Rose" and "Milord," Yves Montand, Georges Brassens and Charles Trenet. I heard the songs so often I knew the words by heart.

I read *Bonjour Tristesse*. I loved Françoise Sagan because she dared say anything she wanted, and she didn't care. Sagan knew who she was. I didn't have a clue who I was and spent all my time trying to make myself liked and trying to fit in, while at the same time doing everything I could to flaunt authority.

Everything French was better: French food, French wine, French music, French literature, French men.

Although Capitaine Charlot was a womanizer, he was smitten by my mother. On one visit he gave her a bottle of scent in a red heart-shaped box. It was sitting on the coffee table when I came in.

"Bonjour, ma chère!" He jumped up as usual and kissed my hand.

"I'm going to the kitchen to have tea," I said to my mother, feeling *de trop*. When I got to the door, I turned around with a smirk.

"Lights on or off?"

Bear-nahr gave me an odd look. I went red. He'd understood!

Bear-nahr had a wife, a daughter my age and a son age six, Hubert (pronounced "Ew-bear"), who had inherited his father's charm and sly humor. Our families often spent the day together. Capitaine Charlot's daughter and I had a little in common, and our friendship, conducted entirely in French, was awkward. I wasn't sure whether I should address her as *tu* or *vous*.

One Sunday we all went to lunch at the French Officers' Club. It was by the Havel, where bodies thrown in by the Russians at the end of the war still washed up on the shore from time to time, fourteen years later.

It was a dazzling, clear sunny day, with the scent of pine trees in the air, and we had lunch outside, on a terrace overlooking the river. I looked at the blue, serene Havel, imagining that a swollen lump might suddenly pop up in the water, misshapen, unrecognizable, someone's father, mother, friend, lover, child . . .

The children were seated at a separate table from the grown-ups. Baguettes of French bread were broken and passed around. No butter was offered. There were seven children ranging in age from six to sixteen, and each of our places was set with a wine glass. The waiter poured a little red wine into each glass, even those of the six-year-olds, and then filled it up with water. I refused the water and just had the wine.

Six snails sizzling in a dish were placed in front of me. They were served in their shells, soaked in melted butter and reeking of garlic. This was diabolical!

I thought of the snails in Ganga's garden, creeping over the leaves of his vegetables with their tentacles out, leaving slimy tracks behind them. What would Ganga have made of this? He'd have Fletcherized them, shells and all.

The wretched little Ew-bear kept his eyes fixed upon me as I dug out a snail with the little fork that was provided. I picked up a piece of bread and buried the horrible creature inside. I put it bravely in my mouth.

Ew-bear waved his hands in the air. "Maman!"

I froze.

"Maman! *Regarde!*"

All heads turned from the grown-ups' table to look as he pointed at me.

"Truc boit son vin sans l'eau!" (" 'Thing' is drinking her wine without water!")

Truc!

Truc went ahead and swallowed. At least I liked garlic.

When my Berlin friends and I were on holiday, we were determined to have a good time. Within a couple of weeks we had formed the Gang, a tight-knit band of around a dozen teenagers, all of whose parents were in or connected to the British military. Our experiences were similar; we were multilingual, changing countries every couple of years, and used to leaving our families abroad when we went back to our English boarding schools. Over the two years our parents were posted in Berlin, we led a life of luxury that had nothing to do with the reality of their bank accounts. We passed the time going to the movies, dancing and fooling about in the Olympic Stadium swimming pools. Military stables provided horses for us to ride in the woods by the stadium whenever we wanted. We had two cinemas to go to: the Jerboa in the British sector, and the Outpost Theatre in the Clayallee in the American sector, which showed English language movies every night.

Every holiday each one of us gave a dancing party. The invitations went out engraved with our parents' names (crossed out) or simply reading "At Home," with the space underneath left blank for the host's or hostess's name. At the bottom, unnecessary information was penned in: "Dancing, supper, dress informal."

The parties were innocent affairs, involving kissing and hand-holding, games like Murder in the Dark and Spin the Bottle. There was a great deal of jiving to Buddy Holly, Ray Charles, the Everly Brothers and the Platters. At my parties I'd bring out my Elvis collection and we'd jitterbug to "Heartbreak Hotel" and "Don't Be Cruel." Louis Armstrong and Bobby Darin singing Kurt Weill's "Mack the Knife" were the closest we got to German music, apart from a singer called Camillo who sang the slow, sexy ballad "Sag Warum" ("Tell Me Why") in a throaty baritone while we danced, nervously pressed up against each other, cheek to cheek.

My friends and I met most days at the British Officers' Club, lounging around in the gardens of the large, white villa in the Thüringer Allee, which had red clay tennis courts, a swimming pool and a restaurant with an outdoor terrace. On Saturday nights there were dances with a band, attended by subalterns, and dinners of shrimp cocktail, steak and Black Forest gâteau. When we weren't at the Officers' Club we were at the swimming pools in the Olympic Stadium complex (where Hitler's hopes for Aryan victory in the 1936 games were famously dashed by the American sprinter Jesse Owens). Since 1945 the complex had been occupied by the British Army. It also housed the offices where my father worked. The immense outdoor pool, used by the soldiers for laps, was presided over by a mammoth iron statue of a cow with horns. The indoor pool took up the better part of a monolithic red brick building that had soaring frosted windows, banks of spectator seats and a top diving board fifty feet high.

The Olympic Stadium was the only one of Albert Speer's buildings that wasn't destroyed at the end of the war. He was now serving a twenty-year sentence in Spandau Prison, a forbidding red brick fortress flanked by guard towers in the British sector that contained most of the British Army barracks. The prison housed just three of the political prisoners who were sent there after the trials at Nuremberg. The other two were Rudolf Hess, Hitler's former deputy, who was serving a life sentence and had reputedly gone mad, and Baldur von Schirach, leader of the Hitler Youth and later Gauleiter of Vienna, whose mother was American and whose grandfather had been a general in the Civil War.

While we splashed around in Speer's swimming pools and played at cowboys riding his iron cow, Hitler's favorite architect was passing the time tending the Spandau Prison garden, where he planted fruit trees and flowers and made fantasy treks across the world, planned with the help of library maps and guidebooks. When he was released in 1966, along with von Schirach, he'd covered over twenty thousand miles of imaginary travel that took him from China to Mexico, across the Sahara, the Balkans and all the way to India.

All four occupying forces took turns guarding the prisoners. Once a month the vacating power would serve lunch at the prison for the other three Allies. No drinks were served at the American lunches, ever since a visiting congressman had expressed outrage at the idea of fraternizing with Communists under the influence of alcohol. The British laid on plenty of drink, but their food was mediocre. The French provided Champagne, of course, and a splendid four-course lunch with red and white wines.

But the Russians outdid everyone, even the French. They served vodka and Crimean champagne, borscht, chicken kiev, beef stroganoff and, best of all, loads of beluga caviar.

ے

"GO AND WASH YOUR FACE."

"I can't."

"Don't be silly." My mother glared at me. "Just go and wash it off, and mind you wash your hands properly too, with soap."

"Mummy, it won't come off."

"You can't walk around like that. You look like Groucho Marx."

The family was seated around the table on a Saturday morning and my father was carving a ham. We were about to have my favorite lunch: boiled ham, stuck with cloves and glazed in the oven under a layer of Old Brown, served with parsley sauce and boiled new potatoes.

My father, always averse to scenes, calmly continued to place slices of ham on the plates that were stacked in front of him and pass them around the table. If he saw the storm coming he did not show it. His calmness was always in inverse proportion to my mother's agitation.

"I can't wash it off."

The full horror of what I had done slowly began to register on my mother's face. Philippa watched the scene with an expression of schadenfreude.

By some odd genetic trick, my sister and I had inherited our Irish grandmother's coloring. I would have preferred to look like my mother, who had auburn hair. Since my father's hair was also dark brown, all through our childhood Philippa and I were told that our hair would eventually turn dark. But our blond hair was Scots-Irish, as immutable as Ian Paisley's Ulster Orangemen. It went with white eyelashes and eyebrows, one step away from albino, and skin that reddened and peeled in the sun. My sister described herself as looking like a boiled egg. I felt that I looked like those portraits of Queen Elizabeth I, eyes like two holes in a white blanket.

Meanwhile, hairdressers would cluck over our hair, holding up the golden tresses to the light and say what a shame it would be when they darkened. We waited for the day in vain. I was now fourteen, and nothing had changed.

But that morning, the day of a party that was of the utmost importance for me, I had taken matters into my own hands. There was a *Friseur*, a hair salon, conveniently located near the women's changing rooms at the swimming pool in the Olympic Stadium. One afternoon I'd paused to look at the list of things you could have done. *Augenbrauen und Wimpern Tönen*. When I broached the subject at home, my mother vetoed the idea at once.

At the hair salon, after the beautician had dyed my eyelashes and brows black, she removed the cotton wool from under my eye-lashes and wiped off my face.

"Öffnen Sie die Augen!"

Staring back at me from the mirror I'd been confronted with someone who looked like . . . Groucho Marx.

My mother stood up from the table. "You're not having any lunch until you get rid of that stuff and you're not going to any party looking like that. What will people think?"

Always worried about what people thought. She went to bed for the rest of the afternoon with one of her stomachaches.

My father and I looked at each other. By this time I was in tears.

"I'll drive you to Roseneck and we'll see if we can find something at the chemist's."

Roseneck was a small shopping center near where we lived in the Grunewald. As we entered the chemist's a little bell chimed at the door and a silver-haired man in a lab coat came out of the back. My father, who was fluent in German, explained the problem. The pharmacist was unfazed. The situation was easily remedied. He went into the back and returned with a bottle of hydrogen peroxide that later turned my tarry eyebrows a light brown.

Next to us a woman reached over the counter to pay for the things she'd bought. She had a row of numbers tattooed on her arm. I was horrified and quickly looked away. Amid all the anguish and foolishness of being a teenager, it brought me up short. She couldn't have been more than thirty years old, and had probably been the same age as me when a concentration camp guard had given her that tattoo.

I couldn't get the image of the tattoo out of my mind. And here I was, worrying about dyed eyebrows.

❧

KHRUSHCHEV WAS STEPPING UP his threats about Berlin. He told the American ambassador to Moscow that if it came to war over West Berlin, Russia would swallow their troops "in one gulp."

The British kept up their morale with military displays in the Sommergarten of the Funkturm, the radio tower that was built in the 1920s and had miraculously escaped being bombed. Thousands of people showed up for the Beating of the Retreat, which had a searchlight display by the Berlin Infantry Brigade dressed in scarlet, blue and gold uniforms that stood out against the vivid green grass of the arena. Trumpeters of the Queen's Royal Lancers and the King's Royal Hussars opened the show with a fanfare, followed by the bands of the Royal Scots, the King's Own Scottish Borderers, the York and Lancaster Regiment and the pipes and drums of the Scottish regiments. After Eightsome Reels and a tattoo beaten by the scarlet-clad and bearskin-capped soldiers of the Grenadier Guards, a solitary bagpiper stood at the top of the bandstand and ended the ceremony with a wailing "Lament."

"Take that cat out of here!" whispered my father.

One of my best friends came to the parade, Nick Newton Dunn, a handsome charmer who, although barely fifteen, already had a well-developed interest in the opposite sex. His cousin Charles had come to stay; a wily boy who used to put bacon under his shorts when he was caned at school so he didn't feel the sting.

A few days later the three of us went to the Outpost, the American movie theater, where I took my seat between the cousins. After the lights went down, Nick reached out to hold my hand at the same time that his cousin tentatively reached out his. They sat during the entire film, quietly massaging each other's palms across my lap, unaware that the hand they were holding was not mine.

Nick knew what the used condoms lying on the sidewalk outside the American cinema had been for. He soon gave up on me and turned his attention to Carolyn Hamilton, the daughter of a brigadier, who was a year older than the rest of us, sultry-looking and, I thought, rather "fast." She became one of The Gang.

The reason for my reckless dyeing of eyebrows and eyelashes was a passion that went nowhere and haunted me for years. Patrick Robertson Macleod. "My son is a devil," his father had said before

Patrick was due to come out to Berlin for the first time. "He's very dark and very good-looking, and God knows, he'll be even more of a devil when he's grown up."

What more could a father say to arouse immediate interest in his son? I wrote down his words in my diary.

Patrick, who was at Eton, was better-looking than I could ever have imagined. He was like a young Alain Delon, with straight black hair that fell in a lock over his forehead and blue eyes framed with thick, long, girlish eyelashes that must have caused heartbreak for many a predatory older boy at Eton. But he was also young and skinny, with a squeaky voice. A fifteen-year-old boy is fifteen. A four-teen-year-old girl is fourteen going on twenty-five. Nevertheless I fell for him right away. He was high-spirited, with a mischievous grin and a sly way of looking at you, making you a co-conspirator in his games.

My friends and I hung around outside Spandau Prison one day when we knew the Russians were on duty, straining our eyes for signs of life. All we could see were the shadowy figures of the sen-tries up in the watchtowers. Patrick wolf-whistled at them and stuck out his tongue.

To impress Patrick, I learned to wolf-whistle between my teeth. The day the Russians landed a rocket on the moon, The Gang made a bus trip to the Havel. I took the microphone and, pretending to be Eartha Kitt, sang "Smoke Gets in Your Eyes." Amazing what a mi-crophone does for a voice. Patrick did Buddy Holly singing "That'll Be the Day." Then Angela, Nick's sister, grabbed the mike and an-nounced that Patrick and I were engaged. Nobody gave the moon landing a second thought.

Later we played Murder in the Dark and Patrick and I hid in a cupboard under the stairs. Just as I thought he was about to "do something," there was a shout from the hall. Nick was the detective and he'd found the "body."

The next day all of us went to the cinema again. This time I sat next to Patrick, whose proximity gave me delightful goose pimples. I wrote in my diary: "We both had our arms on the chair with the hairs touching."

He hadn't seemed to notice. Unlike Nick, Patrick was not yet ready for girls. Nick, on the other hand, most certainly was. You could see it in Carolyn's face.

One afternoon when we all went for a swim at the Olympic Stadium, Patrick dared me to jump off the top diving board. It was fifty feet high. Hardly anyone, even the soldiers, ever climbed up that far just for a look; forget about jumping or diving off.

I was like a tipsy person that day. I gave a self-assured laugh. "I'll do it right now."

My friends followed me up and up a series of ladders like a pack of mountaineers. At the top, I looked down at the pool below. It was the size of a matchbook. But there was no turning back now. I imagined myself an Olympic diver, ready to take home the gold medal for England, and I jumped.

I did it twice. When my mother heard, she said if I jumped off the top board again, I would not be allowed back in the stadium. But I didn't get the chance. My father was posted to London. I never saw Patrick again after we left Berlin, even though we wrote to each other for a while. But many years later Nick Newton Dunn's brother Bill sent me a clipping from the *Daily Mail* about the men Camilla Parker Bowles had dated. There was Patrick, looking very suave in black tie, holding a glass of Champagne.

MORE THAN THREE DECADES LATER I revisited Berlin one summer with my son, Alexander, who was then fifteen. The Outpost movie theater where Nick and Charles held each other's hands over my lap is now an Allied museum, with a transport plane from the Berlin Airlift parked outside. When you walk into the auditorium the first sight that greets you is a bank of wooden card files about six feet tall and six feet wide on either side of the aisle. Each drawer is labeled with a white card inside a metal frame printed with letters of the alphabet. These are the notes on de-Nazification, with information that could have sent one person to prison, another to a job interview. The seats have been removed from the auditorium and replaced by glass-covered cases displaying airlift memorabilia, cookbooks, uniforms and pamphlets about programs for reeducating Hitler Youth. Photographs of American military officers hang on the theater walls.

I'd told Alexander about the time I jumped from the fifty-foot diving board in the Olympic Stadium and I wanted to see it again. So one afternoon we trekked back and forth around the stadium in the rain, trying to find the entrance to the pool where I used to swim, until at last a guard told us it was being renovated. No admission to the pool. *Geschlossen* to outsiders. No more privilege of the occupiers now.

Alexander and I stayed in Berlin for ten days. While we were there, we ate more German food than I probably did on all my Berlin school holidays combined. At the Café Einstein on Unter den Linden, not far from the Brandenburg Gate, we sat on brown leather banquettes and had hot chocolate and apple strudel served by waiters in long white aprons. We stopped at a kiosk outside the Zoo railway station, near the ruined Kaiser Wilhelm Gedächtniskirche, for a curry wurst, a pork sausage slathered in ketchup flavored with curry powder. In the restaurant of the restored Charlottenburg Palace we had *Windbeutel* for dessert, puffed up like popovers, with lingonberries and whipped cream. Afterward we took a train to the Grunewald to find my old house.

It was a clear, sunny evening as we strolled along wide leaf-dappled streets, past old villas spared by the bombs and brand-new houses. Around a corner, we came upon a small lake so calm it was like a mirror. Two men were fishing from a boat.

When you go back after many years to a place where you lived as a child, it often seems smaller than you remember. But our house looked bigger. It was now painted white instead of gray. In front, an obsessively neat patch of lawn was decorated with four tiny topiary trees placed primly at each corner. The ruins across the street were gone. In their place was a characterless white apartment building, surrounded by second-growth trees.

I rang the bell at the front gate of our house, where a huge and pompous brass letter box had been installed. No answer. Then I noticed that the two front doors were no longer painted dark green. Instead, the new owners had put mirrors under the iron latticework.

I stood gazing at my reflection as I stared into the past, thinking what a charmed life I had led in this once devastated city, and how when you are young, you think you have all the time in the world while the very days are running away with you. You never believe that those you thought you would love forever will become ghosts whom you try to make out in the twilight, as you stare into the mirrors on a door.

I SAW MY GRANDMOTHER EVERY WEEKEND at Penrhyn when I was back at boarding school. She and I cooked and talked, digging our hands into the flour bin and rolling out pastry, shaping brandy snaps around the handles of wooden spoons before baking them (and never piping whipped cream into them afterward; for once Granny liked something better without cream). She coated Rice Krispies or cornflakes in melted chocolate and set them to harden on sheets of greaseproof paper as a treat for Philippa, who was now also a boarder at the school and disliking it as heartily as I did.

To make scrambled eggs, Granny would crack eggs from the Burkhardt sisters' farm into a blender and add the equivalent of a stick of butter, softened at room temperature and cut in small pieces. She'd put in two extra yolks, keeping the whites for a souf-flé. Then she'd season the mix with salt and pepper and set the blender at top speed, whipping the butter with the eggs into a froth. She melted more butter in a saucepan and poured in the eggs, stir-ring them over low heat until they were soft and creamy. The eggs were spooned onto buttered toast. Scrambled eggs for a coronary. But I've never tasted better.

While we cooked, we talked about religion, politics, science and literature. Much of the conversation centered around Ireland. It was forty years since my grandmother had moved to Sherborne to escape the Troubles, but she was still passionately involved.

Her ancestors were Protestants who emigrated to the north of

Ireland from Scotland in the time of Queen Elizabeth I. My grandmother didn't want a united Ireland because she feared the Catholics in the north would overrun the Protestants and take away their land, as they had in the south. She was sympathetic to their cause, however, and felt that they were badly mistreated. But she loathed Sinn Feiners ("You can tell them by the way their hair grows on the back of their necks!"). They were the Irish Nationalists who had fomented rebellions in the south. As for the IRA, as far as Granny was concerned, they were nothing but mindless killers.

When we talked, she'd use a rolling pin, a wooden spoon or a saucepan—whatever was at hand—to drive her point home, like Khrushchev banging his shoe on the table at the United Nations.

One day I came home from the cinema in Yeovil to find her in the kitchen making dinner. In those days, before a film began, the national anthem brought the audience to its feet. I boasted that my friends and I no longer bothered to stand.

"Bah!"

She slammed down the lid on the pressure cooker with a bang. The aluminum compartments, which were filled with potatoes to be boiled in their jackets, jangled noisily against the sides. My grandmother had an Irish temper.

"You'd think differently if every time you stood up for the national anthem, you knew you might get shot in the back!"

I felt ashamed. After all, she was lucky to be alive.

It was a story she told often. Sunday morning near Dungannon in County Tyrone, where she taught math and science at a boys' school from September 1916 (a week after she married) to July 1919, she and my grandfather went to the Officers' Club for Sunday breakfast. They had arrived early, and since it was a beautiful morning they decided to go for a walk. While they were out, the Sinn Feiners arrived at the club, killed all the officers, and blew the place up. My grandfather had been on their death list, but they were gone by the time he and Granny returned to the club. "The dirty devils couldn't wait for us. They had to get to the church in time for confession."

My grandmother was a crack shot, trained by her father, who used to sleep with a gun under his pillow. "He could pick the Sinn Feiners off one by one when they tried to climb in over the roof."

But he'd never shoot a man in the back.

Eamon De Valera's Sinn Feiners had murdered two men from her hometown of Ballycastle and buried them by the ruins of Bunemargie Abbey, near the driving range of the links where she played golf.

"The Sinn Feiners had a camp in the Cushendall Mountains near us. The men were taken there and shot because they wouldn't join them. Their bodies were found by the church when a wall was being repaired. Their murderers had brought them there at night so they could be buried in consecrated ground! Bah!"

When she was a student at Queen's University in Belfast, one of the young men in her chemistry class (she was the only woman) used to leave a red rose in her test tube every morning.

"I would walk into the science lab and pluck the rose out of the test tube and toss it into the wastepaper basket," she said. "I wouldn't even look at him."

When she told this story, she would draw herself up, hold her head high and flick an imaginary rose in the trash. I imagined her striding magnificently into the classroom dressed in her mannish white shirt and tie and long skirt, over which she wore a black university gown with a yellow stripe around the collar. She wore her red hair, which she later bobbed, piled on top of her head.

She met my grandfather in a boys' math class. She wasn't part of the class at all, but she sneaked in at the back of the room, where she sat quietly listening. She learned enough to get into physics classes (where there was no female competition), and in 1910 she became the first woman to graduate from Queen's University in science.

She was the only person in her class of twenty-five students to survive the First World War. Everyone else was killed.

"Don't you feel sorry, Granny, that you threw away that poor boy's roses?"

"No!"

According to my mother, Granny's marriage to Ganga was a mistake, the first of many misfortunes (most of them financial) that befell my grandmother during her life. When Ganga came home on leave from the war in 1916, he sent her a telegram asking her to marry him. She was out when it arrived.

The telegraph boy stood impatiently at the door waiting for an answer. The reply was prepaid. So one of Granny's sisters answered it for her. "Yes," she wrote and handed the reply back to the telegraph boy.

So there it was. How could my grandmother have undone the damage, what with Billy, my grandfather, going back to the war?

One of Granny's Irish heroes was Lord Carson, the man who had defended the Marquis of Queensberry and brought down Oscar Wilde. Granny saw Carson as the savior of Northern Ireland because he'd successfully campaigned against Home Rule for Ulster.

I was obsessed with Oscar Wilde. I was enthralled by his wit, his brilliance, his florid prose and, of course, the fact that he was a tragic figure, misunderstood by the world. I would have stuck by him, like his friend Ada Levinson, whom he called "the Sphinx." "Any man can make history," he wrote; "only a great man can write it."

I read his books, his poems and plays, and all the literature I could find pertaining to his life, from *My Life and Loves* by Wilde's friend and biographer Frank Harris, to J. K. Huysmans's decadent novel *A Rebours,* which had been the inspiration for *The Picture of Dorian Gray.* I burned "with a hard, gemlike flame," as Wilde's mentor, Walter Pater, put it. I was Wilde's "sentimental cynic and superstitious atheist," and always ready with annoying quotes such as "Punctuality is the thief of time," "When people agree with me I feel

I must be wrong" and "Only dull people are brilliant at breakfast." I painted his portrait in art class.

I told Granny that at the Old Bailey, Lord Carson had read out loud one of the poems Wilde had written to his lover, Lord Alfred Douglas. " 'Your slim gilt soul walks between passion and poetry,' " he proclaimed, adding, "That is a beautiful phrase?"

"Not when you read it, Mr. Carson," Wilde had replied. "When I wrote it, it was beautiful. You read it very badly."

She slammed down the frying pan.

"You know what they do, don't you?" she burst out suddenly.

"What?"

"They go up people's behinds!"

"Of course I knew that."

They did what? I was shocked.

This explained some of the puzzling references in the book I was reading at the time, *The Trials of Oscar Wilde* by Montgomery Hyde.

As we argued over Oscar Wilde and the Irish Question, my grandmother and I worked on soufflés, marveling at their height, a phenomenon of chemistry. Our conversations became punctuated by the whir of the eggbeater and of the mixer spraying unreachable parts of the ceiling with stuff.

We made soufflés with Mould and Edwards' best aged Cheddar, accompanied by curried tomatoes and chips. Coffee soufflé was flavored with Nescafé and served with double cream. In our hands the hot chocolate soufflé came out perfect. (Nanny's had been piebald. "Well, the recipe said to *fold* in the eggs.") Granny also made a cold version, decorated with chocolate drops and walnuts. She served lemon "fluff"—a chilled soufflé made with egg yolks, lemon juice and whipped egg whites, topped with whipped cream—in crystal glasses. The trick was not to end up with a lump of gelatin on the bottom, but to get it fluffy all the way through.

Of course, she wrote the recipes down in her book.

Cheese Soufflé

1 ounce butter
¹/₂ ounce flour
¹/₄ level teaspoon dry mustard
¹/₄ pint warm milk
3 large eggs
4 ounces grated, well-matured, sharp Cheddar cheese
Salt and pepper

Grease a 1¹/₂ pint soufflé dish. Melt the butter in a saucepan, stir in flour and mustard and cook for 2–3 minutes. Gradually stir in milk and cook further for 3–4 minutes, stirring. Separate the eggs and beat the yolks. Add them with the cheese and stir until smooth. Season with salt and pepper.

Whisk the egg whites and fold into the cheese mixture. Turn into the prepared dish. Bake at 350°F for about 30 minutes, until well risen and golden brown. Serves 2.

For a seven-inch (2-pint) dish to serve 4 use half as much again with 4 large eggs or 5 small ones. Bake for about 45 minutes.

The uncooked soufflé may be left in the fridge covered with foil for one to two hours and then baked in a preheated oven as above for ten minutes longer.

Hot Chocolate Soufflé

4 ounces unsweetened dark chocolate
3 tablespoons sugar
6 eggs, separated

In a double boiler, melt the chocolate carefully without burning it. Stir in the sugar and cool.

Beat 4 of the egg yolks and stir them into the mixture. Set aside the extra yolks for scrambled eggs. Beat all the egg whites until they stand in stiff peaks. Gently fold the whites into the chocolate mixture until blended.

Butter a 2-pint soufflé dish. Pour the chocolate mixture into the dish and bake at 400°F for 15 to 18 minutes. The soufflé should be risen but the center should be runny. Serve with cream. Serves 4.

Chilled Lemon Soufflé

5 large eggs
1 envelope (1 tablespoon) unflavored gelatin
$^{1}/_{2}$ cup sugar
Juice of 2 large lemons
Grated peel of 1 lemon
1 cup thick (heavy) cream
$^{3}/_{4}$ cup toasted slivered almonds

Separate the yolks and whites and place them in two mixing bowls. (As a precaution in case a yolk breaks into the white, crack the eggs one at a time into a cup before adding them to the bowl.)

Dissolve the gelatin in $^{1}/_{2}$ cup warm water.

Beat the egg yolks with the sugar until light and lemon-colored. Beat in the lemon juice and grated peel. Pour the mixture into a double boiler. Cook the mixture, stirring constantly with a wooden spoon, until it has the consistency of a custard, about 15 minutes. Do not allow the mixture to boil or the eggs will curdle.

Remove the lemon mixture from the heat, stir in the softened gelatin and let the mixture cool to room temperature.

Meanwhile, whip the egg whites until they stand up in stiff peaks. In a separate bowl, whip the cream.

Fold the lemon-egg mixture into the egg whites. Fold in the whipped cream, reserving about $^{1}/_{2}$ cup for the top. Pour the

Taken when "on leave" from Mesopotamia in June 1918

W.S. Hamilton

Bombay

ABOVE LEFT: My Irish grandmother, Harriet MacAlister, on her wedding day, September 6, 1916
ABOVE: Harriet at her graduation from Queen's University in Belfast
LEFT: William (Billy) Hamilton, my Irish grandfather, in Bombay, June 1918

RIGHT: Billy (Ganga to his grandchildren) in plus fours
BELOW RIGHT: Ganga and my mother, Lyla, at the seaside, 1938

LEFT: Lyla, in her formal Sherborne School for Girls dress, 1936
BELOW: My mother and father on their wedding day, July 23, 1944
BOTTOM LEFT: My mother and father on the ship to Egypt

ABOVE: Ahmed, our cook
ABOVE RIGHT: Nanny, pouring
out tea
RIGHT: Me dressed as the Old
Woman Who Lived in a Shoe,
with Nanny
BELOW: The house in Egypt

TOP LEFT: My mother helping me blow out candles on my fourth birthday
TOP RIGHT: On the balcony with my mother
ABOVE: Good morning in Egypt
LEFT: Into the desert with my father

LEFT: Christmas tea in
Egypt
BELOW: On the beach in
Cyprus
BOTTOM LEFT: On the
beach by the Suez Canal
BOTTOM RIGHT: Jumping
into the Suez Canal

ABOVE: My parents at a formal reception in Beirut
LEFT: My mother, ready to go out

ABOVE: Up a tree in Lebanon
LEFT: The freighter home from Beirut, 1952
BELOW: My paternal grandfather, Sir Edward Hodgson, with Queen Elizabeth and Prince Philip a month after her coronation, at a game of bowls at the Civil Service Sports Ground in Chiswick, July 20, 1953. My grandmother Gertrude is one person away to the right. She wore black ever since the death of Edward's brother Robin some thirty years before.

ABOVE: A quiet evening at home in Sweden
LEFT: The house in Djursholm
BELOW: Another quiet evening at home

TOP: Class picture at the Couvent des Oiseaux, Saigon
ABOVE: In class at the Couvent des Oiseaux
LEFT: Me in Saigon, by the door of the living room, hoping to be a ballerina

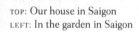
TOP: Our house in Saigon
LEFT: In the garden in Saigon

RIGHT: The journey home, aboard the *Victoria*
BELOW: *Victoria* menu, October 3, 1957
BOTTOM RIGHT: *Victoria* daily events program, October 7, 1957
BOTTOM LEFT: *Victoria* menu cover

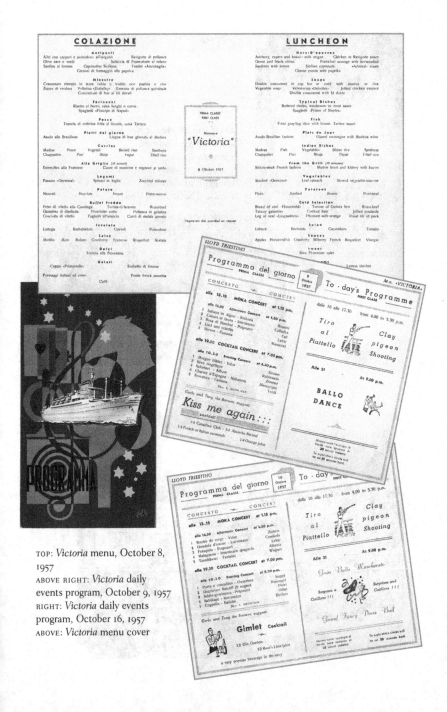

TOP: *Victoria* menu, October 8, 1957

ABOVE RIGHT: *Victoria* daily events program, October 9, 1957

RIGHT: *Victoria* daily events program, October 16, 1957

ABOVE: *Victoria* menu cover

LEFT: Grandmother at Sherborne School for Girls summer commemoration
BELOW: Set to drive to Berlin through East Germany
BOTTOM: The house in Berlin

DO NOT CROSS THE AUTOBAHN

LEFT: Family in the garden in Berlin
BELOW: My military ID card
BOTTOM: Family at table in London, 1984

The person to whom this Card is issued is entitled to the protection afforded to members of the Allied Forces by Allied legislation in force in Berlin.

Le titulaire de la présente carte a droit à la protection accordée aux membres des Forces Alliées par la législation alliée en vigueur à Berlin.

Предъявитель сего пользуется покровительством Союзных Законов действительных в Берлине и оказываемым военнослужащим Союзных Держав.

Der Inhaber dieser Ausweiskarte ist zu dem Schutz berechtigt, der den Mitgliedern der alliierten Streitkräfte durch in Berlin gültige alliierte Gesetze gewährt wird.

Period of Validity Stamp

Surname   HODGSON
Christian Names Moira
Official Address c/o External Department,
British Military Government, Berlin
                 Tele. No.
Passport No.   168501
Signature of Bearer Moira E Hodgson
Signature of issuing Official
Date of Issue   4 September, 1958

The Roofer, Sutton Court Road W4, painting by Philip Hodgson

lemon mixture into four glasses or individual soufflé dishes. Spread the tops with the remaining cream. Cover with foil and chill until set, preferably overnight.

Just before serving, sprinkle with almonds. (Do not do this ahead of time or they will become soft.)

ye

IN THE FALL, my father was posted to the United Nations in New York. My parents couldn't afford to fly Philippa and me to New York for the Christmas holidays, so more than ever, Penrhyn was home.

That summer was the end of my last year in the sixth form at Sherborne. Each girl in the class was given the opportunity to read the lesson at school morning prayers for a week. I decided not to choose texts from the Bible like everyone else. Instead I read from Pierre Teilhard de Chardin's *The Phenomenon of Man*. My grandmother had suggested it. She loved Teilhard de Chardin, a Jesuit and a paleontologist who believed in evolution and the integration of scientific thought with religion.

As I read passages from Teilhard de Chardin, the girls glazed over and Granny beamed with pride in the front row. DRH, dressed in a long black cassock with a purple sash around her neck, was seated at her prayer desk, which was next to the lectern. For five days I was able to enjoy the sight of the dark flush that crept up over her neck during my readings.

But DRH was not finished with me yet. She delivered her final sally when I came to say goodbye at the end of term. I sat as usual outside her office in the school hall, where the lightbulb above the door glowed red. The door opened and one of the girls emerged, clutching the familiar white handkerchief embroidered with DRH's white initials. Five more minutes, then presto! The lightbulb over the door turned from red to green and I went in.

"Bless you, my dear, if you don't pass your exams, *shirley* we can put that down to the meningitis, can't we?"

I told my grandmother what she'd said. It was the last straw.

Granny's ancient black Morris Minor swung down Richmond Road in a fury. I don't know what she said to DRH, but a letter of apology arrived for my grandmother the next day. DRH was very sorry if there had been a misunderstanding. She never meant to imply that the meningitis had affected my brain. In closing, she mentioned that there was going to be a concert at the school that night. "But I expect Moira has told you about that too."

da

PHILIPPA AND I, now thirteen and seventeen, respectively, traveled to New York first class on the *Queen Mary*. We hadn't seen our parents for over six months. On board ship, I wore my mother's hand-me-down dresses and Winklepickers with stiletto heels, and I smoked Sobranies: Black Russians with gold tips and "cocktail" cigarettes that came in pastel colors. The look was completed with sunglasses (worn indoors) and a long black cigarette holder. We were trailed by young American men who danced with us and bought me drinks. They had Coca-Cola. On our last night, they stopped buying the drinks and whipped out their Bibles. They were Mormon missionaries. That night none of us went to bed. We stayed up to see the ship sail into New York Harbor at dawn. The buildings of the city sparkled as the sunrise broke over the windows.

Once we had docked, the illusion was shattered. The streets were narrow, filthy and in perpetual shadow from skyscrapers. There was trash everywhere, the likes of which I had never seen. New York was in the middle of both a garbage strike and a newspaper strike. We drove up to our apartment, 1185 Park Avenue, a large building with an indoor driveway at 93rd Street. I changed clothes and my mother took me to lunch at the Oyster Bar at Grand Central station while Philippa took a nap.

I'd never had oysters before. I sat at the counter in a daze, wondering how I was going to meet the challenge of half a dozen bluepoints served on the half shell. We ate the oysters with a glass of cold white wine (my parents were oblivious of underage drinking laws and had served me wine with dinner since I was twelve, sailing home from Vietnam on the *Victoria*).

"Your grandfather once dropped a live oyster into a glass of brandy to see if the two would mix well in the stomach," said my mother. It had rolled itself into a hard ball.

To my surprise, the first oyster slid easily down my throat. I felt I'd just dipped my head in the sea. The oyster wasn't so strange, after all. It was just a quivery thing, like jelly, blancmange or Bird's custard. The food of my childhood.

After swallowing half a dozen oysters, I tasted my first cheese-cake, which was nice but weird, being both cheese and cake. Then my mother and I went upstairs into the Pan Am Building where Richard Lippold was installing a sculpture. It was made entirely of threadlike wires that lay on the floor in a mess of tangles. We left him to it and went to the United Nations, where my father was sitting with the United Kingdom delegation on the Security Council. The topic under discussion was Cyprus. I sat in a pleasant blur in the visitors' gallery until my eyelids began to lower and I fell asleep.

PART TWO

I SHOULD HAVE BEEN STARTING my first semester at a university in the fall of 1963. Instead, I was dressed like a Pan Am air hostess. I wore a dark blue tailored skirt, matching tight-fitting waisted jacket and black high-heeled Charles Jourdan pumps. My lapels were decorated with two gold United Nations wreaths and my last name was embroidered above my breast pocket. I was standing in the visitors' section of the Security Council addressing a group of unruly high school students who were just a few months younger than me. I attempted to hold their attention by asking them questions.

"The United Nations was established by the five major powers who won the last world war. Can you name them?"

Hands shot up. "United States!"

Pause. "England? France?"

Long pause. "Germany? Japan?"

Minutes later I was pointing to the pipes and ducts overhead in the Economic and Social Council chamber.

"The unfinished ceiling by the Swedish architect Sven Markelius is to show that the work of the United Nations is never done."

For three days a week, I was a UN guide. The other two days I worked in the press section on the third floor of the Secretariat building for Louis B. Fleming, the correspondent for the *Los Angeles Times*.

I had these two part-time jobs thanks to my father, who was a press officer for the United Kingdom Mission to the United Nations. I'd failed math, so if I had wanted to try for Oxford or Cambridge, I'd have had to go back to Sherborne for another term. Not a chance. I told my parents I'd rather skip university altogether and stay in New York. So they made me take a typing course.

Now I possessed a letter from the Geneva School of Business ("advertised as air-conditioned") stating that in addition to typing and shorthand, I had "excellent personality traits and skills." The school was in a run-down building on 86th Street near Broadway, a grungy room filled with long tables set with typewriters. I'd managed to secure the only typewriter that had uncovered letters on the keys.

"Hunt and peck!" said Lou, my boss at the UN office of the *Los Angeles Times* when I typed my first letter for him. He was from Pasadena and reminded me of Jimmy Stewart. Lou was tall and thin, with horn-rimmed glasses, and he always wore a bow tie. As for the shorthand, the only symbol I could remember was "Dear Sir," which was also the symbol for "desire." "Dear Sir desire," I would think to myself as I started a letter, dreaming of the person, preferably French, with whom I would fall in love and marry. For my birthday Lou gave me a copy of John le Carré's *The Spy Who Came in from the Cold,* which I thought was an odd choice.

The guides were much in demand socially. In those sexist days only women between twenty and thirty years old were accepted as guides (I was two years too young, but an exception had been made because of my father). We were supposed to have a college degree (many of us didn't) and speak another language (some guides spoke as many as six or seven). We were from forty different countries and were chosen for our looks and personality. In between tours we would relax in the guides' lounge in the basement of the building under the General Assembly hall, gossiping and smoking. The names would be called on the loudspeaker: "von Gersdorf. Cazenave. Laffont. Czernin . . ."

In the afternoons I worked for Lou, who was a lax boss, hunting and pecking and covering press conferences he was too busy to attend. I found the UN exhilarating. I felt I was at the hub of politics and international affairs, and it was enthralling to be there in the fall, when virtually every important head of state came to address the General Assembly, including President Kennedy and Fidel Castro. Lou and I shared an office with CBS for my first year; then we moved in with Prensa Latina, the Cuban press agency. One day Che Guevara came and sat on my desk and flirted with me until he had to leave because he was about to address the General Assembly. After he'd gone Cuban exiles fired a bazooka across the East River. They'd hoped to hit Che, but instead it landed in the river, just short of the Secretariat building, where I was working on the third floor.

Sometimes I joined my father before lunch in the Delegates' Lounge. A great deal of the august body's daily business, it seemed, was conducted around the bar. After a gin and tonic or two we would go upstairs for lunch in the Delegates' Dining Room, which was on the fourth floor, overlooking the river. The food was mediocre except for one dish: lamb chops. They were huge, double-thick and grilled over high heat so they had a dark brown crust. When you cut into them, the meat was like butter. No mint sauce. They came with watercress and french fries, French style. They were the only thing we ever ordered.

One morning we heard that a member of the British delegation had been detained at the airport. In those days one of the questions on the immigration form was "Do you intend to assassinate the president of the United States?" He'd written "sole purpose of visit."

Even though many Americans wanted the U.S. out of the UN, an organization that they considered little more than a nest of Communists and illegal car parkers, a small body of New Yorkers went out of their way to entertain foreign diplomats. Through the UN hospitality committee, we were invited to parties and given free tickets to the theater, opera and ballet. I was amazed by how rich the Americans were, with Manets and Picassos on the walls of their apartments on Fifth Avenue and Sutton Place, laying on Sunday tennis parties and cocktails around the pool at their mansions in Greenwich, Connecticut, and sailboat outings on Long Island.

In Greenwich one day I stood with the hostess in front of her blazing six-foot-tall fake Tudor fireplace, clutching a small napkin made of antique Belgian lace that had been handed to me by the butler to hold around my drink. In midconversation, absentmindedly, I scrunched it up and tossed it in the fire. I realized by the look on her face what I'd done. It was too late. Ever the diplomat, she went on talking as though nothing had happened, so I said nothing either.

Another hostess, Mrs. Schaefer, had a cat, Hector, who was forced to play the piano at her parties. She would hoist up the cat, his legs splayed out rigid like four sticks as he mewed loudly, and prompt, "Go on, Hector! Play chopsticks! Go on!"

Her husband would stand at the other end, holding out a shrimp on a toothpick. And Hector would slither discordantly across the keys and leap off the piano, the shrimp in his mouth, to general applause.

At the time there was a popular advertising jingle on the radio: "Schaefer is the one beer to have when you're having more than one!" On the way home in the car, my father would sing it, replacing the word *beer* with *wife*.

At last we had a television, because it came with the apartment (along with a twenty-four-hour police guard at the entrance to the building because, my father said, there was a "hanging judge" who lived there who'd condemned men to death). When Philippa was on vacation from school, she and my father would stay up late watching Hammer horror movies, to my mother's disgust. I didn't like them then much either. She and I liked to watch Julia Child, whose *Mastering the Art of French Cooking*, published two years earlier, was on our kitchen bookshelf, well-thumbed and gravy-spattered. I remember Julia holding up a suckling pig and announcing in her plummy voice: "You take a pig. You draw him and you quarter him. . . ." Not so different from a horror movie.

My mother didn't make suckling pig for the United Nations diplomats. For lunch, she made *vitello tonnato,* using chicken instead of veal because it was cheaper, and she served cold baked salmon trout with a thick green mayonnaise flecked with herbs. She went through a phase of making pâtés and terrines from pork belly, veal and pig's liver with brandy and white wine, seasoned with juniper berries and mace, or with chicken livers and Madeira. She had a terrine dish over a foot long for this purpose and she would fill it with the mixture, cover it with bacon, place it inside a larger baking pan filled with water and cook it in a slow oven.

For an elegant dinner, she served canned consommé madrilène—chunks of ruby red jelly topped with sour cream, chives, salmon caviar and a sliver of lemon. Salmon caviar was cheap then. When we had dinner for just the family, she baked pork chops in a casserole in sauce made from Campbell's mushroom soup. She made braised celery and braised endive, my father's favorite cooked vegetables.

Like my grandmother, she kept a recipe book. She also made notes in cookbooks where she felt the instructions were wrong. "When making *daube de boeuf* with olives don't add until the dish is reheated. If left overnight they make it far too salty."

Noilly Prat white vermouth went into everything—into the sauce for sole and chicken, and into the *coquilles St. Jacques,* made with scallops and mushrooms, topped with grated Gruyère and browned in their shells, which were washed and used again.

For cocktail parties she made angels on horseback, which in England in Victorian times were served as a savory at the end of a meal (on toast of course). Sometimes she used prunes instead of oysters, in which case they were called devils on horseback. Either way, there were never any left over.

Angels on Horseback

24 shucked oysters
12 thick slices streaky bacon, cut in half
Freshly ground black pepper

Preheat the broiler or grill.

Wrap each oyster with a strip of bacon and thread it onto a toothpick. Season with pepper.

Place the oysters on a hot grill or under a broiler. Cook, turning once, until the bacon is crisp (about 2 minutes on each side) and the edges of the oysters are curled (hence the name "angels," for they look as though they have wings).

MAKES 24

Like the cocktail parties they'd given everywhere else in the world, those my parents gave in New York rarely ended at the conventional hour of eight. Guests stayed on long after the dinner hour, so my mother would make a couple of dishes in advance to be heated up for the stragglers. Coq au vin. Boeuf bourguignon. Veal stewed with tomatoes and garlic, strewn with bread crumbs, parsley and lemon peel, and served with rice.

For pudding, she'd serve green grapes rolled in sour cream and sprinkled with Old Brown, or Granny's cold lemon soufflé. She cut apricots or peaches in half and sprinkled them with sugar and kirsch or brandy and dotted them with butter. They'd emerge from the oven soft and juicy, their edges caramelized. A jug of thick cream was served with these. And pears, simmered in red wine.

Baked Peaches

6 ripe peaches
2 tablespoons butter, at room temperature
2 tablespoons sugar
1/2 cup brandy

Preheat the oven to 350°F. Drop the peaches into boiling water
for a few minutes, remove with a slotted spoon and peel off their
skins.

Grease a baking dish with the butter (a round dish looks
attractive). Halve and pit the peaches. Cut them into slices
1/2 inch thick and arrange them in the baking dish. Bake for
30 minutes or until the edges of the peaches are lightly
browned.

Heat the brandy in a small saucepan. Pour it over the peaches
and set it alight. Serve immediately with whipped cream.

SERVES 6

There was one dish my mother wrestled and wrestled with until she
got it right: burnt cream, also known as crème brûlée (a recipe from
Trinity College, Cambridge). All too often, it curdled when it was
browned under the grill.

Burnt Cream

Boil 1 pint thick (heavy) cream for 30 seconds. Pour
immediately onto four well-beaten egg yolks in a bowl and
whisk all together. Return to the pan and heat until thick
but DO NOT BOIL.

Pour into a shallow gratin dish. Chill overnight. Sprinkle with an even layer of caster sugar and brown under a very hot grill.

SERVES 4

NOTE: *Caster sugar is a superfine granulated sugar poured from a caster or sugar sifter. In England, grill also means broiler.*

γ

We had many Arab friends, and our apartment echoed with the plaintive strains of Oum Kalsoum and the Lebanese singer Fairuz, records my parents had bought in Egypt and Beirut. Sir (pronounced "Seer") El Sanousi, a Sudanese diplomat who was tall and skinny, with long, tapering fingers and a high giggle, would prepare lavish Sudanese feasts. He cooked most of the dishes himself: *ful medames* (dried fava beans cooked with olive oil, garlic and parsley), stewed okra, lamb and chicken in spicy sauces scented with coriander and cumin, tomatoes stuffed with rice and beef and piles of flat bread to scoop it up. When he served the food he would announce, "No animal fats!" He used only oil.

He would stand over the table, matchbook in hand. "Curse not the darkness, light the candles!"

Sanousi was a poet and after dinner he would recite his poems, in Arabic. The poems were unintelligible to me, except for one very long tract he would recite with welling eyes. The last word of every line was a plaintive cry, "Veee-ennn-aah!" Vienna had been his previous post.

At these parties a musician from Nubia played the oud and our Arab friends would wipe their eyes as he sang tearful songs about his village, washed away by Nasser's Aswan Dam.

MY PARENTS HAD A RULE. Every time a young man invited me out, he had to come to the apartment for a drink first. The purpose was to give him pause. If he had nefarious plans, he might think twice after meeting my father. Often the young men stayed on, lounging on the white sofas in our sitting room, which had a view of the East River and the red Pepsi sign in Queens. They didn't want to leave. They'd be offered a second and a third drink, and we'd be late for dinner. They liked my mother because she was charming and flirtatious. My father was easygoing and joked with them. My parents were very young, after all. I was eighteen; they were forty-one.

When my parents approved of a suitor, he was known as a White Horse. A popular ad for a whisky showed a white horse standing alone in a grand drawing room. Underneath was the slogan: "You can take a White Horse anywhere." There weren't many white horses among the motley group of young men who showed up for cocktails at 1185 Park.

Anthony, a stockbroker, announced that he wanted to leave it all, live on an island and write nonfiction. "Any particular kind of nonfiction?" my mother inquired archly. Tassos, a young government minister from Cyprus, boasted as we sat in a nightclub drinking gin that he'd been an Eoka terrorist but regretted the murder of two soldiers from my home county of Dorset. Digvijay, a maharajah, sent me a photograph of himself, rifle in hand, with his foot on a dead elephant he'd shot in India, thinking I'd be impressed. Narendrah used to place an ironing board on a slant at the foot of his bed; every evening, before he went out, he would lie upside down on it and meditate. Eric, French, good-looking and effeminate, always chided me about my clothes. *"Je n'aime pas ta blouse, Moira."* He was right. It was an ugly, cheap blouse, shiny black with gold stripes. I stopped seeing him when I discovered he was anti-Semitic. I knew he had a crush on Audrey Hepburn, so I told him she was Jewish. At Château Henri IV, a French restaurant on the Upper East Side, Bartle, an attorney, took a menu from my hand and told the waiter, with supreme

WASP self-confidence, "She'll have the artichokes and the chicken vol-au-vent." He never bothered to ask what I'd like (and it was doubly annoying since his choice was exactly what I would have ordered myself if I'd had the chance).

My grandmother got a look at some of the suitors when she came to visit during the school holidays. She terrified them. One evening after dinner the doorbell rang. It was François, a tall angular Frenchman who worked in advertising. It was not a profession my grandmother respected. François and I were going dancing at Le Club. I brought him into the living room to say good night. My grandmother shook his hand and looked at her watch. "Eleven o'clock! It's a bit late to be going out now, isn't it?" She gave him one of her most withering looks. He slunk out after me through the front door like a chastened schoolboy.

She was very taken, however, with Peter Barnett, a young journalist who worked at the Australian Broadcasting Corporation. He used to call me "a fiendish femme fatale journaliste" and described himself as a hopeless old bastard. He took me to my first fancy restaurant, which he could ill afford, booking a table in the name of Sir Peter. It was La Côte Basque, where I had my first taste of *quenelles de brochet* with lobster sauce.

Jean, a photographer from *Paris Match*, managed to elude the parental cocktail hour. A mutual friend introduced us at a gathering in an apartment in a brownstone on the Upper East Side. The guests were all French, worldly, glamorous and terrifying. We stood in the kitchen and drank Champagne. A poster of a famous work by Bernard Buffet—sad, white-faced clown with a red nose, painted on a blue background—hung on the wall by the refrigerator. When there was a lull in the conversation, to fill the silence and to please the host, I said that I liked the painting. I did like it, in fact, and I had a postcard of it at home.

"Qu'elle est chouette!" exclaimed Jean. *"Elle aime les peintures de clowns!"* ("Isn't she sweet; she likes clown paintings.") Everybody laughed.

I wished the floor would swallow me up. How was I to know the apartment was a sublet and the host hadn't chosen the poster. After the party we all went for dinner at the Brasserie in the basement of the Seagram Building. I ordered steak tartare. The waiter produced a plate of raw hamburger. I stared with mounting horror as he emptied the meat into a bowl, tossed it with various seasonings, and proceeded to break a raw egg yolk over the top. More tossing, a vigorous dusting of black pepper, and it was returned, viscous and raw, to my plate. It was like the escargots in Berlin all over again. Thank God the French always had plenty of bread on the table. But the trouble with the French, I thought to myself, is that they don't always serve potatoes with the main course.

ِ ِ

I WAS NINETEEN and I needed a recipe—for my life. But I was floundering. I copied poems by Shelley and Keats into my journal. "Oh, lift me as a wave, a leaf, a cloud! I fall upon the thorns of life! I bleed!" I was full of desire and longing. For what? I copied out T. S. Eliot and Yeats. I read all of Huxley. From *Doors of Perception*: "Most men and women lead lives at the most so painful, at the best so monotonous, poor, and limited that the urge to escape, the longing to transcend themselves if only for a few moments, is and has always been one of the principal appetites of the soul."

So I decided to lose myself on stage. I'd always been interested in acting. I got the role of Alison in the United Nations production of John Osborne's *Look Back in Anger*. I loved being someone else. I cried real tears when Jimmy berated me and was thrilled when I heard a woman in the audience sob.

After the performances I received a call from a talent agent named Anthony Soglio. When I showed up for the interview at his office on Madison Avenue, I was astonished to see my father waiting outside the building. "I just wanted to make sure it was on the up and up," he said. How had he known where I was going?

Soglio was indeed on the up and up. He looked me over as if I were a racehorse. He found me a role in a touring company that was doing a comedy called *Boeing-Boeing* by Marc Carmoletti. It had run for two successful years in London. I was to play one of three air hostesses. It would mean traveling around the country for several months. But I didn't want to leave New York. I did some modeling and found it excruciatingly dull, so I let that drop too. And I started to chafe against the uptown life of cocktail parties and nightclubs.

Then I found the recipe, downtown. My parents unwittingly planted the seeds of revolution when they took me to the East Village to hear Thelonius Monk at the Five Spot. I was swept up by his music and excited by the presence of the artists, writers and musicians gathered in the long dark room. These people were real. The young diplomats who took me to tourist traps such as Café Wha and the Figaro in the Village were out of place with their short hair, suits and ties and conventional ideas. I longed to be among the hippies who loitered in the doorways on the steps, their unkempt tresses, beaded headbands, sandals and bell-bottomed jeans signifying their rebellion against conformity. Theirs was the life I wanted, not living on Park Avenue in an elevator building with a doorman and going out with boring conventional men. The entry to this life was provided by a man I met in, of all places, a ballet class.

At the UN I had made friends with Maria Casanueva, a guide from Chile. She was *jolie laide,* with a page-boy haircut, a clotheshorse figure and a teasing, flirtatious personality that charmed everyone she met. After work she took ballet classes at Ballet Arts studio in Carnegie Hall. So one day I showed up at the six o'clock beginner's class dressed in a brand-new black leotard, pink tights and pink ballet slippers.

"Is this right, Maria?" I would whisper to her at the barre, my shoulders hunched, my arms bent like twigs and my feet hanging down like kippers, as the pianist thundered away at Chopin and Tchaikovsky. Maria also took me sunbathing on the roof of the Secretariat. We got out of the elevator at then Secretary-General U

Thant's office on the thirty-eighth floor, climbed a flight of stairs and spent lunchtime stripped to bikinis, with foil reflectors under our chins. The next day I couldn't go to work. I was burned so badly I could barely open my eyes.

Maria wanted me to meet a friend of hers from Chile. He was a ballet dancer, wild, she said, totally unreliable, but so much fun. I was going to adore him.

I first saw Claudio (not his real name) in Vladimir Dokoudovsky's professional class. The Duke, as he was known, conducted class with a cigarette permanently hanging from the corner of his mouth, which he flicked from time to time into a stuffed ashtray that sat on top of the piano. He had large, sad, dark eyes and straight black hair that hung in a lock over one side of his face. He wore old-fashioned classic Russian ballet teacher's clothes: high-waisted black Dutch boy's trousers caught at the ankle, black lace-up character shoes and a white open-necked shirt with loose floppy sleeves. He walked stiffly because of arthritis and carried a stick that he banged on the floor and sometimes even on a student's shin. Dokoudovsky had danced with Colonel de Basil's Ballets Russes and the Ballet Russe de Monte Carlo but hadn't been a *danseur noble* because he was too short. He'd been deeply scarred by the disappointment. But his class was a terrific workout, and many of the dancers who came to it were stars.

Claudio wore gray knitted wool tights, a white T-shirt, scuffed white ballet slippers and a red bandana tied around his head. He had broad shoulders with slender, narrow arms, beautiful legs and arched feet. His face, with its delicate features, reminded me of Montgomery Clift: thick black eyebrows, long eyelashes over cornflower-blue eyes, a small turned-up nose. He affected a winning, deliberately crooked smile and had white, even teeth. The bandana concealed the fact that he was prematurely bald. On stage he wore a toupée instead of the bandana and stuck it down with glue.

He was a sensual, liquid dancer. It always looks better if you're slightly behind the beat, he said. If he made a mistake in class, he would stop dead and clench his fists, breaking the mood.

On our first date Claudio took me to his favorite place, an Italian restaurant on Thompson Street called Fellin's that stayed open until 2 a.m. Old men were playing bocce in the back, posters of Naples adorned the walls and the tables were set with red checked cloths and candles in Chianti bottles.

Claudio recommended the "spaghetti with green sauce," which cost $1.85. He seemed taken aback when I said I'd like to start with an order of baked stuffed clams as well. But he ordered it anyway, along with a carafe of the house red, which was heavy and dark, from Sicily, and cost $1.50.

I'd never had green sauce before. It was a pesto, but not authentic because it was made with parsley instead of basil. I didn't know. There was so much garlic in it, I thought it was great. This was Claudio's favorite dish, not the least because it was the cheapest thing on the menu.

But when the bill came, he didn't have enough money. The clams had driven it over his limit. I was used to going out with men who picked up the bill without question. It had never occurred to me that Claudio was broke. The bill was ten dollars, and I gave him two, feeling very grown-up.

Claudio was indeed, as Maria had told me, funny, outrageous and slightly crazy. His English was perfect except that he said "plataform" and "passaport," which I found charming. Maria hadn't meant for me to fall in love with him. She thought we'd just be friends. He was a bit old for me, after all. I was only nineteen and he was thirty-three. As he pointed out, "The same age as Jesus Christ when he was crucified!"

But I was swept up by the romance of him and of the ballet. I stopped going to the cocktail parties so much and started going regularly to Ballet Arts instead. I loved the structure of the classes, the routine, the fact that if you just worked at the same thing over and over, you progressed. After a few months, Miss Lee, the director, suggested I move up to an intermediate class. It was usually taught by Nina Stroganova, a Danish ballerina from the Ballet Russe who wore a hairnet and was married to Duke. They didn't get along because he was having an affair with an English dancer from the Met who took his class every day. Stroganova was a kind and undemanding teacher. Sometimes the Duke took her place.

I had dreamed for years of the day when I could go on point. So one day I thought, why not, and bought myself a pair of pink silk pointe shoes. I sewed pink ribbons on them, and before I put them on I tried to crack them to soften them up as I'd seen dancers do. The shoes were like boats, stiff and unyielding. As Duke walked around banging his stick on the floor, I teetered painfully in the center of the studio trying to stop tears springing to my eyes with the pain.

Duke looked at my feet. "How to go on point in one easy lesson!" he commented dryly and moved on to the next student.

It must have been depressing teaching the ragtag bunch of students who showed up for these intermediate classes. One girl careened across the floor doing grand jêtés when her hair came unpinned. "Wot you think you are doing?" Dokoudovsky screamed at her. "The mad scene from *Giselle*?"

Later, as I stood with my leg extended in an arabesque, I looked sideways in the mirror to check myself out.

Duke stared at me. "Are you advertising baking soda?"

In the mornings a plump old woman who wore her gray hair in a bun and dressed in a black tunic with a skirt would place herself front row center, where the professionals stood. I felt sorry for her but also annoyed. I asked Claudio, "Who does that woman think she is that she can stand front row center?"

"She thinks she's Agnes de Mille," he replied.

Who was Agnes de Mille? I'd no idea I was looking at one of the most famous American choreographers of the century—the woman who'd created *Oklahoma!*

ONE MORNING IN FEBRUARY 1965 my father came into my room and grabbed me by the feet to wake me up. "The Americans have bombed Vietnam!"

The fact that he, normally so reticent and calm, was in such an emotional state shocked me. I had never before seen him so upset about anything.

A couple of months later, with the Vietnam War still very much on my mind, I went to Washington to visit Peter Barnett, who'd been posted there as a White House correspondent after leaving the UN. He was an enthusiastic supporter of my efforts in the kitchen, and had asked me to cook dinner at his apartment for the Washington hostess Perle Mesta and Dan Rather, who was covering Washington for CBS, and his wife. Peter very properly put me up in the mansion of a rich old lady in her nineties, who acted as sort of a chaperone. I gave him a list of ingredients and that evening, in his modern, well-equipped kitchen, I made, courtesy of Julia Child, *suprêmes de volaille à blanc*—chicken breasts baked in a fireproof casserole and coated with a sauce made with vermouth and cream—which I served with a gratin of potatoes dauphinois, and zucchini cut into chunks and browned in olive oil and butter.

The conversation centered on Washington, Johnson and politics. When the Vietnam War came up, we were on dessert, my grandmother's cold lemon soufflé. Mrs. Mesta wanted to look on the bright side.

"I have a wonderful millionaire friend who is in the waterbuffalo-canning business," she said. "He just had the most beautiful idea. He's from Texas and he's arranging to have our planes fly over villages that have been bombed and sprinkle them with bluebonnet seeds."

ح

Suprêmes de Volaille à Blanc
(Breast of Chicken with Cream)

4 suprêmes *(boned breasts from two fryers)*
$^1/_2$ teaspoon lemon juice
$^1/_4$ teaspoon salt
Big pinch white pepper
A *heavy, covered, fireproof casserole about 10 inches in diameter*
A *round of waxed paper 10 inches in diameter and buttered on
one side*
4 *tablespoons butter*

FOR THE SAUCE

$^1/_4$ *cup white or brown stock or canned beef bouillon*
$^1/_4$ *cup port, Madeira, or white vermouth*
1 cup whipping cream
Salt and pepper
Lemon juice as needed
2 *tablespoons fresh minced parsley*

Preheat oven to 400°F.

Rub the *suprêmes* with drops of lemon juice and sprinkle lightly
with salt and pepper. Heat the butter in the casserole until it is
foaming. Quickly roll the *suprêmes* in the butter, lay the buttered
paper over them, cover casserole and place in the hot oven. After 6
minutes, press top of *suprêmes* with your finger. If still soft, return
to oven for a moment or two. When the meat is springy to the
touch it is done. Remove the *suprêmes* to a warm platter and cover
while making the sauce (2 to 3 minutes).

Pour the stock or bouillon and wine into the casserole with the
cooking butter and boil down quickly over high heat until the
liquid is syrupy. Stir in the cream and boil down again over high

heat until the cream has thickened slightly. Off the heat, taste carefully for season-ing, and add drops of lemon juice to taste. Pour the sauce over the *suprêmes*, sprinkle with parsley, and serve at once.

SERVES 4

NOTE: *From Julia Child, Louisette Bertholle, and Simone Beck*, Mastering the Art of French Cooking, *Volume One. New York: Knopf, 1961.*

༽

MY BOSS, LOU, went back to California, where he became foreign editor of the *Los Angeles Times*. I sold my UN badges for ten dollars to a Texan on one of my tours (that was a lot of money for me in those days). I was now twenty, and I'd found a job in the travel sec-tion of the *New York Herald Tribune* as a secretary, even though I could barely type. The editor, Barney Laschever, knew I badly wanted to write, and he let me do some travel pieces. I loved my job at the *Trib*. The paper was in its heyday, with Clay Felker in charge of the magazine, publishing writers such as Tom Wolfe, Kurt Von-negut, Jimmy Breslin and John Gruen. I was a published writer too! The composing room sent up a copy of my first story (a short, rather sarcastic travel piece on Atlantic City). They'd printed it on a board and sprayed it gold for me as a memento. I wrote my stories in long-hand, like school essays, on sheets of lined foolscap and typed them up. Try to learn to write on the typewriter, said Barney when he saw me laboriously transcribing my efforts.

I didn't know the first thing about wine when I went upstate to do a piece on Widmer's winery in the Finger Lakes. But I did know that Prohibition had had a devastating effect on the industry. (Wine-makers used to turn out grape juice with warnings on the bottle: Caution! This grape juice may ferment and become alcoholic.) Now the vintners were trying to make a comeback. When I arrived at the winery I was offered a glass of Scotch before I tasted the wines. One Scotch on the rocks later, they seemed fine to me.

Widmer's Wine Cellars sent me a case of all their different wines afterward. My parents and I tasted them without a palate-cleansing glass of Scotch beforehand. My father said they weren't even fit for making sauces. (We didn't know then that you shouldn't use a bad wine for sauce because the taste is even more pronounced without the mask of alcohol.) New York State wines, including Widmer's, have come a long way since then.

Things were going well at work, but at home events took a sudden downturn. Out of the blue my mother had to make a trip to Sherborne. My sister, following her elder sibling's footsteps, was in trouble at school. So my father and I were left on our own. One night, after dinner with Claudio, I came home at 4 a.m., and to my astonishment, I met my father coming up in the elevator at the same time.

My mother returned to New York a few days later. I told her my father and I had been to a couple of cocktail parties where people who didn't know us laughed when I said I was his daughter. She wasn't amused. Perhaps she was just tired.

The next morning, when I went into the kitchen to get a cup of coffee, my father emerged from the maid's room in his dressing gown. The bed had been slept in. I didn't ask why and he said nothing as we drove to work.

That night my mother got very drunk, beginning with pink gins and going on to a second bottle of red wine at dinner. "While I was in England looking after Philippa your father had an affair with some woman called Shacklady! He's very pleased with himself."

My father said nothing but continued calmly eating his food.

After dinner my mother, who was weaving unsteadily, came into my room and told me that their marriage had been a mistake from the start. She'd tried to get him to talk, but on their honeymoon she'd suddenly realized that his silences weren't deep thoughts, but lack of interest. He was always looking at other women. In restaurants he'd get a glazed expression because he wasn't listening to a word she was saying, but was focused on the woman at the next table. She'd wanted to leave him, but she was already pregnant. "Besides, it would have devastated Granny."

I brought her a hot Scotch with lemon and went to bed. Then I cried myself to sleep. Because of me, her life had been ruined.

Shacklady? I looked it up in the phone book the next day. There was no one by that name. Who was the woman? What became of her? I never found out. Until then, I had believed my parents were happy together, and now the illusion had been shattered. I didn't want to be around them.

So the next night I told my parents I was staying over with Claudio. If they hadn't had that fight, I wouldn't have considered it. I'd never rebelled against my parents before; I'd had enough to rebel against at school. But now, I didn't care, and I made my first step toward leaving home.

Claudio lived on the fifth floor of a tenement on Thompson Street at the corner of Prince Street, in SoHo before it had a name. In those days the entire neighborhood was Italian. His apartment, which he'd painted white, was a tiny studio with a shower, a two-burner stove, a sink, four chairs and a rickety table. There wasn't space for a sofa. A partition made with bookshelves he'd put up himself divided half the space into a bedroom that had a view down Thompson Street. At the end of summer, the place pulsed with noise from the Feast of San Gennaro a block away, where we would buy greasy sausages and onions stuffed into loaves of Italian bread.

Claudio's friends, many of whom were from Chile, were painters, musicians and writers. We'd sit up until three in the morning, drinking pisco sours and eating quantities of empanadas, the Chilean national dish of pastries filled with ground beef, raisins, onions and a boiled egg. The host or hostess would say, Oh! Do we have a treat for you. Out would come the empanadas. We would also buy them at an Argentinian place on MacDougal Street and eat them in the street.

Pisco was a white *aguardiente* made with muscat grapes that the Chileans claimed as their national drink—and so did the Peruvians. You mixed it with limes and lemon and sugar for pisco sours. We drank a lot of those.

On weekends I'd take class in the morning, then Claudio and I would have lunch in a diner in the corner of the Carnegie Hall building: Western omelettes made with American cheese. In the evenings we would sometimes eat at Maria's, where she taught me to make *manjar blanco*. You put a can of condensed milk into a large saucepan of water and boiled it for four hours. When you opened the can after it had cooled, the milk would have metamorphosed into a thick caramel, which we spread on bananas.

Claudio wrote plays, painted, took photographs, played the violin and made films. He'd gone to ballet classes as a boy in Santiago because his sister took them, and he'd shown serious talent. He also loved to sing. When he was a soloist at the Metropolitan Opera Ballet, the dancers sometimes got swept up in the music and couldn't help joining in the singing during a performance. If they were caught, they were fined. He had also danced with the Ballet Russe de Monte Carlo and in Broadway shows, such as *Milk and Honey* starring Molly Picon. Now he'd begun teaching at Ballet Arts in Carnegie Hall, which paid practically nothing. He also had a part-time job making prints for the photographer Hans Namuth, with whom he was constantly at loggerheads. Namuth had made a brilliant film of Jackson Pollock, shot under glass on which the artist was making a drip painting. But Claudio always made fun of Namuth, mimicking his heavy German accent behind his back, *"Ach!* Hansie!"

Claudio was tortured by his lack of success, and he constantly threatened to go back home to Chile, where he'd be appreciated. He had many talents but some terrible streak in him led to failure. His charm and humor belied the fact that he was often on the edge of despair, full of rage at the world, and this rage often came out when he drank.

My parents didn't know what to do about Claudio. My father

said nothing. My mother made waspish remarks. They hoped I'd get tired of him and he'd go away.

But I didn't tire of him, although I still spent time at home and went to uptown parties and dinners without him because he couldn't stand those conventional people. This was hardly surprising. He was broke and all but jobless.

Meanwhile, my father had returned to the main bedroom and despite occasional sniping from my mother over the dinner table, they appeared to be getting on. Then the following spring, my parents were posted back to England. I didn't want to leave the *Tribune* or Claudio. I wanted to stay in New York.

Before my parents left Claudio came up for a farewell dinner. It was an awkward evening and everyone drank too much. My father had placed an empty cardboard Brillo box he was using as a packing case by the fireplace. Its presence led to a discussion about Andy Warhol that soon boiled over into a row. "How can you call that art?" my father shouted at Claudio, who was holding up the Brillo box and admiring it. "Bollocks!"

My father hated himself for having been baited. Claudio was highly amused. I was furious with him—and with my father's narrow-mindedness. There is something about the English—a lack of drive and ambition, self-deprecation, a willingness to accept what's handed out without question—all this I'd grown up with, and it had become ingrained. With Claudio I'd turned into one of those long-suffering, acquiescent English girls I'd read about in novels. I wasn't convinced at the time the Brillo box was art, but I defended Claudio.

I was just twenty when my parents sailed away on the Cunard Line's *Carinthia*. They had a miserable trip, asking themselves whether they had done the right thing to leave me behind with Claudio. He was no white horse.

WITHIN DAYS of my parents' departure, the *New York Herald Tribune* went on strike. I had worked there less than a year: no benefits. Now I was without a job—and without money, in a new apartment in Greenwich Village.

Just before my parents left, they had moved me into a narrow, seven-story building on Tenth Street between Fifth and Sixth Avenues. I'd found the apartment in the *Village Voice*. The building, dated 1905, had originally been a boardinghouse, and the name Marlborough Arms was still etched in stone over the ugly modern entranceway. There was a store on the ground floor, a boutique that hung a flag emblazoned with its name outside the building: Femme Fatale.

My apartment had a large living room, a bedroom behind French doors, high ceilings, molding and an ornately carved marble fireplace. The fireplace worked nicely if you put a piece of foil over the top third of the opening to stop it from smoking. We kept the sagging single beds the two old German ladies who had lived there left behind, and we bought furniture from the Salvation Army. The color scheme, picked out by my mother, was a conservative Wedgwood blue and white, very Robert Adam. My father put my painting of Oscar Wilde in a gilt frame he made himself and hung it above the marble fireplace.

The view from the bedroom and bathroom windows had been blocked in the 1950s when the Beaux-Arts artists' studios next door had been torn down to make way for a hideous red brick apartment building. The view was now of a murky well that regularly sent up stale cooking smells and echoed with the noise from other apartments. As for my kitchen, it had no window at all. (That's not quite true. It did have a window; it was above the refrigerator and opened a couple of inches into the bathroom.)

I couldn't afford the rent on my own (even though it was just $125 a month), so Kay Wilmette and Carmen Hylton, dancers who took class at Ballet Arts, moved in. I found them thrillingly exotic and beautiful. Kay was tall and dark, with long straight black hair and legs that extended up by her ears when she danced. She was from Washington; her father had been from the Potawatami tribe in Oklahoma and her Portuguese mother a former nun. Carmen was black, from Chicago; her mother had danced with Carmen de Lavallade and been in the movie *Cabin in the Sky*. Carmen had performed with Alvin Ailey and in Broadway shows and was also a singer. But between us we could barely meet the monthly rent. Kay came with a cat, Willow. It was the first time I'd lived with an animal apart from the tortoises. At last, no one was going to tell me I couldn't have a pet.

Our three beds were lined up in the small bedroom so it looked like a hospital ward. In the morning the alarm would go off at seven. Kay would wake up, turn over, light a Camel and smoke a few puffs, staring at the ceiling before she pulled herself out of bed. Then she'd trudge into the kitchen and Carmen and I would lie there, trying to go back to sleep while we smelled the coffee as it burbled away in the percolator. Neither of them had jobs as dancers. Kay worked for a motorcycle messenger service called Coleman Younger. Carmen worked for a telephone answering service. They took class at the end of every day, and so did I.

Now that I was unemployed, Maria, the Chilean friend I'd made while working as a guide, found me a job as a storeroom clothes model for a firm she worked for called Mister Pants. The only problem was that my legs were too long for the pants. When I walked around in front of buyers from Saks and Altman's I had to bend my knees to make the trouser legs cover my ankles.

At last, Mr. Stuart, the obstreperous owner whom we loathed, called me into his office. "You look like an abortion!" he screamed. "I'm going to have to let you go."

"Go where?" I asked.

It was the first time I'd seen him at a loss for words.

I packed up as many skirts, blouses and jackets as I could fit into two large shopping bags and left.

My next job was as a waitress at the Figaro, a bohemian coffee shop on Bleecker Street that was frequented by writers and folk singers. I thought it would be fun, but it wasn't. Men would try to pick me up and then take off without leaving a tip when I didn't respond. So I got a part-time job at Antartex, a midtown boutique that sold sheepskin coats. The coats were heavy, and it was tiring work hauling them down from the hangers and onto the backs of the customers. One day Alton, a stockbroker friend who looked like Woody Allen, showed up at the store and said, "I'm taking you to Lutèce." I was wearing jeans and the rust-colored sweater my mother had knitted for me when I was in the hospital with meningitis. I'd just noticed it had moth holes. I couldn't possibly go. But the woman who owned the store overheard our conversation and said, "Lutèce! You can't miss the chance! Go ahead and have fun."

At Lutèce Madame Soltner didn't look twice at my clothes but sat us smack in the middle of the dining room. André Soltner in his toque came bobbing down the hallway. "I will make you something."

And what a meal it was. Snails flavored with white wine and served in little ceramic pots, terrine of crawfish with Nantua sauce, quail stuffed with foie gras, young chicken braised with tomatoes, wild mushrooms and artichoke hearts, and hot raspberry soufflé. The topping on the apple tarte tatin was like a sheet of glass.

⚜

Tarte Lutèce

6 ounces pâte brisée
8 apples, Golden Delicious or some other baking apple
Juice of 1 lemon
8 tablespoons (1 stick) unsalted butter
$1/2$ cup sugar
$1/2$ cup heavy cream

Preheat the oven to 350°F.

Roll out the pâte brisée to a 9-inch circle and bake it on a baking sheet in the preheated oven until it is light brown and cooked through.

Peel and core the apples and cut them into 8 sections. Moisten them with the lemon juice to prevent them from turning brown.

Raise the oven temperature to 375°F.

Put a large skillet or frying pan over high heat. Add the butter and sugar and stir until the mixture turns a golden caramel color. Add the heavy cream and still over high heat, continue cooking and stirring for another 2 minutes.

Add the apples. Make sure that each slice is coated with the caramel mixture. Cover the pan with aluminum foil or with a well-fitting lid and put it in the oven for 10 minutes.

Remove the pan from the oven and arrange the apples on the pastry in a tightly assembled pattern of rings within rings.

Heat the caramel that remains in the pan for another 2 to 4 minutes, until it thickens. Pour this caramel over the apples. Serve hot.

SERVES 5 OR 6

NOTE: *The tarte may be prepared in advance and reheated the same day. From André Soltner and Seymour Britchky,* The Lutèce Cookbook, *New York: Knopf, 1995.*

༠

Now that I was without a regular job, I signed up for morning classes at the Art Students' League on West 57th Street. I'd done one good painting, the portrait of Oscar Wilde. Maybe as a painter at last I'd "burn with a hard, gemlike flame." But where to begin? I didn't know what kind of painting to do.

My teacher, Robert Brackman, was a portrait painter and figurative artist of Russian origin. He'd been famous in the thirties, but his work was now out of fashion. He was in his late sixties, short and stout, and wore a fisherman's cap and brown overalls. He smoked cigarettes nonstop, letting the ash build up and fall, sometimes onto a pupil's work.

I had never been taught how to paint in oils. I stared, embarrassed, at the skinny model who was perched naked on a chair in front of us, ribs showing. She was an anorectic ballet dancer whose hair had been scraped back into a bun for so long that she was partly bald. I wondered how to begin. I looked over at the person next to me and saw what to do. You primed your canvas with white gesso. You sketched with charcoal and then painted over that, using a light brown paint. The morning sped past.

Just before noon, Brackman appeared behind me. He looked at my work in silence, the ash building up on the end of his cigarette. At last, he removed the cigarette from his mouth and let out a deep sigh. "Oh brother!" he said in a low mournful voice, cigarette ash dropping onto the floor.

He stared some more. "Oh boy . . ."

Then he turned to me. "Why don't you just paint on paper so you won't waste canvas?"

I painted on paper. Then I painted on canvas. I loved it. There were days when I'd start out with a picture that looked quite good, and by noon I would have destroyed it. But I stuck with it.

Brackman stopped by again. "These young girls come in knowing nothing, and then . . ."

I was thrilled. But by then I'd realized how hard it was going to be if I was ever to be any good. I didn't think I'd make it, so at the end of the semester I gave up painting. Instead, I cooked.

I had loved the physical act of painting, the mixing and layering of colors, the creamy textures and the smell of linseed oil and turpentine. I found a similar pleasure in cooking. It was instant art and more appreciated. I had barely enough money for rent and I bought my clothes in thrift shops. But I began giving dinner parties.

MY KITCHEN WAS IN a disused closet off a long, narrow hall. The refrigerator was set directly alongside the stove, which in turn was jammed against the sink. When the oven heated up, the side of the refrigerator buckled. Over time it developed a dark burn, which I covered with a piece of fireproof oven pad. There was no work surface unless I put the dish drainer on the floor in the hall. And if I fried anything, I had to open the front door to let out the smoke.

I approached my first dinner party with trepidation that turned out to be well founded. I made all the classic mistakes. I included several last-minute dishes that kept me nervously occupied in the kitchen while my guests passed the time by themselves. I served too much food. There was chicken liver pâté and toast (mother's), jellied consommé madrilène topped with sour cream and chives (mother's), then salmon steaks with hollandaise sauce, asparagus and steamed potatoes, followed by cheese and salad.

When the guests were on their consommé I broiled the salmon steaks, putting the hollandaise in the oven to keep warm. It was a gas oven and the broiler was underneath. I was unaware that when it was turned on, the oven temperature soared to about 400°F.

I put the asparagus on to boil with the tips in the water and the stalks in the air. I figured that since I was used to eating asparagus with my fingers, there was no real point in cooking the end that you held.

Of course, when I went to get the hollandaise, I found scrambled eggs. One guest undertook to eat the asparagus with knife and fork. I was mortified as he tried to slice the uncooked ends. The salmon was so overcooked it had dried out. The boiled potatoes were perfect (thanks to my grandmother).

The coup de grâce was a chocolate mousse with green Chartreuse. I had made the mousse the night before and something strange had happened to the chocolate: no sooner had it melted than it congealed into a dry lump. I didn't know what was wrong so I added warm water. Almost immediately it lumped up again. I took it off the heat and added more water and about a cup of Chartreuse from a bottle left over from my parents' duty-free liquor cabinet. The mixture tasted strong and strange. Undaunted, I pressed on and beat in the egg whites, poured the mixture into six glasses and refrigerated them, hoping a miracle would occur overnight. I didn't realize that I had burned the chocolate.

But I liked being a hostess and I became good at it. I followed my mother's mantras. Don't finish the food on your plate until the last person at the table has finished theirs. Always take a second helping first so your guests feel free to do so. Bohemian though my new life felt to me, I would set the table with the engraved place mats I'd grown up with, Buckingham Palace and the Tower of London, which my parents had given to me before they returned to England. Old habits die hard.

I gave dinner parties as often as once a week. The guests were artists, poets, writers and many hangers-on stopping by for a free meal. Above the marble fireplace, under the gilt-framed portrait of Oscar Wilde, was a handwritten notice. "Anecdotes 50 cents. Anecdotes about yourself $1."

Underneath it was a box for the money.

Dinner party conversation was to be serious—about ideas. But the anecdote box filled up. Too many stories. Too much wine.

In that kitchen I did the research for cookbooks and food columns and prepared dinner for as many as forty people at a time. Julia Child nearly destroyed me. I faithfully followed her recipes in *Mastering the Art of French Cooking,* Volume One, using every dish and pan in the kitchen, piling them up in the hall. Roast duck with orange sauce. *Crêpes farçis.* Even *quenelles de brochet.*

One day I followed to the letter Elizabeth David's recipe for *car-*

ciofi alla giudea in her book *Italian Food*. After heating up "a deep pan nearly full of very hot oil," I plunged in four artichokes, pressing them down with a wooden spoon so the leaves spread out. "Now dip your hand in cold water and, keeping as far away as possible from the stove, to avoid the spluttering of oil, shake a few drops of water over each artichoke. This operation has the effect of making the artichokes crisp and crackling."

I did just that. There was a sudden "whoosh!" and flames shot up several feet high over the back of the stove, leaving a black, sooty trail all the way up the wall and over the ceiling.

Soon I had the apartment to myself. Carmen moved in (temporarily) with her boyfriend. Kay got a job as a stewardess on a Norwegian freighter and sailed away to the Middle East. Her cat, Willow, a sleek Persian gray, started looking as though she was carrying a pair of saddle bags around her middle. Next thing, I had five kittens in the closet. The first who dared to walk out of the closet and across the floor, mewing and still blind, I named Bully. He had thumbs. He was also extremely smart and had a voracious appetite. (One evening he leaped down from the top of a bookcase onto the dining table and actually swiped the steak off a guest's plate.)

Now I had six cats. I used to go to a Ukrainian butcher in the East Village to buy beef lung, which I cooked for them. The smell was awful.

My walls were hung with electrified op art paintings by a Chilean artist named Ivan Vial. They had overlapping circles painted in straight lines, and when they were plugged into the wall they made dizzying shapes. Peter Barnett was making a documentary for Australian television on the bohemian life of Greenwich Village. He filmed me one afternoon as the paintings went around and the cats crawled all over me because I had a bowl of cat food hidden in my lap.

Then at last I got a real job again—assistant travel editor at *Mademoiselle* magazine. It didn't pay much. Condé Nast expected you to come from the sort of family that could afford to chip in with the bills. Hah!

The job sounded good, however. Some writing, some travel, some office work. But my duties turned out to be of a different order. The editor would go on press trips and return with the notes for me to turn into a story that came out under her byline. I took her clothes to the laundry and did her Christmas shopping. I mixed up the purchases by mistake and her mother, who was size 16, received a size 6 nightgown for Christmas. The editor tossed her personal letters into my mailbox and told me to answer them for her on the magazine's hideous pink stationery. I also ghostwrote a travel column that appeared under her name in the *World Journal Tribune.*

While I worked at *Mademoiselle,* Claudio was teaching a morning class and had the rest of the day free. One evening, I found a long black hair in his bed. And another time, a silver earring shaped like a fish, with scales. Claudio laughed when I confronted him. "Poor thing!" He wrote a schedule of his daily activities for me.

At last Claudio got a job, a soloist with the Ballet Russe de Monte Carlo. He had danced with the troupe before it was disbanded in 1962. Now the company had been revived by Sergei Denham and Boris Trailine under the patronage of Prince Rainier of Monaco with Léonide Massine, who was seventy-one and wore a black cape, as ballet master. The troupe consisted mostly of young French dancers and included Nina Novak, Denham's lover, and Massine's son Lorca. A couple of weeks later, Claudio left for Monte Carlo. He asked me to come with him, but I couldn't afford to leave my job at *Mademoiselle.*

One day when my boss was out of the office, an editor I'd known at the *Trib* called. He said he wanted to ask her to do a column on shopping in Paris. "I can write it for you," I said.

And I did. I'd never been to Paris.

After I was fired from *Mademoiselle* a few days later, my shopping piece came out in the *World Journal Tribune*'s Sunday magazine under my name. I wasn't proud of what I'd done, but I'd had to get even with my boss for all those months of ghostwriting. The following week, leaving Carmen, who was now back in the apartment, to look after Bully and the other cat I'd kept from the litter, Jason, I went to Paris for the first time.

CLAUDIO WAS LIVING TEMPORARILY on the top floor of a six-floor walk-up on the Rue Bonaparte, near the Café Les Deux Magots. I arrived on a cold, drizzly morning in February 1967, hardly through the front door when the telephone rang. It was my father. He'd found Claudio's number, even though it was unlisted. It was nearly a year since my parents had sailed away on the *Carinthia*. They were hurt that instead of going to London first, I'd gone to Paris. But my father didn't say anything about that at the time. He said he wanted to be sure I was all right.

I was all right, but not for long. The apartment had belonged to Claudio's brother, an architect, who had gone back to Chile. It had been redone inside so that it was modern, charmless and plain, and there was very little furniture left. There was, moreover, virtually no heat. I'd never been so cold. Even the most arctic nights at Penrhyn weren't as bad as this. Plus the lights kept going out as you climbed up the stairs.

Claudio had rehearsals, so I went for a walk after breakfast and found myself in the food market on the Rue des Epices. I wandered around in a daze, awed by the displays of vol-au-vents, sea urchins, scallops with their roe, snails packed into buttered shells, fish I'd never seen before, crottins of goat cheese sprinkled with ash, and so much else that I wanted to buy there and then.

I noticed a shop that had a carved horse's head hanging over the front door. Arranged in the window were the rosiest pieces of meat

I had ever seen. I couldn't believe the prices, so I bought two thick steaks.

Then I went into a wine shop. An elderly man in a business suit and tie emerged from the back. I wanted to buy two bottles of wine, one white and one red. In those days in Paris you could get a cheap bottle for twenty-eight cents. When I told him that was the sum I was willing to spend, the man didn't show me the door. Instead he asked what I was serving for dinner. I told him I'd bought steaks and planned to start with oysters.

"What kind of oysters?"

I looked at him blankly. I remembered only bluepoints, the ones I'd first tasted at the Oyster Bar in Grand Central station. He told me to come back when I'd bought the oysters and then we'd choose the white wine.

There must have been two dozen different kinds of oysters on display in the market, some of them, amazingly, even available in different sizes. Round belons, green-tinged Marennes, *huitres creuses* (rock oysters), *fines de claire,* Bouziques, Arachons and huge *"speciales de Normandie."*

What were all these kinds?

The oyster man suggested belons, which were priced some-where in the middle.

The wine merchant was pleased with the choice. A Macon-Lugny from Burgundy would go nicely.

Most days, Claudio went to get his wine bottles filled from a wagon that came to the neighborhood. They didn't have labels and the wine was rough. This would be a treat.

I went back with my shopping and made garlic butter as my mother had taught me. I chopped parsley, tarragon and garlic and mashed the mixture into butter, which I seasoned with salt and pepper. I shaped it into a cylinder and put it in the refrigerator. I pounded peppercorns in a bag with a hammer and pressed them into the sides of the steaks.

That night Claudio came home and opened the oysters. They were very different from the ones I'd had before, with a wonderful smoky, metallic taste. I sautéed the steaks in butter so they were browned, but rare and juicy. I sliced the cold garlic butter, put a couple of pieces on top of each steak and brought them to the table. Claudio had one mouthful of steak and started laughing.

What was so funny?

He asked me to describe the butcher shop.

It had a very pretty carved head of a horse outside.

The meat had a strange texture and was gamier than beef. Slowly the truth began to dawn. I, who worshipped Pat Smythe, the British show-jumping champion, I who in Sweden used to ride at a stables every other day between ballet lessons, bringing sugar lumps and carrots for my chestnut steed Gajo, was eating horse.

The lightheartedness didn't last long in my relationship with Claudio. I was only too aware that among the ballet girls, being one of the few straight men in the company, Claudio was a fox loose among chickens. Like all lotharios (and true to his Latin temperament), he was also violently jealous. He'd once poured a glass of red wine down the dress shirt of an architect he thought was making advances to me at a party. Just walked over and calmly emptied his glass down Clive Entwistle's starched front without saying a word.

Claudio knew that in New York I often went to Max's Kansas City, where you could fill up with dried chickpeas and a hamburger and meet artists. He had never enjoyed going there. Too much competition. He began to grill me about the past couple of months. At last, I made the terrible mistake of confessing to a fling with a painter.

What followed was a haze of recriminations, shouting, hysterics and rage, culminating in Claudio's dramatic exit, off to spend the rest of the night God knows where.

After he'd gone, I stood against the bathroom door, which was painted fire engine red, and stared at myself in the mirror. Without makeup, my white eyelashes and eyebrows made me look washed out. Ten years old. I'm mentally stuck at ten, I thought, and this is where I'll remain forever.

The next morning I went to a café for breakfast. The cobblestones were flying in all directions under my feet as I crossed the square. I sat down shakily at a corner table, ready for a cup of coffee.

An elderly waiter, napkin over his arm, came to take my order.

"Mademoiselle veut un couvert?"

Because I'd been to French schools, my conversation was fluent and I had a good accent. But I'd never heard this expression before. I thought when he said *couvert* he was asking if I'd like a tablecloth (a cover). I didn't want to put him to any trouble, so I shook my head and said no thank you.

He gave me an odd look and walked away. After I'd waited for about ten minutes I called him over and asked if I could have a cup of coffee and a croissant.

"Alors!" the waiter shouted, *"Mademoiselle veut un couvert!"* As he spat out each word he slammed down a knife, a spoon, a plate and a napkin, which he picked up from the next table.

I burst into tears.

He looked at me in astonishment. He leaned over and patted me on the shoulder. *"Ne pleurez pas, Mademoiselle, s'il vous plaît, ne pleurez pas!"*

He rushed over to the counter and got me a croissant and a café au lait. *"Voilà! Ne pleurez pas, je vous en prie!"*

He refused to accept payment. That was my first lesson in how to deal with rude Parisians: burst into tears.

Even Paris failed to alleviate the misery of the next two weeks. I spent a great deal of time alone since Claudio was rehearsing. I was distraught and passed my days at the movies, wandering around the museums by myself, and having coffee in a ridiculous place called Le Drugstore, which had famous people's lips, ears and eyes sculptured in bronze on the walls. I went into the expensive antique shops and the art galleries of the neighborhood. The exhibit in one was foam rubber carpet that had life-size foam rubber cabbages "growing" on it. I would have liked to have shown it to Claudio and made him laugh. I strolled along the stalls of the booksellers on the Left Bank, taking pictures. *"Photographiez la Seine, pas moi!"* screamed one of them, a limp-haired woman in a dirty long brown coat. I wandered around Les Halles, which was in its last throes as a market. I took a photograph of a fruit vendor and she hurled an orange at my camera, missing it by an inch and hitting me in the face.

At last, Claudio came back and we made up over a sad dinner in a couscous restaurant near St. Germain before I flew to London to see my parents.

That summer I went with him on a tour of Spain with the Ballet Russe de Monte Carlo. We toured the country by bus for six weeks as part of the Festivales de España. The program included *Raymonda, Les Sylphides,* and the white scene from *Swan Lake.*

After the performances, which didn't start until eleven o'clock at night, the dancers were hungry. Most of them were French and took a dim view of Spanish food. Too much olive oil and garlic. We would go to tapas bars and have plates of serrano ham, stewed octopus and *bacalao croquetas,* eaten with plenty of bread and cheap red wine. We'd get to bed at three o'clock in the morning, and then we'd have to be up at seven and on the road again. Claudio and I were so broke that we slept in the bus. He was the only one of the dancers who spoke Spanish, and he used to chat to the driver and make him laugh. So when the driver was in his hometown near Málaga, he invited us to stay in his house, and his wife made us dinner.

The dish I remember most vividly from Spain is not paella, serrano ham or even anything we had from the tapas table. It is the salad we were served at the driver's house: raw onions and tomatoes with olive oil. The onions, cut in thick ivory slices, were strong and sweet. The olive oil was dark green and fruity. I'd never had tomatoes that tasted like this, so different from the hard, pallid ones sold in cellophane-covered plastic boxes in New York.

The next day the company took a ferry across the Strait of Gibraltar to perform in Morocco. I couldn't afford to go so I stayed with the bus driver's family for another night. The following afternoon the dancers were back on the bus, due to perform the white scene from *Swan Lake* in the caves of Nerja, a small town near Málaga. Some of them had bought hashish, which they had packed into their makeup boxes so it looked like dark pancake.

The caves of Nerja were famous for their prehistoric paintings, which dated back to Cro-Magnon times, and for their stalactites and stalagmites, which soared hundreds of feet. In the summer, the largest cave became a theater.

Just before the performance several of the dancers smoked a joint, including Claudio, ever the mischief maker, who persuaded many of the young corps de ballet girls to join him. I stood watching from the wings as the white swans assembled on stage. The dancers cringed as hundreds of squeaking bats came swooping down over their heads.

Nina Novak, who had not smoked any hashish, was dancing Odette/Odile. The orchestra was very bad and played extremely slowly—so slowly that Nina, who was not the greatest of dancers at the best of times, was barely able to do her pirouettes without falling off her toes. She was on the verge of tears and so, meanwhile, was the corps de ballet. The hashish they'd taken was strong enough to bring them close to hallucinating. In their white tutus with feathers around their ears, they wobbled across the stage, their legs extended in arabesque. The already painfully slow music seemed even slower, and it took a lifetime to go across the stage. The bats flew around the cave all evening long. To make matters worse, not only were there stalactites hanging from the ceiling, there were even a couple of stalagmites on the stage itself.

After the performance we went to a tapas bar and drank Terry cognac (the very cheapest brand) and spent the rest of our money on platefuls of langostinos, tiny red crayfish, before we went back to sleep on the floor of the bus.

Alas, this was the last tour of the Ballet Russe. The company was unable to raise enough funding to go on and when we arrived back in Paris, it was disbanded.

CLAUDIO AND I were now both out of jobs, and we decided to live in London for a while. We could stay with my friends from Sherborne, Liz and Chris Wilcox, who had married very young. Liz was already pregnant and Chris was working as a doctor at St. Mary's Hospital in Paddington. They lived in a rambling apartment in Hammersmith.

I found a job at a bistro in Mayfair called the Mad Ox. The waitresses were advertised as "miniskirted goddesses" and our uniforms—long-sleeved red paisley-print dresses six inches above the knee—came from a boutique on Carnaby Street. I also wore false eyelashes and white eyeshadow with black eyeliner behind the lid, like Twiggy, and ironed my hair, which was halfway down my back.

My parents were not at all happy about my new occupation. "You're never going to make anything out of your life! It's time you got a proper job!"

I hoped whatever I did would make useful material for my writing—if I were ever going to become a writer. Meanwhile, I certainly didn't write much. But I did at least learn something about food.

The Mad Ox was on the ground and basement floors of a small building on Maddox Street, just off New Bond Street. Most of the customers were lunchtime shoppers who ordered salads or businessmen who came in for steak and *pommes frites*. One man, a tough-looking Scot with a crew cut, was a regular, and a table was kept for him in the window. He always attracted a small crowd looking in from the street, since he wore a live cobra around his neck.

The restaurant was managed by a young Persian, Houshang,

who was nice to the waitresses but insisted we work a split shift, from 12 to 3 p.m. and then 5:30 to closing time. The hours were long and the money was pathetic. But the pastries we served for dessert were baked fresh every day at a nearby patisserie, and at the end of the evening shift, we were allowed to take the leftovers home. I would come back late at night, laden with éclairs, strawberry tarts, napoleons and slices of chocolate cake, and when Chris came back from work at the hospital we would sit at the kitchen table and gorge ourselves.

The Mad Ox kitchen was run by a tyrannical young German of classic Aryan blond looks called Wilfried. He lost his temper if we kept the food waiting even for a minute. He'd stand at the service window of the kitchen, which was in the basement, threatening us with his knife. "Hey shtoo-pid!" he would yell. "You want me to die waiting for you? You want to kill me? I kill you first."

He was not a great cook. The most popular first course on the menu was angels on horseback, oysters wrapped in bacon, served on toast points instead of toothpicks as my mother used to do. They were also the most expensive—and they were bought frozen. The only reliable item that emerged from Wilfried's kitchen was steak. We used to try to wheedle minute steaks out of him, and once in a while, if he was in a good mood, he'd even send us out a sirloin.

The Americans who came in were shocked by the small size of the portions we served. "If that's a steak, it must have come from a mouse!" So we used to give them two—and charge them double. Still, it was a bargain by American standards in those days.

One of our miniskirted goddesses, flame-haired Ruth, was covered in even more freckles than I was, thanks to her childhood on the beach outside Sydney. She was so overweight that her stockings hissed as her thighs rubbed against each other when she walked. But she was the fastest worker in the restaurant, taking the stairs up and down like a sprinter until two or three in the morning. I asked her how she managed to keep such a pace.

It was the pills her doctor had prescribed to depress her appetite. Ever since she'd begun taking them, she'd had the energy of an Olympic athlete, an unexpected and welcome side effect. She started sharing the pills with me. I found I could keep going until four in the morning on a Saturday and not feel the least bit tired.

The Mad Ox didn't have a sommelier, so Houshang made the waitresses responsible for the wine. If we made a mess of the cork, we were allowed to keep the bottle "for the kitchen." As a result, I developed a taste for Châteauneuf du Pape, which was one of the most popular bottles on the list and often had a difficult cork.

One evening a group of rowdy Yorkshire businessmen came in late for dinner. They were rather drunk, and they ordered well-done steaks "and a nice bottle of Sauternes."

They finished the first bottle fast and ordered a second. Ruth, legs hissing, sped away with the empty bottle and returned a minute later. She uncorked the bottle and poured some wine into a glass for one of the men to taste.

He looked at the glass. "Hey! This wine is pink!"

It was indeed.

Ruth didn't flinch. "Of course it's pink," she said. "It's another year."

When I was cleaning up after they'd left, I found a steak underneath the banquette.

"I'm not surprised," said Ruth. "What do you expect from people who order Sauternes with steaks."

"And well-done steaks at that!"

"Serves them bloody well right. But who stacked a rosé d'Anjou in with the Sauternes bottles?"

Frenchmen weren't as easy to please as the English. One day four of them, thick-set provincial businessmen, came in for lunch. They ordered salads and steaks "à la minute."

Boni, the salad maker, was from Spain. In his previous job he'd been a dresser for the singer Shirley Bassey. He was gentle and campy, full of gossip. Wilfried couldn't stand Boni simply because he was gay. Boni would spend hours in the prep kitchen making elaborate, baroque, beautifully arranged salads, dressing them with as much care as he must have lavished on Miss Bassey herself.

When I told him I was serving a table of four Frenchmen, he lost his head. He embellished their green salads with slivers of tomato, radish flowers, scallions snipped into curly fringes, sliced beets shaped like stars, petals of cucumber with scalloped edges, diced hard-boiled eggs and sprigs of watercress. I brought the salads to the Frenchmen, who looked down at them with disdain.

Typical French, think they're so superior, I thought as I walked away.

A few minutes later, one of the Frenchmen hailed me.

"Meez! Take a look at this!" He pointed to his salad plate. There, resting on top of a slice of tomato, was a slug.

I whisked the plate away and went downstairs to Boni. Avoiding the eagle eye of Wilfried, I asked Boni to make another salad. It took a while and at last I delivered it upstairs to the Frenchman.

Two minutes later: "Meez!"

Another slug had emerged from under a leaf of lettuce and was playfully waving its horns in the air.

"Oh, dear," I said. *"Ce sont des escargots à l'anglaise!"*

The Frenchmen weren't charged for their salads, but they left without leaving a tip.

Wilfried screamed and waved his knife at Boni, who walked out for good.

The next morning I couldn't get out of bed. My arms and legs felt like lead and my eyes felt as though they'd been glued shut.

"What are those pills you've been taking?" Claudio asked.

When I made it back to work a day later, I found out. Dexedrine. A nice cocktail when mixed with Châteauneuf du Pape.

CLAUDIO AND I RETURNED to New York and I got a job coediting *Horizontes de Viaje,* a travel supplement to *Visión,* a Latin American news magazine. I wrote in English and the articles were translated into Spanish and Portuguese. Meanwhile, at a cocktail party a friend introduced me to a literary agent. A publisher was looking for a book on Chinese cooking with American meals. Fusion cuisine way before its time. But I'd lived in Vietnam, and we'd had a Chinese cook. Those credentials were enough, it seemed, and my outline for the book was accepted.

The agent said he would take 50 percent. "Let's split it down the middle, OK?" I hadn't the first clue what agents normally took, so I agreed. I was a writer at last! Well, a cookbook writer.

I split what was left of the money with Raeford Liles, an artist friend from Alabama who'd worked at one of the bars Claudio used to frequent. He loved food and agreed to test the recipes with me. Raeford, who was in his mid-forties, had been a fighter pilot in the Pacific during the war and later an engineer with NATO, spending seven years in Paris, where he'd studied with the artist Fernand Léger and developed a taste for French food. Now he lived on his military pension in a crumbling tenement overlooking the Lincoln Tunnel, one of the few remaining buildings on the block that hadn't been torn down. His studio was stacked with canvases painted in Day-Glo colors and decorated with neon bar signs and an inflated plastic jeroboam of Moët & Chandon Champagne. The room was choc-a-bloc with things he used to buy at job lots on Canal Street: aluminum fish poachers, fake Georgian candlesticks, rice cookers, battery-operated pepper mills, wind-up toys and giant Lego bricks he made into sculptures that stood three and four feet high. There was no stove in his tiny apartment, which had a bathroom down the hall. He did all his cooking in an electric skillet. It served as our wok.

The idea behind the book was to encourage non-Chinese Americans to add a couple of Chinese-inspired dishes to their menus.

The ingredients were to be available at supermarkets all over the country (not a lot of choice in those days). The food was economical too, another selling point. Instead of cooking a steak, you could buy a small amount of beef and stir-fry it with vegetables.

Raeford, an inventive cook, had two sides to his personality. One used to "come up from the basement" and make him say and do crazy things. The other was well-behaved and responsible. Raeford sautéed tiny shrimp in the skillet and piled them on newspaper. We'd eat them for lunch with a bottle of white wine, peeling them as we went along and dipping them in a homemade mayonnaise. He'd lay on a spread of sea urchins to be eaten from their shells with a plastic spoon. He cooked soft-shell crabs in ouzo, setting them alight. He added dried tangerine peel to stir-fried beef. But then his wild side would get the better of him, and he'd make a dish such as tripe stewed with rabbit in apple cider.

We'd meet a couple of times a week at lunchtime, do our shopping in Chinatown or at the markets on Ninth Avenue and test the recipes. Our book was embarrassingly naïve, but to my astonishment, it went into the Literary Guild book club and sold quite well. It was in its way, I suppose, ahead of its time.

Then came another innovative work, the *Quick and Easy Raw Food Cookbook,* which included my mother's recipe for jellied consommé madrilène with red caviar and sour cream. Since these were the days before salmonella became a household word, there was also a recipe for a popular Japanese dish—blanched, raw chicken on skewers, served with wasabi. I was photographed for a full-page article in *Newsday,* eating sushi. Raw fish! That was practically unheard of in New York then.

Things were not going well with Claudio. He kept threatening to go back to Chile, where he would find work, be treated decently and not have to do demeaning jobs like dancing at the Latin Quarter or drudging in the darkroom for Hans Namuth. In June he went to Florida on a tour with a small group of dancers. I took a trip to the

Caribbean for *Horizontes*. At a hotel in Guadeloupe, I ate four dozen marvelous oysters the size of thumbnails that were served on the all-you-can-eat buffet. The next morning, I came down with a throat infection. *"Mademoiselle, vous avez des champignons sur la gorge,"* said the doctor ("you have mushrooms growing on your throat"). So I cut the trip short and returned to New York. The next day I was invited to a Fourth of July party for the Chilean poet Nicanor Parra given by a Chilean pianist, Carla Hübner. I didn't feel well, but I didn't want to miss it.

There weren't enough chairs in her small apartment so I sat on the floor. A man in a blue cotton turtleneck was talking to someone about poetry, and I thought he was probably gay since he was wearing blue beads, which even in those hippie days seemed a bit excessive. He sat down beside me and asked if I was English. He'd lived for a while in London, he said, and he was a poet. He introduced himself, William Merwin. The name meant nothing to me.

"The worst thing about parties uptown is that there's never anything to smoke," he said.

"Yes," I replied, "isn't it just the worst thing?"

"Shall we leave?"

For lunch a few days later, William made me one of his favorite things: steak tartare. The meat had been ground to order by the butcher at Jefferson Market. William mixed it in a bowl with two kinds of mustard and—the secret ingredient—a quarter of a teaspoon of curry powder. The curry powder made all the difference, he said, and it worked for scrambled eggs too. We had the steak tartare with toast and cold beer. My ordeal at the Brasserie, when I'd ordered this dish expecting a grilled sirloin, seemed very long ago.

Steak Tartare

1 pound prime sirloin, ground
    to order
2 tablespoons capers, drained
1 small onion, chopped
2 tablespoons olive oil
One 2-ounce can anchovy filets,
    drained and cut into small
    pieces
Worcestershire sauce to taste
Tabasco to taste

$^1/_4$ teaspoon powdered Colman's
    mustard
$^1/_2$ teaspoon Dijon mustard
$^1/_4$ teaspoon curry powder
Sea salt and freshly ground
    black pepper
1 tablespoon red wine vinegar
1 egg yolk
$^1/_4$ cup chopped parsley

Combine all the ingredients in a large bowl and mix together
carefully. Serve immediately.

SERVES 4

NOTE: *Now that raw eggs carry a small risk of salmonella, use organic
eggs and make sure they have no cracks in their shells and are very
fresh. Also have the meat ground to order.*

MY RELATIONSHIP WITH CLAUDIO ended painfully, but I had no doubts that William was the one. He was eighteen years older than I and in an unhappy marriage. Yet in spite of the guilt and anxiety I felt about seeing a married man, we spent the rest of the summer and the next seven years together.

William's last two books of poems, *The Moving Target* (1963) and *The Lice* (1967), had been among the most influential of his generation. Now he was working on *The Carrier of Ladders,* a collection of poems that was to win the Pulitzer Prize. (He donated the prize money to the anti–Vietnam War effort.) He was also translating Pablo Neruda, the aphorisms of the Italian poet Antonio Porchia, and, with the scholar Clarence Brown, the works of the Russian poet Osip Mandelstam.

By observing William and listening to him, my awareness of things became sharper and richer, my attention clearer and more intense. Through him I was to receive an extraordinary education.

That first summer together William and I walked the hot streets of the city, browsing through the Eighth Street bookshop, wandering around the East and West Village and Chinatown, and eating in bistros and cheap Indian, Japanese and Italian restaurants. We went to the Elgin Cinema on 18th Street every other night for a month. For two weeks we saw a Bergman double bill, followed by two weeks of Kurosawa. Afterward we'd eat at a French bistro on Perry Street where you brought your own wine and where they played Edith Piaf and didn't mind if you pushed back the chairs and danced. We'd go for boiled artichokes vinaigrette and *linguine alle vongole* at a dumpy Italian trattoria called the Little Place on West Fourth Street. We had huge plates of moussaka and well-done roast lamb from the steam table at Molfeta's, a Greek cafeteria on Ninth Avenue and 44th Street. And I cooked meals in the tiny kitchen of my apartment on Tenth Street.

One day Allen Ginsberg took us to see W. H. Auden's apartment on the parlor floor of a townhouse in the East Village. (Auden was away, spending the summer at the house he shared with Chester Kallman in Austria.) The mess was staggering. The ironing board stood in the middle of the living room; dusty piles of outdated phone books were strewn around the unswept floor; jelly jars were heaped in the tub.

A few days later, William and I had dinner with Elizabeth Tingom, a pretty, blonde California girl who worked in the poetry department at the *New Yorker,* and her then husband, the writer Robert Hemenway, who was a friend of Auden's. The previous year they'd landed his place in the East Village as a summer sublet. They had seen every foot as a historic site where immortal lines were actually written, inspired or nurtured, however indirectly. To be able to restore everything faithfully to its original position upon his return, they made a careful map of where everything had been left, down to the ironing board, before it was folded up and put away in a closet.

At the end of their first day in the apartment Elizabeth climbed respectfully into the bed that was normally slept in by the aging, overweight poet, who once said that his face looked like a wedding cake left out in the rain. She hesitated for a moment, but she couldn't resist. She opened the drawer of the bedside table. In it she found a one-pound jar of Vaseline and two pairs of castanets.

A friend of mine at *Horizontes,* Marilyn Hoffner, told me about a cabin near her summer house. It was in the woods up a mountain near Fishkill, about an hour and a half from the city near the Hudson. William rented the cabin for a pittance. We took the bus from the Port Authority to Fishkill and went on foot from there, carrying shopping bags filled with food and wine. We walked up the hill along a winding gravel road, past wooden summer cabins that looked like gingerbread houses hidden among the trees. They had been built out of logs by Ukrainian immigrants in the forties, decorated with curlicues and ornate porches that were set with boxes of marigolds, geraniums and impatiens. When the road came to an end, we hiked through the woods and crossed a stream by jumping on large stones that had been placed across it. The path led to a glade where sunlight dappled bushes of mountain laurel that were covered with white blossoms and humming with bees. The cabin had one room. There was no plumbing, just the stream, which was clean and clear, where we bathed and got our drinking water. We camped in sleeping bags and cooked over an open fire outside. For dinner we ate corn on the cob, dipped in water in its husk and roasted over the flames; potatoes baked in the ashes; sweet and spicy Italian sausages grilled until they hissed and burst through their skins; steaks and chops I bought at Washington Beef Market near the Port Authority before catching the bus to Fishkill. I'd get swordfish or mackerel at Central Fish Market a few doors down, where Raeford had introduced me to sea urchins.

After dinner William would read his new poems and I would listen, awestruck. He made me a reading list. *The Maxims of Chamfort,* poems of Cesar Pavese, James Wright, William Blake, the stories of Isak Babel. He was translating *Voices* by Antonio Porchia. "They will say you are on the wrong road, if it is your own."

In the ensuing months, William and I traveled around the country where he gave readings at colleges, so that eventually I knew many of his poems by heart. In California we stayed with Galway Kinnell, who'd been at Princeton with him. He told us that after one of his readings a woman in the audience rose to her feet with a question. "Was that last poem a real one, Mr. Kinnell? Or did you just make it up?"

The following summer I went to London to see my parents, and William went to his house in the southwest of France. I read and reread the letters he wrote me until they were creased and falling apart like old road maps. Then in the fall he was back, Carmen had moved out, and I was cooking dinner for him again on Tenth Street.

The blue and white Adam color scheme that my mother had picked out when I first moved in had never looked right on the leprous walls and paint-gummed woodwork of my apartment. So I'd covered the walls with a rust-colored fabric, printed with gray and blue flowers on yellow vines. I'd painted the moldings dark red and upholstered the sofa and armchairs in pale gray-green brocade. The marble fireplace was six feet long, carved with a profusion of grapes and vine leaves by Italian workmen nearly a century ago, and even though it had been described in the lease as "as is," it worked. When someone threw out a mirrored door from one of the mansions on Tenth Street one day, I carted it up six flights of stairs. It made the living room, with its high ceilings, twice as big. French doors opened onto the dark green bedroom, which was lined with bookshelves and hung with lace curtains and a framed poster of Marcel Proust. Somehow, between freelancing and advances on cookbooks, I managed to scrape together the rent.

A round table is the best shape for entertaining (as long as it's not too big, like those tables at benefits, where you can talk only to your immediate neighbors). My table, a battered oval drop-leaf from the Salvation Army, was covered with a round wooden top, another treasure I'd found discarded in the street. It seated eight if you squeezed in and was set with silver Georgian candlesticks (my twenty-first birthday present) and a white lace cloth from a job lot on Fourteenth Street. Under candlelight, the cloth looked just fine. Overlooking the table was a wall of paintings and framed photographs, among them sepia portraits of my grandparents, a poster of a bathrobe by Jim Dine, a faded, hand-colored photograph in a beat-up black wooden frame of the Argentinian tango singer Carlos Gardel looking soulful in a fedora and a white silk scarf, and a Hans Namuth photograph of Jackson Pollock sitting on the running board of an old jalopy just before his death, printed by Claudio.

My place had a patina. "Your apartment's like the edge of Bohemia," said one of my friends. "It transports you to another place and time." Indeed, with a stretch of the imagination, you could pretend you were in a Russian dacha or a London drawing room in the 1890s. The only hint you were in New York was the view through the window gates over the fire escape. Above the rooftops of the brownstones across the way, the top of the Empire State Building was visible, a needle pointing at the sky.

In the evening my apartment felt like a salon; people of all ages and professions sat around the table drinking wine until late, and after dinner we would often dance and play charades.

That winter, William and I gave a dinner for twenty-four people, mostly poets. I made the ambitious decision to roast a suckling pig. I'd never cooked one before. Among our guests were James Merrill, Richard Howard, Howard Moss, John Ashbery, David Kalstone, the writer John Gruen and his wife, the painter Jane Wilson.

At Washington Market the butcher wrapped up the pig in brown paper, secured it with string and put wooden handles on top. I took the pig home on the subway as though I were carrying a suitcase.

The recipe said to cut the eyes out with a pair of grape scissors. All well and good. But grape scissors weren't in my Greenwich Village *batterie de cuisine*. I had only an ordinary knife, which I used to an effect that would have gone down well in a Polanski movie. Feeling like Catherine Deneuve in *Repulsion,* I dumped the pig in the bath where it lay overnight, soaking in cold water as the recipe instructed. When I came in the next morning, half asleep, I gave a shriek. It was floating in the tub like a drowned corpse.

I stuffed the pig with a mixture of bread and apples, sewed up the cavity and put a ball of foil in its mouth. Then I placed it on a rack on a roasting pan and put it in the oven. The head stuck out of the door.

I was frantic. I had twenty-four people coming in less than five hours. The pig was too big to go in the oven.

Finally I sawed it in half. I covered up the sawn-off parts with foil and put the head and shoulders on the top rung, the tail and the middle part underneath. When it was roasted I served it with a belly band of flowers wrapped around its middle. "It's like a Hawaiian luau," said Jimmy Merrill admiringly. "What a lovely idea!"

No one was any the wiser. The pig was great.

I think it was that night over dinner that someone told a story about the time Robert Lowell and Caroline Blackwood were invited to see the Queen Mother. There were strikes in London and frequent blackouts. The lights went out the evening the couple was due at Buckingham Palace. They had to get dressed in the dark, Caroline rooting in the back of the closet for one of her thrift shop numbers and Cal, as Lowell was called, searching on the floor for his socks. By the time they reached the palace, the lights were back on. Lowell was invited to take his place on a dais next to the Queen Mother. When he sat down, his trousers rose over his ankles, revealing to the assembled gathering that he was wearing one black sock and one red. As he leaned forward trying to get his trousers to cover his ankles, the Queen Mother beamed at him. "Oh, Mr. Lowell, I am so delighted to meet you at last," she said. "One of my favorite poems is 'The Waste Land.' "

The next year William went to France again for several weeks, but he met me in July in Paris, looking tanned after a couple of months at his house in the Lot. We were going to travel to Lapland. He'd bought a new Volkswagen bus, which had arrived from Germany, all shiny and blue. We planned to sleep in the back on air mattresses and cook our meals in the open.

In Amsterdam, there was no camping site, so we decided to stay in a bed and breakfast. I'd been to see my parents before we set off and my father had given me his Sam Brown, the army belt he'd worn at Arnhem in the war when he swam the Rhine. I thought it would be a cool thing to wear. It was the seventies, after all. So I'd packed it in my suitcase, which was known as "the monster" because it was so big. The monster was too wide to take the corners of the stairs of the old canal house, so we left it with the rest of our luggage in the VW bus. I thought nothing of it; Amsterdam was full of flowers and houseboats and cheerful friendly hippies wearing beads and bell bottoms and smoking dope. That night the town proved not so friendly. Thieves broke into the VW bus and took everything we'd left in there, including "the monster." I never forgave myself for losing the Sam Brown.

In Norway we ate *Gammelost,* a rich, caramel-colored cheese that is sweet like a piece of candy, sort of like a solid version of the *manjar blanco* Maria taught me to make. It's aged under the mattresses of elderly people and invalids, said the Norwegian shopkeeper, hence the name, which means "old cheese." We ate slivers of it with cloudberries as we sat on a beach watching six dignified-looking oyster catchers staring out to sea.

On the road, William would often stop the car to look at birds. He kept a small pencil and notebook in his pocket. He liked short pencils. We'd pull up at the side of the road while he made a note about something or peered through his binoculars. Through mine, I'd make out a black speck in the sky. William, however, would identify it at once, and bring out his Roger Tory Peterson for confirmation.

In Finland people shouted "Deutschland!" at us as we drove past, and threw stones. Some youths even tried to drive us off the road. This went on until William realized that because the VW bus had been shipped directly from the manufacturer, the license plates were German. So he bought Union Jacks and pasted them on the sides and back of the bus. He didn't want to be seen as an American because of the Vietnam War.

It was surprising to come across so many German tourists in a country where the Nazis had wrought such devastation. The war was still fresh in people's memories. In 1944 the Nazis had burned every house and barn they could find in Lapland. Some of the shells were still standing. Now the German invaders wore blue track suits and traveled in elaborate caravans, complete with TV antennae and netted sunporches. In the saunas you could hear them slapping themselves with birch branches and singing songs.

Outside the state liquor stores, which looked like clinics, we'd see local men stone-faced, staring and drunk. Drinking didn't make them happy. They were silent, weaving glumly about the streets, and then throwing up against the wall of a building.

"Ah! We've passed the watershed," William said one day, coming out of the bathroom. Of course. The water went down the sink the other way. He noticed everything.

On the way up north we would stop to pick wildflowers. William identified them, and I pressed them on the pages of my journal: marsh orchids, butterwort, bog pimpernel, chickenweed, wintergreen, alpine bistort, cheddar pink (a rarity!). On July 4, our second anniversary, rosebay.

In the supermarkets I stood in line with Lapps and bought fish baked inside loaves of bread, boat-shaped potato-stuffed Karelian pies, rye bread, stuffed cabbage, smoked reindeer, a pâté made from liver and barley, and fresh cottage cheese. With a pestle and mortar made from Finnish juniper I ground coriander seed to sprinkle on a salmon cooked over an open fire. I served it with hollandaise sauce I managed to make from scratch without it curdling. The mosquitoes were in my hair and my nose and falling into the food. The Lapps were immune to them; they walked around with mosquitoes on their faces and didn't bother to flick them off.

Every night, the Lapland sun crossed the horizon without setting, bathing everything in a flat, white light.

THAT FALL, I WAS INVITED to cover the opening of the Hilton Hotel in Caracas for *Horizontes*. William had returned from a month in France and came with me. The Hilton, a modern high-rise in the center of the city, was not his sort of thing. Upon our arrival at the hotel, moreover, we had to negotiate our way through a phalanx of guards armed with machine guns. We found Caracas ugly, the restaurants pretentious and expensive. I wrote a piece that parroted many of William's opinions, which he'd expressed in no uncertain terms. Because I had published other articles in the same issue of *Horizontes*, "New Hotel in Caracas" was unsigned. My story was illustrated with a drawing of a donkey standing in front of the town, an attempt to be endearing that was taken entirely the wrong way by the citizens of Caracas. They saw the article as a Colombian plot to discredit the country and ruin its tourist trade. Alas, the president of *Horizontes'* editorial board was Alberto Lleras, the ex-president of Colombia, and by sheer coincidence, the same issue of the magazine had run a glowing article about his native land. Lleras, deeply embarrassed, announced that the "señor" who'd written the Caracas piece was a freelancer and would not be used in the future.

Now I had no job. This worked out fine, since William was ready to leave New York for a while. The city offered too many distractions. He needed a place where he could work without interruption. In November he fetched the blue VW bus, which he'd shipped to New York, and we loaded it up. (Once again, I left the apartment with friends who looked after Bully and Jason.) We were going to Mexico for the winter. Some friends of William's, Danny and Charles Bell, had bought an old farm in the Spanish colonial town of San Cristóbal de las Casas in Chiapas, near the Guatemalan border, and they'd found us a house to rent for the winter.

We made a fleeting trip through Pennsylvania, Virginia and the South, via Louisiana and Texas. Since it was too cold to sleep on air mattresses in the bus as we'd done in Lapland, we checked into motels. I'd get out a hot plate and fill the hallways with the smell of onions and garlic while William stood on his head and did yoga exercises to recover from the day in the car. We traveled well together, and I was excited at the prospect of spending a few months in Mexico, where neither of us had ever been.

I also liked the challenge of the makeshift motel meals. Makeshift they were. It was hard to find anything in the supermarkets but prepackaged beef, pork or chicken, frozen vegetables and iceberg lettuce. William called it "foodite." There was no fish, no free-range or organic anything. But there was a good deal of beef raised in feedlots, pumped with hormones and antibiotics. I made stir-fried dishes I'd learned on Raeford's hot plate when we worked on the Chinese book: beef with mustard greens, chicken with almonds and fried zucchini, sautéed chicken livers and mushrooms. The only state where we found good food was Louisiana. And at the house of the poet and ecologist Wendell Berry in Kentucky.

We spent a couple of days at his farm near Lexington. Wendell was tall, lean and good-natured, a clean-shaven President Lincoln with protruding ears and a strong Kentucky accent. He had a pretty wife, Tanya, and two children, Den and Mary, aged twelve and eight. When we arrived, Tanya served us meatloaf with squash, greens and potatoes, all homegrown, homemade bread and stewed rhubarb for dessert.

The Berrys didn't have a vineyard, of course, but they did have homemade wine. After dinner Wendell brought out dandelion and cherry wines he'd made. The sinking feeling induced by the prospect of such cordials was dispelled with the first sip. The conversation centered not around poetry but gardening and compost heaps.

The next morning the sun came through frosted windowpanes in the bedroom. It was a cold, cloudless day and after a breakfast of eggs from the Berrys' chickens, bacon from the homegrown pigs, sorghum molasses on homemade bread, homemade jam and honey from his bees, Wendell took us around the farm. They had a cow, a horse, rabbits, veal calves and many chickens. As we walked up a creek riddled with stones, he and William knelt down and scooped up handfuls of dark, moist earth. Wendell had built himself a study looking out over the river, and he'd carried a stove all the way there on his back. "Anyone who'd walk that far to see me would be welcome."

After another great farm meal for lunch—thick veal steaks—Wendell drove us around the neighborhood. I was reminded of Sherborne, where everyone around was "kin" to everyone else, and their families went back for generations. He introduced us to tobacco growers in overalls who were tying up long orange leaves of tobacco that were hanging from the rafters of a barn. They were in their sixties, with bony, lined faces, and they spat on the floor. Developers had been by again, scoping out the land for houses. They'd put little red flags all over the place and had even come up with names for the street, such as Canvasback Alley.

"There are no canvasback ducks in Kentucky!" said Wendell angrily. We walked through the woods and ripped out all the red markers we could see. "I'm going to have to try to raise the money to buy the land myself."

"A lot of readings," said William.

As I lay in bed that night I heard Wendell laughing with his son, Den. He was reading him a story about Pogo, the possum.

The family scene at Wendell's filled me with longing. I'd be content living off the land like that, wouldn't I? I'd be happy spending my days baking bread, feeding chickens and putting up jams made from the fruit I'd picked in our orchard. If I could only have a child to read stories to at bedtime.

But William didn't want children: "I have no desire to be a pater familias." I didn't realize then to what extent his life was inextricably bound up with his work. He was not interested in "the pram in the hall," as Cyril Connolly once put it, nor would he ever be.

The next morning we were on the road again. In Tennessee we

stopped at a trading post called the Pioneer. It looked as though it had remained unchanged for a century. An ancient floor-to-ceiling glass-fronted icebox, painted white and black and decorated with a pair of bullhorns, stood next to the counter. Hanging on a line of hooks in the ceiling were country hams, gnarled and black-brown, like the fossilized burls of a tree. "These were dried in tobacco barns and smoked over hickory," said the storekeeper, an old man in overalls. We bought one, all eighteen pounds of it.

The store also sold patchwork quilts for ten dollars, old books, and jars of arrowheads 3,500 years old. In the back I noticed a box covered with a dusty cloth that reached to the floor. When the hawk-faced storekeeper saw me staring at it he walked over. As he drew back the cloth his eyes glittered. A skeleton was curled up inside the box.

"That's our nigra!" he said.

He pointed outside to a free-standing cage. "There's the jail they took him from to lynch him fifty years ago."

We couldn't wait to get away.

A few days later we found a motel that had not only a kitchenette, but a baking pan large enough to hold the ham. I scraped off the mold, placed the ham in the pan with a few inches of water, and baked it for several hours. This ham was nothing like the pressed, plumped-up, watery hams I knew from the supermarket. It was strong, salty and dry, reminiscent of the serrano hams I'd had in tapas bars when Claudio and I had traveled around Spain. And there was an infinite supply. During the rest of the trip I sliced the ham for spaghetti carbonara, folded it into omelettes, slathered it with a sauce flavored with mustard and herbs. I fried it, secreted it under poached eggs on toast, shredded it, put it in salads. When we crossed the border to Mexico, I hid it in tortillas and masked it with hot sauce. I disguised it in enchiladas in a spicy filling of chiles and tomatoes with onions, garlic and cream. But there was always more.

We had a brief respite from the country ham when we reached

Oaxaca. At El Tule, a restaurant overlooking the square where a marimba band was playing, we had *chicharrónes* (fried pigskin) wrapped in tortillas, sweet tamales and enchiladas with mole sauce. We were entranced by both the food and the town, which was in a high valley surrounded by desert and overlooked by the pyramid of Monte Albán.

Now this was a place where I could live. William liked it too. We were both so delighted with Oaxaca we decided that if San Cristóbal wasn't right for us, we'd come back. I was thrilled by the market, the tropical fruits and exotic vegetables I'd never seen before: paddles of cactus stripped of their prickles and already cooked, fresh chiles of every color and hue, dried fish, scarlet shrimp, cheeses wrapped in corn leaves and tortillas—big wide yellow ones the size of dinner plates, and small pale versions, thin as a crêpe. I'd packed a Mexican cookbook by Elizabeth Lambert Ortiz and the *Time-Life* cookbook on Latin American food. I couldn't wait to get started. But did I really think that we were going to have a life like the Berrys when we got to San Cristóbal? I didn't, but still, I hoped it was a first step to something, although I wasn't sure what.

In Chiapas, PRI (Partido Revolucionario Institucional, Mexico's ruling political party) signposts lined the mountain road from Tuxtla Gutiérrez to San Cristóbal. They were riddled with bullets. Clusters of makeshift crosses littered the deep ravines on the side of the highway to mark the spots where cars and buses had gone over. It wasn't hard to believe, as I read in the guidebook, that not long ago, this part of Mexico had been accessible only by mule. I tried not to shut my eyes as we sped along.

All of a sudden, we rounded another sharp bend, and San Cristóbal lay beneath us in the valley of Jovel. It was surrounded by mountains as though in a bowl. We were nearly seven thousand feet above sea level, and the air was thin and smelled of pine. White churches stood on a hill at either end of town, like a pair of sentinels. Small gray puffs hung over the town, frozen in the air like gun smoke in seventeenth-century paintings of battleships fighting at sea.

It was early December and the temperature dropped rapidly as we descended into the bowl. The dense evergreen oak and pine forests gave way to clearings where we could see wattle huts with thatched roofs, carefully tended cornfields and rows of cabbages, carnations and lilies, planted incongruously side by side. There was a sudden flash of red or blue as an Indian woman herding sheep or working in the fields flitted behind a rock to avoid being stared at. The women wore thick black woolen skirts with red and green sashes, and rectangles of black wool were folded over their heads with red tassels hanging jauntily down the back. The men were dressed in white wool *chamarras* (ponchos) and leather belts. Their high cheekbones and hooked noses were straight out of the pictures I'd seen of Mayan murals.

Our first stop was Na Bolom, where Danny and Charles were staying while their house was being renovated. As we stood in the courtyard of the house, we heard a booming female voice speaking with a German accent, her sentences punctuated with "god-dammit!" as she complained about the deteriorating conditions in San Cristóbal. "The *basura* [garbage] everywhere . . ."

That was my first introduction to Trudi Blom, or Doña Gertrudis (pronounced "Hair-troodis") as she was called by the locals. She was a small Swiss-German woman in her late seventies with cropped white hair, dressed in an embroidered Indian shirt and white trousers. She was made up like a film star from the 1940s, with black penciled eyebrows, scarlet lipstick and large silver earrings. She introduced us to a smiling boy, who had long hair and wore a white shift and leather sandals. Young Chank'in. He was a Mayan Indian from the Lacandon jungle.

"He wants to wear jeans, get a motorbike and go to Mexico City. I told him, you do that and you'll be nobody, goddammit!"

Trudi was the widow of the Danish anthropologist Franz Blom, with whom she had come to Chiapas in 1943. She ran Na Bolom, a former seminary that had been turned into a guesthouse with a museum and a library. Trudi and Franz had made it their life's work to save the last remaining Lacandon Indians from extinction. There were about four hundred left; they had been the least colonized of the Mayans and lived deep in the rain forest, which was now being threatened by roads, mahogany cutters and ranchers.

We followed Danny's car up a hilly cobbled street lined with low white-washed adobe houses that had red-tiled roofs and small barred windows. At last we stopped in front of a heavy wooden door. It opened onto a flower-filled patio. There was a larger house up a few steps to the right, and on the left, a smaller, one-story building.

A short, bandy-legged man with a big wide grin came running down the stairs of the main house to greet us. It was our future landlord, Ralph, an American from Michigan known locally as Don Raffa.

"He looks like the joker in a pack of cards," said William.

I wondered if the joke was on us. The day was sunny, but the house was like a cave. There were two dark, dank rooms, and the front door had to remain open to let in the light. Ralph had built a brick fireplace in each room, halfway off the ground. "Only gringos have fireplaces," he said.

"What do local people do?" I asked.

"At night they just go to bed."

There was also a charcoal brazier. "If you use it," said Ralph, "keep the door open."

William made a fire with pieces of *ochote*, a resinous wood brought in by Chamulan Indians who carried it into town on their backs. The fire didn't heat the room very well, and we went to bed. As we lay there we could hear a barrage of fireworks. Saturday night: a cause for celebration. Those mysterious clouds we'd seen from the car as we drove into the valley were *cuetes*, fireworks made by Chamulan Indians.

But I didn't feel much like celebrating. I wished we'd stayed in Oaxaca.

In the morning, we awoke to the sound of crowing roosters, gobbling turkeys and yapping dogs. The scent of charcoal filled the air, which rang with explosions of more *cuetes,* fireworks celebrating mass. I opened the front door to a thick mist. It was even colder in the house.

The following days and nights were punctuated by explosions of fireworks. The Indians and Ladinos (residents of mixed Spanish and Indian descent) set them off at any hour—to celebrate weddings, fiestas, funerals, christenings, Christmas Eve, Easter, Sunday, going to work, coming home, lunchtime, getting drunk, returning from the market.

"More money is spent on fireworks," Ralph told us, "than the entire annual budget of the town."

By Thursday, the *cuetes* had reached a crescendo. It was the Fiesta de Guadalupe in the domed blue and white church that was perched on top of the hill at the end of San Cristóbal's main street. A more pagan Catholic feast would be hard to imagine. The blue and white steps leading up to the church were lined with stalls selling *refrescos* (soft drinks). Many of the children were dressed up as Indians and one even brought a chicken into the church, holding it under her arm and stroking its brown feathers. A marimba band competed lustily with the church choir, the church bells, the jangle of a merry-go-round and rock music from the square below. The fireworks continued throughout the day and well into the night.

There was not much peace inside Ralph's house either. A sweet, generous man with a permanent big, friendly grin, he was hopelessly in love with Gregorio, a macho young Ladino workman who strung him along. Gregorio wore a white plastic cowboy hat, a black nylon shirt and pointed cowboy boots, and tied a red kerchief around his neck. He taunted and teased Ralph, singing him love songs on his guitar. At night they'd get drunk on beer and tequila. There'd be shouts in the courtyard. Ralph would beg Gregorio to stay over. Gregorio's wife would come banging on the door in the middle of the night, shrieking for him to come home.

And so here we were having driven all this way, living in two cold rooms, with no peace, under lowering skies. William had had enough. "I haven't had a moment to myself since we've been here."

So he rented a room in an empty house, a few streets away, owned by Doña Catalina. He would leave after breakfast and work there undisturbed. At least, until people began to find out where he was and came hammering on the garden door whenever they felt like it. At first I didn't mind his going off for the day. I was working on a cookbook and trying to learn Spanish. I wrote long, detailed letters to my grandmother, who sent back pages filled with her musings on just about every subject, from Arnold Schoenberg and Edward Heath to the meals she'd eaten and her memories of scientific experiments long past (the excitement at seeing my grandfather on a television screen in 1928, his lips moving as she heard his voice ask, "Are you there, George?"). Nevertheless, the days began to seem rather long.

After William had left in the morning I would go to the market. The Indians from the outlying areas came there every day to trade. Some of the men looked like the archangels of Michelangelo, dressed in white shirts gathered at the neck and embroidered with squash blossom motifs, diaperlike pants folded through their legs, red sashes and straw hats with wide round brims. They were Huaxtec. The Zinacantecos wore pink and white striped *chamarras* and shorts that revealed well-muscled legs and high-backed Mayan sandals, just as you saw in the frescoes. Wide-brimmed straw hats were tilted down over their eyes and streams of colored ribbons flowed down their backs. Chamulan women with babies wrapped in shawls on their backs sold fresh peas and fava beans already peeled, piled in neat heaps on the cloths spread on the ground. They shouted, "Sst-sst *chula! Qué vas a llevar?"* ("What are you going to buy?")

I bought eggs that had thick, stained shells from a Chamulan woman who had carefully wrapped them in her black woolen shawl and trekked them all the way on foot from her village. They were sold by the piece and she placed them one by one in my basket. The yolks were deep orange and flecked with red. My grandmother would have been impressed.

There was no butter in the market, but a Chamulan woman sold unhomogenized milk. I would pour it into the blender and run it at high speed until the curds separated from the whey. The butter was light, pale and sweet, full of air because it had been whipped.

William said that if you ate yogurt every day, its bacteria would replace the bad bacteria in your stomach. So in New York he'd bought a yogurt maker, a white plastic tray that heated four glass-covered dishes. We made up for the thin local milk by adding a cup of powdered milk to the mix. It thickened the yogurt and made it more nutritious. We ate it every day with homemade granola. (A few years later I took one of these yogurt makers to my parents in London. I forgot that the voltage was twice as strong, and by the time they came down to breakfast in the morning the plastic tray had dissolved into a Claes Oldenburg soft sculpture. My mother kept the dishes for leftovers.)

My San Cristóbal kitchen library included Adelle Davis's *Let's Cook It Right,* which was a health-food cult classic at the time. I didn't agree with everything Davis said ("Garlic, like makeup, should never be obvious"), but I believed her about the benefits of whole grains and whole wheat. Pan Bimbo was the most popular choice of bread in San Cristóbal, a sliced white loaf that had the texture of Kleenex. But a couple of local bakeries made rolls, and in one of them I found whole wheat flour. Following Davis's recipes, I baked bread, using the whey from the milk I churned for butter. The loaves were as heavy as bricks. I made peanut butter, roasting the peanuts until they were dark, then grinding them in the blender with salt and peanut oil. The smell of the freshly baked bread would bring

William out of his study. We'd cut thick, warm slices and cover them with the coarse peanut butter sprinkled with salt. Until one day, I decided I was getting fat.

ﷺ

DESPITE OUR ORIGINAL MISGIVINGS about the town, William decided to buy the house where he had been working during the day. It was white, with two huge windowless rooms, flagstone floors, a red-tiled roof and a front porch that faced west. Over the high adobe walls that surrounded the shaggy, tangled garden, you could see blue mountains in the distance. After dinner we would walk down the hill from Ralph's and take a stroll around our new place. One night we laughed as *cuetes* were being set off to celebrate the full moon. It sounded like the London Blitz.

Workmen were hired, and following William's designs, they built plain, white fireplaces for each room and put in large windows. William's study had a view of the garden, and our bedroom doors opened onto a terrace. In the back of the house was a narrow, cell-like study for me with a small fireplace and a high barred window. The sill was on the same level as the sidewalk, so that you saw people's feet as they walked past. William would have built my study at the front of the house if I'd wanted, but I thought that the kitchen should go there. It would be nice to look out over the garden in the evenings when I was cooking dinner.

I continued studying Spanish, reading *Don Quixote* aloud every day with Charles, who spoke it with a strong Southern accent. I had picked up the local accent from Soyla, the maid, who was just sixteen and worked for us every day. So my Spanish, combining Cervantes' seventeenth-century prose and the inflections of a young Chiapas peasant girl, was also something to hear.

One night we learned that *The Ritual,* a Bergman film William and I had missed in New York, was playing at the local cinema with Volker Schlöndorff's *Der Junge Törless.* It seemed an odd choice of films for San Cristóbal. The theater was a rambling flea pit smelling faintly like a latrine, with walls covered with pictures of Mexican movie stars from the forties and fifties. The seats were hard and it was cold. As if on cue, the second the movie started, small boys began running up and down the aisles clinking bottles and shouting, "*Refrescos! Cacahuetes!*"

This refrain was kept for the entire performance. Every time the projectionists changed reels, for no apparent reason they would turn down the sound so that it was inaudible. William took them beer as a bribe to get them to turn it up. There would be a loud thud—a reel change—and the soundtrack was inaudible again. So much for the movies.

There wasn't much else to do. I read Joseph Campbell and struggled through *The Cloud of Unknowing*, *The Upanishads* and Norman O. Brown. I read *Incidents of Travel in Central America, Chiapas and Yucatan* and books about the Spanish explorers. I did research on the Mayan Indians in the library at Na Bolom and worked on articles about them. But tension was mounting between William and me. Sometimes he would emerge from his study in a highly irritable state of mind. He sensed that I was lonely, that I missed being around people, and it troubled him.

Come evening, I threw myself into cooking. Elizabeth David's *Spices, Salt and Aromatics in the English Kitchen* had just come out and I made chutneys and pickles and marmalade with lemons from our tree. And I started to cook Mexican food with the help of our maid Soyla. The first time I asked her to buy some chicken, she brought home two live hens, carrying them upside down by their legs, just as Ahmed had done in Beirut. He'd said it tranquilized them. Still, I was appalled. But what had I expected? I hid indoors while she twisted the necks out on the porch. She laid them on the kitchen table, their eyes already covered by a glaucous veil, their bodies still warm under their feathers. She plucked them and put them on to boil. When I brought out the blender to grind spices for the sauce, it was her turn to look horrified. A *licuadora!* For mole?

Soyla used a *metate,* a piece of heavy volanic stone shaped like a three-legged table that's also used for grinding spices and corn. I'd bought it in the market at Oaxaca, along with a collection of pots, glazed and unglazed. Soyla ground nuts and spices in the *metate:* pepitas (pumpkin seeds), walnuts, sesame seeds, almonds, tomatillos, cilantro and garlic. She heated oil in a clay pot and added the sauce with some of the chicken cooking liquid. She cut the chickens into pieces and added them to the sauce with bread, onions, tomatoes and chocolate that had all been ground together in the *metate.*

I bought fresh tortillas from a woman who lived across the street. She would open the front door of her house and set out a table of hot tortillas wrapped in cloths. So many children crowded around I began to wonder if she was running a school in there as well. "How many children do you have?" I asked one day. Twenty-two.

At dusk, the aroma of frying quesadillas would begin to waft up the hill and the marimba band next door would start rehearsals. *Cuetes* would go off as people returned from work. A dismal orchestra would whoop it up in the *zocalo* (the main square), and the dogs in the street would begin their barking contests.

I would grab a plate and a napkin, put them in my basket and go down to our neighbor's house. She would stand outside in the street huddled over a *comal* (charcoal brazier), making quesadillas as people lined up. She'd pile them on my plate, spooning hot red salsa on the top.

Cheese Quesadillas with Spicy Tomato Relish

1 jalapeño chile, seeded and chopped fine
1 small onion, chopped fine
2 large ripe tomatoes, peeled, seeded and chopped
¹/2 cup fresh cilantro (coriander) leaves, chopped
Salt and freshly ground pepper to taste

¹/2 pound Monterey Jack cheese
8 fresh tortillas
About ³/4 cup peanut or vegetable oil

Combine the chile, onion, tomatoes and cilantro in a bowl. Season
with salt and pepper, mix well and set aside.

Slice the cheese into 2-inch-long pieces. Pour the oil into a
shallow dish big enough to dip a flat tortilla into it.

Heat a heavy frying pan or cast-iron skillet. Dip each tortilla
into the oil, coating it lightly, and fold it over a slice of cheese.
Place the tortilla in the skillet, taking care not to break it in half.
If necessary, press the top with a fork for a few seconds so the
tortilla doesn't open out flat. Fry for 1 to 2 minutes on each side,
or until golden.

Serve at once, spooning a little relish on top of each tortilla as
it is served. Pass the remaining relish around the table separately.

SERVES 8

NOTE: *If necessary, the quesadillas can be kept warm in a low oven.*

꒜

Back home I'd blend some margaritas in the *licuadora,* mixing
tequila with the juice from the strong, small limes they called
"limones" and a splash of Cointreau, then dip the glasses in salt.
We'd sit out on the porch to watch the sunset and eat the quesadillas. That was the part of the day I enjoyed most, talking to William
and listening to him read from his new works. On gray days, when
a *norte* would blow in and heavy rain clouds would hang over the
valley, we'd sit inside by the fire and pour a glass of vino tinto Santo
Tomás, a hefty red that came in gallon jugs and guaranteed a
headache.

There were long, empty days of silence, work and gardening interspersed with (for me) welcome bouts of travel to the Yucatán and Guatemala. In the garden we uncovered a terraced bed around a peach tree, which had been covered with rubble, and there we planted irises. William grew lettuces, radishes, broad beans and strawberries mulched deep in pine needles. Because the house was white, he decided to put only white flowers around it. Colors would have looked garish.

For three years in a row, we spent the winter in San Cristóbal, returning to New York in the spring. But the town, despite its stark beauty, was beginning to wear on us. The mountains had begun to close in, like the high walls that surrounded every garden and the thick bars that covered every window. We both felt trapped. We were always reminded that we were outsiders. In San Cristóbal *adios* was an old-fashioned greeting, not a farewell. But the children had learned a mistranslation of it, and when I walked down the street I was followed by small, piping voices shouting "Goodbye!" and often "Goose bye!" The children would run after me and call out *"gringa!"* Or, since some of them were too young to pronounce the word *gringa*, *"Kinka. Mira la kinka!"*

They were sweet, cheerful children (and far too many of them). But I didn't like being a big blonde gringa. I didn't like the women in the market going "sst" and asking four times the price for their food, but who could blame them? Sometimes kids in the street passing my window would toss their candy wrapper through the bars into my study, and I'd let out a cry of rage.

William and I loathed what was being done to the town, to the landscape and to the Indians. As soon as a family could afford it, steel-framed windows were bashed into the foot-thick walls of their house and the old wooden doors were replaced by steel roll-ups. Because of its colonial architecture, San Cristóbal had been designated a historic district town by President Echeverría. But the mayor of the town had friends, it seemed, in the steel and cement industries. In the three years we'd been here, many of the old colonial houses had acquired second stories made with breeze blocks. They began to sprout a thick forest of television antennae, even though the reception was virtually nonexistent. Bemused Indians would cluster outside the windows of a television and radio shop, watching the snowstorm on the screens.

I spotted a car parked in the living room of a house; it was covered with a white sheet, plastic-covered chairs reverentially arranged around it in a circle. The car was starting to rule the day in San Cristóbal. A *periférico* was being built around the town.

We'd come by car but we hated the car. E. M. Forster said of the automobile, "Healthy, ever in motion, it hopes to inherit the earth." The Indians watched in bewilderment as roads were bulldozed into their *parajes*. They were told that the roads meant employment and hard cash, and that they wouldn't have to work so hard anymore. Chiapas was changing, and not for the better.

After our third year in San Cristóbal, William decided to sell the house. Feeling conflicted and miserable, we packed up. I went to England to see my parents and my grandmother, who was now eighty-two, retired and living with them in London. Despite the small pension she received from the school, she never seemed to have any money, not even enough for her hair appointments. What was she spending it on? My father decided to investigate. He noticed that mysterious plain brown envelopes arrived for her each week and decided to steam one of them open. Football pools. My grandmother spent every penny she had on them. She was certain that one day she'd win and none of us would ever have to worry about money again.

Then one morning she couldn't get out of bed. An ambulance was called and my grandmother was taken to St. Mary's Hospital in Paddington. Chris Wilcox was an intern there and looked in on her every day. But I knew she was dying the night she refused her whisky. Not even a nightcap. She died the next morning.

William and I had been together for nearly seven years. I was almost thirty. I'd grown up, through him. He had become increasingly interested in Buddhism and I was troubled by the way he seemed to be retreating into an ascetic, spiritual life. Was I really such a rationalist?

In the spring of 1975, William and I separated. He went to live in Hawaii and I remained in New York.

IN THE FALL, Elizabeth Tingom, my friend from the *New Yorker,* invited me to a Moroccan dinner at her apartment on Perry Street. The food was cooked by Madeleine van Breugel, a Dutch woman in her late thirties, who lived in Morocco and had invited several Moroccan friends.

Madeleine was tall, slender and elegant, with large green eyes in a heart-shaped face and a chestnut mane of hair under which she sometimes concealed a small green parrot named Chulita. When Madeleine walked through Customs the previous week, Chulita had hidden under her hair without a peep. According to Madeleine, she always kept quiet in airplanes and at border checks. Tonight, Madeleine was dressed in a long embroidered Moroccan caftan. She sat on the floor and ate with her fingers, which flashed with large, valuable rings.

She was one of the oddest cooks I've ever encountered. She never tasted the dishes as she made them. At meals she never ate, she just picked. That night she cooked spicy meatballs, loaded with paprika and cilantro, a chicken tajine with green olives and preserved lemons, couscous and an assortment of salads. One was made with grated carrots and raisins. Another was made with brains tossed with lemon, paprika and cumin.

Madeleine was an impetuous, difficult person, given to high drama, but a loyal and generous friend. She lived in a palm grove just outside Marrakesh. Why didn't Elizabeth and I visit her for a couple of weeks? I could write an article.

I jumped at the idea. I was miserable in New York, pining for William.

On the road to Madeleine's farmhouse outside Marrakesh, Elizabeth and I learned our first and most important phrase in Arabic: *insh'allah*. *Insh'allah* is the core of Islam and the essence of the Moroccan approach to life. If Allah wills it, your plans will be met. You are not a free agent in the matter. There is no point in worrying, for events are not under your control. That was why, I discovered, it was so hard in Morocco to get a direct answer about anything taking place in the future. Between a plan and its being carried out, Allah often had all sorts of other ideas. For example, suppose on your way to an engagement you run into an old friend and decide to spend the afternoon with him drinking tea in a café. The person you've stood up will understand. Most likely Allah willed something else for him too, and he would not have been there anyway.

As we drove through Marrakesh, Allah had planned a *shergi*, the fierce wind that blows up without warning from the Sahara, sometimes lasting for three days. It reminded me of the sandstorms of Ismailia. Elizabeth and I took refuge in one of the cafés along Avenue Mohamed V, the city's main boulevard. The sky was low and ominous; a thick pink dust sent everyone scurrying for cover. Dogs barked; jacaranda blossoms were swept to the ground; people shouted instructions to which no one paid the slightest attention. An intrepid bicyclist covered his head with a plastic bag and pedaled on, determined to beat the weather. The air was filled with a boisterous but fleeting energy. It evaporated as quickly as the storm.

Inside the café, three basic faces—Arab, Berber and African—stared at us with unflinching curiosity. Some of these observers wore European dress, others striped djellabas and canary-yellow slippers with white turbans or red *chechias* on their heads. They watched us languidly, toying with glasses of Oulmes mineral water, black coffee or mint tea. When the storm was over we moved to a table outside. Within seconds we were under attack as shoe-shine boys, an old man in a burnoose selling salted almonds, a hunchbacked dwarf, a rug seller, urchins with postcards and a woman whose child was screaming at the top of her lungs all converged upon us.

Veiled women with kohl-rimmed eyes scrutinized us as they sped past on the back of motorized bicycles, the long caftans they had put on for modesty parting on the side to reveal a large expanse of thigh: underneath they were wearing miniskirts.

Hamdu'lillah, thanks to God, we reached La Petite Maison, Madeleine's little pink adobe farmhouse before dark. It was in a palm grove in Dar Tounsi, just outside Marrakesh. Rose and purple bougainvillea climbed up its garden walls and a yellow Barbary fig tree stood in the courtyard, which was covered in vines.

Nine years ago Madeleine had come here for a week, on her way to Kenya. But she met John Hopkins, an American writer, and she had stayed. They were looked after by Kaftan, the caretaker, and Akhia, who kept house and cooked, and they had five dogs. But now she and Johnny had broken up, and he was moving to Tangiers.

My room was in a separate building from the main house: it had a wooden door that opened in two sections like that of a stable, and gave onto a sandy courtyard. The next morning, I awoke to the smell of coffee and homemade bread. Breakfast was being served in the courtyard outside my room under a canopy of thatched palms. A marble table had been laid with hand-painted blue and white Moroccan pottery and seventeenth-century silver knives and forks from Madeleine's baronial house in Holland. Akhia had set out fresh orange and grapefruit juice in jugs covered with gauze to keep off the bugs, along with a lump of sweet butter on a plate, pots of local honey and Madeleine's homemade jams. There were baskets of figs, peaches and cherries and a silver bowl of white roses from the garden. Each person had a melon the size of an orange.

"Women for duty, boys for pleasure and melons for sheer delight," said Madeleine. "An old Moroccan saying."

The sun speckled the table while we ate the melons, which

Madeleine shared with her parrot Chulita, and drank black coffee flavored with cinnamon.

I felt away from the mainstream (and I didn't miss New York, or care what happened there), but I had a new sense of belonging—to the whole world, not just one part of it. I'd never felt that in Mexico. The palm trees, cactuses, vines, birds' chatter and the gentle silver green of the spreading olive trees around the little farmhouse in Dar Tounsi became images of tranquillity. Sometimes as I would read, the book would slip from my fingers, and I'd sit staring fixedly in front of me with that petrified, vague, absentminded gaze I would often see on the faces of the inhabitants.

The land was flat, meandering in the distance to the foothills of the Atlas Mountains. It was riddled with deep gulleys called *seghias,* which were hollowed into the ground to give the palm trees water. But the earth was so dry that your feet left crusted prints. The stillness hinted of the Sahara, which lies across the Atlas range. When dawn came up, the colors deepened and began to glow. The sun reflecting off the crumbling pink adobe walls brought out the delicate hues of the roses, the sprawling purple bougainvillea and the yellow Barbary figs—a picture held in perfect harmony by a dash of red from a caftan or a distant camel's saddle. A rich, sprucy scent would fill the soft air: mint mixed with pine. In the late morning haze, the mountains became invisible, washed into a metallic sky. When darkness fell, the landscape seemed bereft of life, motionless, frozen. An awesome calm would descend, broken in the middle of the night by the thin voice of the *muezzin,* echoing from the mosque in the distance.

I loved being here so much that when Madeleine asked me to stay on, I agreed. But at night, alone with my thoughts in my room, I was increasingly concerned about my left eye. One evening I sat in bed with a book, drinking a cup of tea. As I read I noticed that the print began to swim up from the bottom of the page, changing sizes. When I covered my left eye, the print was fine. But the right eye didn't focus properly. I looked in the mirror and saw that the pupil was enlarged. It was probably an astigmatism. I was going to England for the month of August to see my parents, so I'd go to an oculist in London before I returned to Marrakesh in September.

Meanwhile, I read Gide's *The Immoralist*: "Rather than recounting his life as he has lived it, he must live his life as he will recount it."

I reread Bowles's *The Sheltering Sky*: "He did not think of himself as a tourist, he was a traveller. The difference is partly one of time, he would explain. Whereas the tourist generally hurries back home at the end of a few weeks or months, the traveller, belonging no more to one place than to the next, moves slowly over periods of years, from one part of the earth to the other."

We took trips all over Morocco: to the Djemaa el Fna in Marrakesh, which was filled with acrobats, singers, snake charmers, dancers and storytellers. A medicine man extracted a tooth with a pair of pliers from the mouth of an elderly Berber, who shouted, "Thanks be to God," and spat blood into a tin. We went to a bakery in the shrine town of Moulay Idriss, where I watched men cut *kif* while boys hauled trays of bread from a roaring oven. We visited the lighthouse of Cap Spartel at midnight, its crystals turning in the blackness as waves crashed fiercely on the desolate shore near Tangiers. We ate sardines grilled on braziers by fishermen in the harbor in Essaouira and held a picnic on a beach near Tangiers by Phoenician ruins, bringing with us only items the Phoenicians would have had: bread, figs, cheeses in round baskets made from dried grass, olives, peaches and wine.

Madeleine seemed to live on a great deal of Oustalet rosé wine, starting just before lunchtime and tippling steadily for the rest of the day. The only thing she ate was seafood. But she wouldn't touch oysters. "I only eat dead fish!"

My birthday in May was the occasion for a feast, and we were going to be hennaed in preparation. Two Berber women with tattoos on their faces painted intricate designs like lace on our hands and feet. They covered them with stockings to protect the henna as it dried. We had to lie back in an easy chair for the better part of the day waiting for it to take. As we lay there, they fed us couscous and Akhia's lamb and tangerine tajine.

Madeleine's Moroccan friends, Omar, a construction magnate, and Mohammed, a movie mogul, had been put in charge of the birthday feast. Or a mass slaughter, as it turned out. They arrived with a sheep, which they tethered in the garden for a day. We could hear it bleating as the henna dried on our hands and feet.

Omar went to Safi for lobsters and returned with six, plus three huge striped bass and a sackful of live pigeons. The pigeons were put in a cage for the night. Kaftan slaughtered the sheep the next morning for a *mechoui*, a Berber version of roast lamb. He dug a pit in the garden and baked it whole over coals. It took all day to cook. Then the pigeons got the chop too, and we saw them piled on a plate on the floor with their livers in a heap and flies frantically hopping from one carcass to another. Some of the pigeons were stuffed with couscous and roasted; others found their way into *bisteeya*.

We began dinner with the *bisteeya*, a round flaky pastry dusted with sugar and cinnamon and flavored with coriander and onion. This was followed by the *mechoui*. The lamb had been basted with butter as it roasted and was golden and crunchy, falling off the bone. I was happily dipping the pieces of meat in salt and cumin when a passing guest was kind enough to point out my serious faux pas: I was eating with my left hand. Even though they used to bind my thumb when I was a child to encourage me to use my right hand, it never worked.

After the *mechoui* we were served a tajine, a stew that was made with chicken, lemon and olives, seasoned with cumin, saffron, ginger and paprika, and cooked and served in a clay pot with a conical lid (also called a *tajine*). It came with couscous. The couscous was the most difficult thing to eat by hand, especially my right hand. While others rolled the grains deftly into a ball that was popped like a marble into their mouths, I was reduced to licking my grain-coated fingers. I had read the instructions in *The Pillars of Hercules,* a book about travels in Morocco written in 1848 by David Urquhart, a Scotsman (who, incidentally, introduced the Turkish bath to London): "With the point of the fingers of the right hand a portion of grains is drawn towards the side of the dish. It is fingered as the keys of a pianoforte til it gathers together; it is then taken up into the hand, shaken, pressed until it adheres, molded until it becomes a ball; tossed up and worked until it is perfect, and then shot by the thumb, like a marble, into the open mouth."

I tried to shoot marbles of couscous into my mouth as we reclined on the carpets that had been laid on the sandy floor of the courtyard. There was brain salad and veal tongue in aspic, all kinds of other salads, wine, Champagne and a chocolate birthday cake from the Mamounia Hotel with one candle in the middle. And an enormous basket of apricots, plums, oranges, tangerines and bananas.

During dinner one of the guests, a rotund and bespectacled visitor from Rabat, stood up. "Moy-ee-rah!" he exclaimed, throwing up his arms like an opera singer. "Moy-ee-rah! Your name is like a wave, *une vague, la mer,* that flows in and out. But Bouazza. That is my name. You hear that and you want to run away!"

That night, with typical Moroccan generosity, Omar and Mohammed offered us the use of their apartment in Casablanca. So a few days later, Elizabeth and I set off, with Madeleine behind the wheel driving in bare feet full blast down the coast road, which was wild and beautiful and ran along vast stretches of unspoiled beach. Banks of thin sand had drifted up into the crusty salt beds and carefully tended tomato plantations that lined the road. Dry stone and cactus walls separated barley and wheat fields where women— bright figures in multicolored scarves, brocade blouses and loose candy-striped bloomers under gathered overskirts—worked with scythes. Tethered donkeys and camels with bandaged eyes walked in small circles, pumping water. Corn, too, was being threshed in circles, the bigger animals on the outside, the little ones trotting in the middle. A camel's lower lip wagged as she munched on a purple thistle, churlishly ignoring the baby that nestled under her belly. A white Mercedes flashed by, packed with men, each in different headgear. We stopped to watch a dung beetle with staring orange eyes roll its load across the hot tarmac.

"Eh! M'si! Donne-moi une cigarette!"

Four small boys appeared out of nowhere and pressed their faces tightly against the car window.

Madeleine shook her head. They shouted at her.

What had they said?

"May Allah rain curses on you, damned Nazarene."

They shook their tiny fists.

"If I'd really wanted to show them I could have shouted, 'May Allah curse you children of a woman who makes water in public places when people are looking!' " said Madeleine.

Outside Casablanca, workmen in red wool caps and blue overalls were snoozing on the grass outside factories and construction sites. Half-finished buildings with wires sticking up from cement pillars were sprawled across the landscape, waiting to house the next generation. With 75 percent of the population under twenty-one, the future looked grim. How much longer before the rest of the country is wrecked, I wondered. I haven't been back to find out. Casablanca was a hint of what was to come.

From the distance, the city had looked all white: white waves, white sky and white modern buildings that rose behind the spray like futuristic toys. But the magnificent old souk had been torn down in the name of progress. At night, the town seemed deserted; the cafés were closed and the streets were empty except for the occasional roving gang of boys.

Omar's apartment was located in the city's most fashionable shopping district. The furnishings consisted of oversized chocolate-brown velveteen cushions scattered around a small living room that boasted a stereo, a glass coffee table, some wooden barrels and a well-stocked liquor cabinet. On the wall were posters of barely nubile ballet dancers by David Hamilton and a blow-up of the singer Donna Summer with a dog collar around her neck. The dog collar motif was repeated on the other side of the room with a picture of a priest holding a naked woman in his arms.

"Where are your books?" Elizabeth asked Omar.

There was no kitchen stove and the cupboards were bare apart from a couple of Armani suits hanging in the wardrobe. There was nothing in the refrigerator except a bowl of olives and, oddly, a packet of potato chips.

"Please don't tell anyone about my apartment," said Omar. He didn't want his parents to know. Despite the fact that he was twenty-eight years old and ran his own firm, Omar was still living at home, eating dinner with his family and sneaking out at night afterward. Few young Moroccan men moved away from their families before they married, it appeared, and he was no exception. We couldn't stand the apartment, and two days later we headed for Tangiers.

I'd wanted to meet Paul Bowles ever since I'd read *The Sheltering Sky* and *A Hundred Camels in the Courtyard,* a collection of his short stories that William had given me. Madeleine knew Bowles, so we drove on to Tangiers, where he lived. We stopped for coffee at the Café de Paris, which was filled with elderly men with dyed hair who sat watching the people, especially the boys, go by. "I wanted to go to America to buy modern art but it's so expensive," I overheard one of these men say languidly, speaking English with a French accent. "I like the Surrealists after Dalí. All we have at home is sixteenth- and seventeenth-century paintings."

Madeleine and I went to dinner at the Natulis restaurant. The waiter wrote down our order: "1 grim salad, 1 mixt, 1 pate voley." Later, over drinks outside in the garden at the Parade restaurant, the ground was uneven and I fell off my chair. "So did Tennessee Williams," said

Madeleine when she'd stopped laughing. "But he said, 'Let me lie here.'"

Paul Bowles held court every afternoon in his apartment. I was surprised when I saw where he lived. Inmeuble Itesa was a gray concrete apartment building surrounded by rubble-strewn fields in an empty no-man's-land prowled by stray cats, many of them pregnant.

You entered the living room through a thick curtain. There was hardly any light because of the tall green plants, a veritable Douanier Rousseau jungle, amassed on a balcony that was closed in by windows. The room was moist and hot, and from the jungle came the chatter of a canary. Bowles, slight and white-haired, with sharp blue-green eyes, was reclining on cushions in the center of the room. He had a mild, slightly given-in face, the face of someone who was spending too much time around people who became measurably more interesting after he'd smoked a good deal of *kif*. He didn't drink alcohol, but pastries were in plentiful supply.

Bowles, surrounded by a gaggle of admiring ladies, smoked nonstop and delivered occasional witticisms while making pleasant, nondescript conversation and telling stories.

"The story that frightened me most as a child was about a man in South Africa. He and a friend heard of a whirlpool at the bottom of which lay diamonds. People would jump in to get the diamonds. Some would return, others didn't. His friend jumped in and didn't come back. The man looked down into the pool and saw his friend whirling around and around like a dervish at lightning speed. His arms had already worn down to a stump. He imagined his friend whirling until there was nothing left of him. At night I would lie awake thinking of this."

Paul's guests were always raving about his tea. One day I followed him into the kitchen. "What's your secret recipe?"

He showed me: a Lipton's teabag and the juice of half a lemon.

I WANTED TO GO to Goulimine. This small, remote town is a port of entry to the western Sahara and a trading post of the Tuareg blue men, nomads who have traveled the desert since the pre-Christian era. They come in camel caravans from as far away as the Sudan, Mauritania, Mali, Senegal and Niger and pitch their black tents near the town. The town was now the last stop for foreigners. All the roads were closed beyond because of Morocco's war with Algeria and sporadic terrorist attacks from Polisario rebels. I saw myself as a modern-day Isabelle Eberhardt, the explorer who at the turn of the century left the dreary suburb of Geneva where she'd grown up for an exciting life among the Arabs in the desert. She dressed as one of them and her hands were always hennaed. I'd find myself a blue man and go off with him into the Sahara.

We were warned not to go to Goulimine. There were mines on the road, kidnappings and *bombes plastiques*. But Madeleine said the stories were exaggerated, and we set off. I wondered, however, as we climbed the sinister mountain pass beyond Tiznit, whether we'd made a wise decision. The forbidding recesses of the sun-baked rocks made a perfect setting for a surprise attack. But we encountered only convoys of Moroccan soldiers. In battle fatigues and dusty black turbans, leaning over the tops of tanks or hanging from jeeps, they waved and smiled, their desert goggles glinting in the sun. There were few other vehicles on the road except for beaten up 1950s jalopies from the U.S. base in Kenitra, painted blue and used as collective taxis.

Beyond the mountains, the land became flat and desolate. Goulimine shimmered in the distance, rising like a mirage out of the coarse, pebble-ridden sand. It was an ugly town, a conglomerate of half-completed buildings and a barracks. An area for target practice and training, when not in service for the military, was taken over by the children as a playground. We saw no other foreigners, only soldiers, walking hand in hand. There were Chleuh merchants, turbans wound around their gaunt faces to keep out the sand and the night cold, and blue men in billowing indigo robes. Sewing machines hummed steadily in the shops in the market as the blue cloth was fashioned into the loose flowing garments known as *draa*. The more the material stains the skin, the more it is prized. The best is like carbon paper.

A caravan had recently arrived, according to the cheerful hare-lipped boy who served us dinner at the Hotel Salam. For the following day a trip was arranged, *insh'allah,* to the oasis where the blue men watered their camels. Ali, a boy who lived there, would be our guide.

The oasis was a dusty twenty-minute drive into the desert along a dirt track. Low mud walls, flanked by palm trees, surrounded neat squares of alfalfa bordered by ditches of running water. Figs, pome-granates, grapes, oranges, lemons and dates were thriving, despite a three-year drought. The houses, made from hand-packed mud, were windowless, built around a courtyard that one entered through a dark, narrow corridor.

We had arrived at the wrong time. It was early afternoon and the village was deserted. The blue men had gone to rest from the heat of the day. But luckily, for reasons that were never made clear, one blue man had pitched his tent with the permission of the village chief in a courtyard on the fringe of the oasis. A blackened kettle was sitting on a charcoal brazier outside the tent, which was made from goatskins and camel hair. Ali went inside to ask the owner if he would receive us.

Moments later a handsome man of average height, dressed in layers of blue robes, emerged from the tent. The blue of his robes had rubbed off onto his hands and feet, giving his dark skin a luminous glow. He wore a light blue turban and a collection of amulets around his neck.

We exchanged a complicated litany of greetings, beginning with *la bas?* ("How are you?") punctuated by much kissing of hands and cheeks, and finishing with *marhaba* ("You are welcome"). We removed our shoes and followed him into the tent, which was cool inside.

His name was Mohammed. He had finely turned hands and

walked with grace and muscle, a catlike walk like a ballet dancer, with the legs swinging out from the hips. His face was serene and gentle, with high cheekbones and a straight nose. His eyes reminded me of a line by Yeats: "the visionary melancholy of purely instinctive natures."

I sat down on a cushion that he placed on the goatskin-covered floor. These bachelor quarters were sparsely furnished: a makeshift bed, an old tin trunk at its head, a camel-hide bag painted in gaudy colors hanging from a peg. Mohammed busied himself making fresh mint tea, producing interminable infusions he sweetened progressively with a big lump of white sugar. He poured the tea from a great height into tiny glasses. *"B'smillah!"* ("Allah grant you good health.") He swigged it back like a shot of liquor.

"Moroccan whisky!" whispered Ali, to show he knew about such things.

As Mohammed talked he worked a string of plum-colored prayer beads. Where was I from?

"England."

Was there any rain?

There most certainly was.

"Hamdu'lillah!"

How long did it take to get there?

For a moment, I was stumped. Then I said, vaguely, "Oh, about seven days."

"Seven days!" He laughed heartily. "That's nothing! It takes me five weeks to travel from Mauritania. Ten more on the way back, when the camels are loaded. Seven days!" He found this highly amusing.

"Where are you living now?" he asked.

"Marrakesh."

He looked blank. "I've never heard of it."

Mohammed had come across the desert with fifty camels, traveling with a friend, two shepherd boys and two slaves. Slaves! Three of the camels had died; two they had eaten. They had sold or traded twenty-five, keeping twenty for the journey home. He had brought six trunks of jewelry and robes to trade in Goulimine for friends in Mauritania. They trusted him because he had *baraka,* grace and good luck.

He unlocked the trunk and from among the clothes inside Mohammed extracted a silver Berber cross. He placed it facedown on a bowl of sand and showed me the four guiding stars that were represented in the imprint. "I travel at night," he explained, "and I use this to guide me."

I asked Mohammed whether he had seen much fighting in the desert. His face grew cold. "No," he answered curtly. "But I heard it. Those men are not good Muslims."

Was he planning to stay here long? "We'll leave soon, *insh'allah.* It's too noisy here."

Mohammed said he was the youngest of five sons. His father used to travel with him, but now he was too old. One hundred and fifteen, Mohammed assured me. Before he leaves home Mohammed sets in a supply of figs, dates, dried meat and milk for his family. He has three sons.

The tea seemed to be having a peculiar effect on me. "How would you like another wife?" I heard myself ask idiotically.

For a second he looked astonished. Then he burst out laughing as I blushed like a schoolgirl.

"But I already have two," he said with a teasing gleam in his eye. Before I could pursue any further my fantasies of vanishing into the desert like the heroine of *The Sheltering Sky,* there was a shout at the door. "Mohammed!" a voice called urgently. "You're late for the mosque."

On the way back from the oasis the sky had gone from a clear bright blue to a muddy color, full of dust particles. The sun was transformed into a gleaming silver disc that cast an iridescent, almost waxy glow on the scrubby, dried-out landscape.

"Once you have been under the spell of this vast, luminous silent country," Bowles has written, "no other place is quite strong enough. No other surrounding can provide the extremely satisfying sensation of living in the midst of something that is absolute."

اﻟﻪ

AFTER WE RETURNED to Madeleine's farmhouse, the parrot Chulita disappeared. She just flew off. Gloom descended over the house. Akhia and Kaftan couldn't keep from crying. To get rid of any *gris-gris,* evil spirits, they burned the blades of the knives over lighted candles. Elizabeth and I drove all day with Madeleine to see a *chouafa,* a seer. People were camped out in two huts in the yard, men in one, women in the other. Some had come all the way from Chad. They had been waiting over a month.

No, said the *chouafa's* man. We won't accept money to let you jump the line.

"That proves she's for real," said Madeleine sadly. "But we can't stay here for a month."

The man told Madeleine to go to Taroudant. Maybe there in the spice souk she could find a charm to get Chulita back.

Madeleine was deeply superstitious. So we set off at once for Taroudant, which is in the Atlas Mountains of southern Morocco.

At first glance, the souk seemed innocent enough. The stalls, built along a narrow lattice-covered alley off the main square, were run by friendly turbaned Berbers in white djellabas. They had a reputation for being hard bargainers, but their prices were low. Baskets piled with cumin, turmeric, cinnamon, ginger, henna and dried herbs were neatly arranged next to packets of soap, shampoo, detergent, horn combs, licorice toothbrushes, wood scrubbing brushes for the hammam baths, brightly painted wooden kohl jars and little glass bottles of colored powdered makeup, along with jars and boxes of incense, musk, kohl, saffron and other spices.

The businesslike atmosphere of the market did not suggest the occult. Few travelers who fingered the amber beads, the gold and silver hands of Fatima, necklaces of horn, the silver coins, shells and corals, or charms concealing verses from the Koran suspected their real purpose. To know that, you must be initiated into the world of *grisgris* and the Evil Eye.

At one of these stalls, nestled on shelves that lined the anterior wall, was a curious collection of skulls, claws, bones, gazelles' horns, dried birds' carcasses, stuffed chameleons, lizards and bats whose mouths were sewn shut with string. Two young Moroccan men in American jeans moved purposefully toward the stall; their request sent the owner, a corpulent old Berber, rustling among the artifacts at the back while they stood awkwardly by. The smaller of the two was wearing a T-shirt that bore the legend "Unforgettable Jimmy" above a crude portrait of James Dean. Judging by the number of men and boys I saw in identical T-shirts, they were a national best seller, even though I imagined that few of those who sported them were likely to have seen any of James Dean's three films.

The storekeeper, who had been rummaging under a table on his hands and knees, emerged with a collection of bedraggled birds' carcasses. They were stiff, faded and bald in patches. He set them out on the counter with the genteel air of a saleslady displaying a selection of gloves. The two men examined the birds eagerly. What, I wondered, were the distinguishing marks that determined their choice?

The charade of bargaining began. The fat storekeeper was insulted: the price they offered was well below what he had paid for such a fine bird, how was he expected to make a living, etc., etc. The two argued, cajoled, walked away, returned and eventually capitulated. At this point I intervened. What was the carcass for?

The boy in the James Dean T-shirt blushed. The storekeeper, who was heaving from the exigencies of hard bargaining, pretended not to hear. He turned his back to replace the unsold skins in their nesting place and the young men melted away. I pressed on with my question, and he finally relented.

"When he gets home he will burn the bird," he explained. "Then he will write the name of his girl in the ashes, and within three days she will be his."

It was as simple as that.

An old woman came up to buy a chameleon. It was for good luck, the storekeeper confided, and dangerous against enemies since it could cause their teeth to fall out. The dried belly of the big, green creature was so distended it looked as though it might blow up at any moment. She packed it into her basket under the tomatoes, eggs and bunches of mint and coriander and shuffled off.

On the way out I spotted the unmistakable tall, slender silhouette of Madeleine, who was surrounded by a circle of curious onlookers. She was arguing furiously with a spice vendor over two baby hoopoes trapped in a makeshift cage. It was so small that the birds couldn't stretch their wings, even though they hadn't yet reached their full height of five inches. One was scraping its beak disconsolately against the bars. Their feathers, fanlike and rust-tinted with black-and-white stripes on the crest and wings, were still covered with down.

"You're not going to buy those birds, are you?" I asked Madeleine. "It will only encourage him to go out and trap some more," I added, in case she should think me mean. I did not know at the time what grisly sacrificial rites lay in store for these unhappy birds. Even Madeleine, who knew something about *grisgris,* had no idea. But she wanted to save the birds.

The Berber knew his customers. He insisted on the outrageous price of thirty dirhams.

Madeleine snatched up some black horn bracelets hung with coins.

"We'll take these too," she said.

He shrugged.

"And we'll never buy from you again."

After she delivered a short lecture on the humane treatment of animals to the amusement of both the storekeeper and the small crowd that had gathered, we drove away. We'd seen no sign of Chulita. We hadn't found a charm for her, and she never returned.

The hoopoes were very quiet as we wound our way down the mountains back to Marrakesh. On the way Madeleine suggested we stop at the palace of an Italian friend, the Princess Ruspoli. The princess had a large library with many books on Moroccan lore that she would certainly be pleased to let us see. She was also an international breeder of salukis, Arabian hunting dogs that look like greyhounds.

The princess was a thin, voluble woman in her fifties. She had two large bedrooms given over entirely to racks of trousers, arranged like a display in a department store. "I've had all these trousers since I was a teenager, and I'm still the same size!"

The rest of the house was given over to salukis. There must have been at least thirty, and they had the run of the place. Guests had to fight the dogs for seating privileges and pretend not to notice as the animals sprang recklessly onto the table during meals. After lunch, we admired a new litter of puppies and made our way along marble halls to the library, accompanied by an enthusiastic retinue that loped over the shredded cushions scattered on the floor and the valuable prematurely dilapidated rugs.

"My favorite author is Paul Gallico," the princess announced as she opened the doors to her collection. Here we discovered two large black dusty volumes entitled *Ritual and Superstition in Morocco,* over 1,500 pages of text compiled by a Professor Liebenthal shortly before the First World War. We looked up *hoopoe.* "The hoopoe is rich in magic and medicinal virtue. After its entrails have been removed it is dried and then worn as a charm. It makes him who wears it feared by others, it protects him against witchcraft and the Evil Eye, it neutralises any spell which has been cast upon him."

The Arabic for *hoopoe,* we learned, is *bled had houd.* The bird, which migrates across the Sahara to Egypt, is quite rare and supposedly protected. It nests from March to June, usually in tree trunks, walls, under roofs or inside piles of stones, and lives off insects and flesh.

We named our birds Houd and Houdni, the latter being a pun on the Arabic for "take me." Our Moroccan friends were much amused.

Kaftan cleaned out the enormous cage that a few months before had housed Ace, a wounded hawk, until he had been well enough to fly. Kaftan was fond of animals. He placed the cage in the kitchen, which was warm, and put the hoopoes inside. They were frightened and hungry and their round black eyes shone at us in terror. I was afraid they would die in the night.

Madeleine had spent a couple of years in Swaziland married to a vet. She knew what to feed the birds and prepared them a mixture of finely chopped horsemeat, powdered milk and water. Holding them in our hands (we could feel their hearts beating under their warm, downy feathers) we prised open their scimitar-like beaks and stuffed their gaping throats with food. We returned them to the cage and covered it for the night.

All was quiet in the kitchen except the hiss of the kerosene lamps, the occasional mouse scurrying across the floor and the distant barking of dogs. Before going to bed I looked in on the birds. Their gray eyelids had closed. Exhausted from the journey and stupefied by the unaccustomed food, they had fallen asleep.

The next morning I was awakened as usual by Marcel, the donkey, outside my window braying with pleasure at Kaftan's arrival with his breakfast. Ours was set up under the vines, and when I came out of my room, I saw that Kaftan had put the cage with the birds in the center of the yard, between me and the breakfast table. As soon as they saw me they began to twitter hysterically, jumping up and down and flapping their wings to get my attention. I rushed to fetch the food, little knowing that I had put myself in the role of mother, and that Houd and Houdni would start to run my life. As I brought the food over, Houdni trilled like a Berber woman ululating. The birds pecked at my fingers and at each other, but they wouldn't take the food. I had to stuff it down their throats; only then would they swallow. When they had eaten, they jumped onto their perch and immediately fell asleep.

After a week, every time I passed their cage, Houd and Houdni screamed for food. From their perch they could see my head outlined through the window grille of my room, where I worked each day, trying to write about my life in Morocco. They kept me on a steady routine from refrigerator to cage, often fooling me into feeding them minutes after Madeleine had already done the job. They were getting bigger by the day and had begun to lose their down.

Madeleine said it was time the birds learned to feed themselves. I left a bowl in the cage but they refused to touch it. Houdni would stare at it and begin a desperate trilling, which she kept up until I fed her myself. After meals they liked to have their beaks and heads washed and to be stroked on the neck and around the eyes.

At last the two birds began to eat by themselves. I had to control the urge to pluck them up and stuff their throats as I used to. I missed the feel of their warm little bodies in my hand and the dull scrape of their beaks as they pecked at my fingers. But the birds were being primed for freedom.

Their next step toward this goal was to learn to fly. The windows of my room had shutters and the ceiling was made from woven bamboo and fronds, held up by palm trunks and bound by plaster. A low beam ran underneath, making a perfect perch. Ants of various sizes and other insects wandered in and out of the plaster and up the whitewashed walls. This room might be a good place for the birds to begin hunting too.

I took down the mirror, closed the shutters and covered the floor and bed with newspaper. I brought their cage into the room, leaving the door open with a curtain in front of it. I pulled back the curtain.

They did nothing. At last I took them out and tried to get them to fly off my hand. They refused to move. Then Houd, the more aggressive of the two, flew up, flapping his wings like a butterfly, chirping and scattering bits of down. He searched for a landing spot upon the beam. Inspired by his example, Houdni followed and they remained on the rafters, heads cocked to one side, staring down at me. Then they carefully looked around the room to get their bearings. They didn't seem the least afraid.

Houd let fall a shower of droppings on the bed where I was lying. He began carefully taking the ceiling apart, searching for grubs. He hacked lumps of plaster off and then set to work on the palm trunk. The birds spent the next half an hour sharpening their beaks, stopping to puff up their crests, deflate and clean themselves. Then they would start pecking some more. Houdni tried very hard to break a necklace made of pink seashells that was hanging from the rafters. Suddenly the tiny gray shields came down over their eyes and they dozed off. But every time I turned a page of my book, their eyes flipped open.

For me, reading was becoming increasingly difficult. I now had to keep my left eye covered in order to stop the print from swimming up the page. I was glad that Madeleine and I were going to leave for Europe in a few days, so I could get some new glasses.

We weren't planning to be away for long, so we decided not to set the birds free until we returned. They were still very young and so tame now they could easily be caught for *grisgris* by villagers coming through the palm grove. The hoopoes thought of human beings as friends. Kaftan would look after them.

The night before we left Marrakesh, Madeleine made a lamb tajine with olives, and we drank a bottle of Oustalet. I didn't pack much. I had come over in spring, bringing coats and sweaters I wasn't going to need in London, where it was quite hot. So I left most of my clothes hanging in the wardrobe.

When I went to bed a lark was singing. I couldn't wait to come back.

❧

Lamb Tajine with Green Olives

2 1/2 pounds boneless lamb
    shoulder, cut into 1 1/2-inch
    pieces
2 tablespoons olive oil
1 teaspoon ground cumin
1 teaspoon ground coriander
1 teaspoon turmeric
1/2 teaspoon sweet paprika
1 onion, chopped fine
2 garlic cloves, minced

1/2 pound cracked green olives,
    pitted
2 tomatoes, peeled, seeded and
    chopped
1 preserved lemon, chopped
Salt and freshly ground black
    pepper
Lemon juice (optional)
1/2 cup chopped fresh cilantro
    leaves

A day before you plan to serve the tajine, trim excess fat from the lamb pieces. Heat the olive oil in a large, heavy-bottomed casserole. Add the lamb pieces and sprinkle them with the cumin, coriander, turmeric and paprika. Sauté for 5 minutes over moderate heat. Add the onion and garlic and sauté for one minute. Add 2 1/2 cups water, stir and bring to boil. Cover and simmer for 1 hour, or until tender. Refrigerate overnight.

On the day of serving, preheat the oven to 450°F.

Remove the fat, which will have accumulated on the top of the stew. Using a slotted spoon, remove the pieces of lamb and place them in an ovenproof serving dish large enough to contain the meat and the sauce. Bake for 15 to 20 minutes, until browned and crisp.

Meanwhile, blanch the olives in boiling water to cover for 1 minute, then drain. Bring the lamb juices to a boil in a saucepan with the olives and tomatoes. Cook until thickened (about 10 minutes) and stir in the preserved lemon. Season to taste with salt and pepper. If necessary, add a squeeze of lemon juice.

Pour the sauce over the lamb, sprinkle with cilantro and serve with couscous.

SERVES 4

IT TOOK ME A LONG TIME to get through Customs when I arrived at Heathrow Airport in mid-July. I'd been hennaed on my hands and feet, I had a henna necklace tattooed around my neck and a henna diamond emblazoned on my forehead. The young Customs officer rummaged slowly through my luggage while my parents waited outside, wondering whether I'd missed the plane.

At last he pulled out a large brown paper bag and opened it. His eyes gleamed. It was filled with a greenish rust brown powder.

"Don't get too excited," I said. "It's only henna."

At my parents' house in Chiswick I unpacked the tajines and other pieces of pottery I'd brought from Morocco. That night I made a Moroccan meal: Madeleine's meatball tajine, with couscous and a green salad. I ate with my fingers, just as I'd done in Marrakesh. My father looked at me in horror.

"I like to feel the food with my hands as well as my mouth," I said.

"Yes, but do you have to use your fingers to eat *salad?*"

The oculist I went to see a few days later couldn't figure out what was wrong with my eye. He sent me to a specialist. But medical science, it seemed, was baffled. I went to one doctor after another, first on the National Health and then, at great expense, on Harley Street, where the names of the doctors were written in Arabic and the waiting rooms were filled with women shrouded in black, accompanied by their male minders. Dr. Casey was stumped. He sent me to Dr. Green, a few expensive doors down.

Dr. Green's reception room was hung with Persian miniatures, and the floor was covered with a Persian carpet. There were copies of the Sunday color supplements on the table. I didn't have to wait long before I was ushered into a consulting room that had French windows giving onto a garden. He was in his midforties, dark-haired and slender, dressed in a Cardin suit—the sort of person you'd expect to see on the dance floor of Annabel's.

We ran briskly through the history of my health. Meningitis, mastoid, blood clot on the brain, all when I was fourteen.

"When I get ill I do it properly," I said. "I don't fool around."

"How old are you?"

"Thirty-two."

"Thirty-two! My God, you're very well preserved!"

I stared at him without knowing what to say.

"Do you exercise?" he asked.

"Yes, I go to ballet class every day."

"Where?"

"Dance Centre."

"Ah." He nodded as though he knew all about it. "I have a couple of patients who are dancers. Whom do you study with?"

As if it could matter less. But I told him, and he wrote it down. He didn't know what was wrong with me either. "You're in perfect health. You've got blood like a man!"

I felt like hurling one of the Persian miniatures at him. Finally he said, "Maybe you should just leave it."

But my old friend Chris Wilcox, who was still a doctor at St. Mary's Hospital in Paddington, wouldn't allow me to "leave it." He sent me to Dr. Jane at the Western Ophthalmic Clinic on Marylebone Road, who started me on a series of tests.

Meanwhile, I stayed part of the time with Philippa, who had a large apartment in Marylebone, just a short walk from the clinic. My parents had rented it when they moved back to London after New York, and they passed it on to her when they bought a house in Chiswick.

It was 1977 and Philippa was managing a folk rock group called Fairport Convention. She also sang with members of the Bonzo Dog Doo Dah Band and appeared on stage dressed like a schoolgirl or in a nun's habit. In the front hall there was a photograph of her as a nun, smoking a joint the size of a cigar. It was taken down when my parents came to visit.

Her apartment had become a magnet for a constant stream of musicians and actors. Meals and cups of coffee, glasses of Champagne, wine and pints of beer were consumed on and off all day and night, beginning with, for some guests, a breakfast special of Guinness, fried eggs, tomato, fried bread and bacon and ending with margaritas and spaghetti bolognese in the evening. Philippa provided most of the food. On Sunday a dozen people would sit down to her generous lunch of roast pork with crackling, Brussels sprouts and big, floury roast potatoes with crisp, golden skins. The guests were mostly long-haired "muzos," many of whom slept over in one of the five bedrooms, on the living room sofa, or passed out on the floor. They twanged away on their guitars and sawed at their fiddles until four in the morning.

Philippa's Roast Pork with Caraway Seeds and Crackling

4 pounds loin of pork, boned and rolled, with skin
Vegetable oil
Sea salt
2 tablespoons caraway seeds
1 quart cider
1 cup crème fraîche
Freshly ground black pepper
6 fresh sage leaves

Preheat the oven to 400°F.

Score the pork skin about $^1/_8$ inch apart with a very sharp knife. (Philippa uses an X-Acto knife obtainable from art supply stores.) Rub it with vegetable oil.

Rub a good amount of sea salt all over the skin and into the score lines. Sprinkle with caraway seeds.

Place the pork in a roasting pan and pour about $1^1/_2$ cups of the cider into the pan. Place the pork in the oven; after 30 minutes reduce the heat to 350°F and cover the pork with a sheet of aluminum foil. Check that there is enough liquid in the roasting pan during cooking and add more cider as it evaporates. Cook for another hour.

Remove the foil and turn the oven up to 400°F. Cook uncovered for 20 minutes longer. Remove the pork from the oven and put it on a serving dish in a warm place.

Put the roasting pan with the cider on the stove over low heat and add the crème fraîche slowly, stirring well. Do not allow it to boil or it will curdle. Season with pepper, add the sage leaves and pour into a heated gravy container. Serve alongside the pork.

SERVES 8

Philippa had a close friend, Luke Kelly, who was the lead singer of the Dubliners. He had an eye-opener of a pint of Guinness each morning. So did the actor Donal McCann, whom I first met sitting on a stool in the kitchen in his underpants at 10 a.m. with a mug of beer on the counter in front of him.

The constant party at Philippa's flat was just the distraction I needed from the increasingly tedious saga of my eye. Dr. Jane persuaded me to have a final consultation with a colleague at the Western Ophthalmic.

The appointment was at 2 p.m., so Luke suggested we all go down to the Pontefract & Castle, a seedy pub on the corner of

Marylebone Road, a few blocks from the Western Ophthalmic, for a glass of Champagne. We were going to celebrate the last of my eye appointments. It was the end of the road at last.

"I'm never going into that place again," I said, with the mixture of resentment and defiance people feel against doctors and hospitals.

I had a pleasant Champagne buzz as I walked down the street to the clinic. Dr. Green had thought it was just a retinal hemorrhage. So I'd have to live with partial loss of vision. I could handle that.

Dr. Jane put in some eye drops and asked me to wait while my pupil dilated. When she returned she said she'd like me to meet a Mr. McFaul.

He was a Scotsman, dour and grave. He looked into my eye. "Hmmm."

I must have reeked of Champagne.

Dr. Jane said, "Can you see it?"

"Yes," answered McFaul. "Hmmm."

"Would you wait outside for a few minutes?" asked Dr. Jane kindly.

All of a sudden I knew something was seriously wrong. It wasn't what they had thought. Not a retinal hemorrhage after all.

I sat in the semidarkness, away from the other patients who had bandaged eyes. They were complaining about being kept waiting.

That's why it's called a waiting room, I thought to myself. You wait. I wait. And I can't read because of the drops that have dilated my pupils, and I'm getting a headache.

At last Dr. Jane came out. She led me into another room and asked me to sit down. Then she leaned forward and took hold of my hand. "I'm afraid you're going to have to lose the eye," she said.

I stared at her with a mixture of horror and disbelief.

"It isn't nearly as bad as you think," she went on. "Lots of people manage very well with only one eye."

But you've got two, I thought.

"You have a tumor," said Dr. Jane. "It's got to come out. We'll give you a glass eye."

My hands began to shake. "May I have a Valium?"

A West Indian nurse arrived with a glass of water and a blue pill. Ten milligrams, but it wasn't enough.

I walked over to the telephone box, put in some coins and dialed my sister's number. When she answered, I couldn't speak. The words wouldn't come out of my mouth. I felt as though I were being strangled. She was saying "Hello? Hello?," and I couldn't answer. Finally I managed to whisper, "Please come."

She arrived right away. I still couldn't speak.

We went back to the flat, and when the Valium kicked in I spent the afternoon copying names from my address book into a new one she had given me as a present. Philippa was always very good at figuring out just what a person needed at a time of crisis. I got many of the numbers wrong. But it helped to see the names of my friends.

Chris came over with more Valium. I was afraid to tell my parents. They would be devastated.

"Better not to see them tonight," said Chris. "Go out to dinner. I'll tell them."

He set off on his motorbike down to Chiswick.

Meanwhile, along with a raucous group of musicians, Philippa and I went to the Italian restaurant around the corner. For dinner we had prosciutto, spaghetti puttanesca and a great deal of red wine.

Afterward, to go to sleep, I took a couple of Mogadons, large flat white sleeping pills etched with two closed eyes.

❧

IT WAS STRANGE to be feeling absolutely fine and yet be told I was going to lose an eye. When Chris told my mother that night he had to catch her to stop her from falling to the ground. But I wasn't giving in without a fight. Roy Guest, a friend of Philippa's who was a music producer, suggested I try psychotherapy. He had been treated by George Frankl, a Viennese Freudian who had successfully worked with cancer patients and had published a book called *The Failure of the Sexual Revolution*.

We called him George Shrinkl. I'd lie down on the couch and George would hypnotize me. "Now, let's have a look at the unconscious, shall we?"

He tried to shrink the tumor through psychotherapy. His sessions would sometimes last over two hours. He kept his other patients waiting until I had a "breakthrough," and even though his office was on Harley Street, he never charged me more than twenty pounds. Under hypnosis I saw the tumor in my eye. It looked like a white slug, and I would imagine squishing it.

"The tumor looks like a broad bean or two peas," said Mr. Chopdar at the Middlesex Hospital, where I went for yet more tests. He'd injected stuff into my veins and looked at it on a screen.

Nearly two months had gone by. All I did each day was go to the dance studios in Covent Garden and take ballet lessons. I would look around at the people on the bus and think, Why me? Dancing calmed me down. It was the one thing that for a couple of hours allowed me to forget William, the tumor and the fear that I was going to die. But the tumor was growing rapidly. So at last I made a date for the operation. Shrinkl was close to tears.

Late on Monday afternoon on November 14, I checked into the hospital. I was there on the National Health, and I shared a ward with four elderly women.

"Miss Argentina was saying on the news that she'd like to look at a historical monument while she's here," announced one of them cheerfully when I came in. She was wearing a bright pink dressing gown and had a bandage over one eye. "Forget about the Tower of London! She should come and look at us!"

She got out of her bed and paraded around the ward with her

arm behind her head, pretending to be a Miss World contestant walking down the ramp.

Dinner arrived. "Oh! Coronation chicken!" said another of the women, lifting up the tin cover of her plate. It looked very nasty.

All I had wanted to do on the night before I was to lose my eye was go out to a restaurant. So I had asked Mr. McFaul if I could have dinner with a friend. (He was the surgeon; in Britain surgeons are not called "Doctor.") When he gave his permission I don't think he had in mind the meal I was going to eat. Roy had invited me to Wheeler's, a famous old fish restaurant that had several branches in London, one of which was right by the hospital. Wheeler's had a men's club atmosphere that I loved—paneled walls, green banquettes, hunting prints and congenial elderly waiters dressed like butlers.

Roy and I had two dozen Colchester oysters, potted shrimp, grilled lobster, Dover sole meunière, zabaglione (whisked to order) and two bottles of Sancerre. The taste of that zabaglione, loaded with Marsala, light and frothy, was still in my mouth when I walked back to the Middlesex.

Before I went to bed, I brushed my teeth and looked in the mirror. Goodbye eye, I said as I covered my face with cream.

I WAS RELEASED from the hospital a week later, three days before Thanksgiving, and went back to Philippa's apartment. Elizabeth Tingom had come from New York for the occasion and to help me out. Together, the three of us made a Thanksgiving dinner—roast turkey, roast potatoes and cranberry sauce (the latter bought at Harrods). It seemed odd to our English friends. Christmas dinner a month early! But I wanted to give thanks I was alive.

The poet Richard Howard called and said the time of mourning is before, not after. I felt a sense of relief that it was over. But I didn't know what to do next. Going back to Morocco was out of the question for now. A wise decision, because I wouldn't know for another three months whether the operation had been totally successful and they'd "got everything." As for Houd and Houdni, I received a letter from Madeleine two weeks later saying they had "caught a disease" and died.

One evening I went to a dinner party where I sat next to the financial correspondent for the *Sunday Times.*

"Did you lose your eye in a Middle East war?" he asked.

"No," I replied, "in the Middlesex ward."

At least I hadn't lost my sense of humor. But I had lost my self-confidence. I was used to being thought of as pretty. I hadn't realized how much I had depended on my looks, not to mention my eyesight. I also had problems with depth perception. This was glaringly evident at the dinner table. People would stare at me, wondering if I was drunk as I poured wine, water or coffee all over the place, missing the cup or glass entirely. I became claustrophobic for the first time in my life, afraid of elevators and subway cars. I suffered from vertigo, which had never been a problem before. In Mexico I used to run up and down hundreds of steps when William and I visited the pyramids. Now I had to test with my foot to see if a step was there before I walked on it. Stairs looked flat to me.

None of that stopped me from cooking, however. There were always plenty of people to feed at Hyde Park Mansions. I calmed myself down by chopping and slicing, putting things on to bake or boil, creating meals in Philippa's nice big kitchen; mindless, therapeutic, Zen-like work that made me feel focused and hopeful.

I went back to dance class wearing an eye patch. The teacher pushed my head between my legs and said, "Come on, your eye's not going to fall out, you know!"

I wrote an article for the London *Observer* on Lynn Seymour, "the greatest actress in ballet shoes," who was at the Royal Ballet. Some ballerina! When I interviewed her she was wearing denim overalls and puffing on a thin cigar.

After the interview was published in the Sunday magazine, a

Coutt's bank check arrived. It came with a bouquet of flowers and a note from the editors saying, "Best wishes for your recovery from *The Observer*" [*sic*]. The check had the bank's logo printed on it: one eye.

I went to Geneva to interview James Mason for the *Sunday Telegraph*. I should never have played a good doctor, he said. It was a bad career move. Women had loved him when he played a villain.

At last it was time to get a false eye to replace the clear plastic retainer I wore in my eye socket. This service, like everything else to do with my illness, was provided for free by the National Health.

With his long white beard, the "ocularist" looked like Dr. Coppélius, the dollmaker in the ballet *Coppélia*. He set down a black suitcase that had his name and Hampstead address pressed onto the side on a plastic strip and snapped it open. Inside was a black velvet tray holding rows of eyes, all different colors and sizes, that stared up at me. There were several layers of trays. He set them out on the table and proceeded to pick out an eye with his spotlessly clean, pink, fleshy fingers. I held up a mirror and tried it on for fit, rather the way one might try on a hat.

"I think that's got a little too much brown in it," he said, staring intently. He chose another. "Try this for size . . . no. That's a little too blue. You need one that has more green in it."

We chose a temporary eye. The final one, to be specially made, wouldn't be ready for another month.

"There's always a rush for eyes over Whitsun and Easter," he said.

"There is?"

"That's when people get married. They like to have a new eye for the occasion."

I hoped that on my next fitting my good eye wouldn't be bloodshot. I must remember not to drink too many margaritas or glasses of red wine the night before.

I could have kept going for a long time doing very little, with people feeling sorry for me. But I realized at last that it was time to put an end to the sleeping pills and tranquilizers. It was time to "get on with it," as my father would have said. Since I had to remain in England for the time being, I needed a job.

Even though I now had a temporary eye, I wasn't quite ready to go out without an eye patch. It was more comfortable without it, but an eye patch was more glamorous than a wonky eye. Philippa, always ready with a great idea, went out to a stationery store and bought a package of gold and silver stars. She stuck them on the eye patch for decoration. "Now that looks more cheerful!"

So I was wearing the eye patch decorated by Philippa when I turned up for an interview at the *Sunday Times*. I was also dressed in black jeans with zippers all over the place and a silver bomber jacket. I was hired on the spot.

Of course. The interview had taken place after my editor had had lunch.

In those days, journalists working on Fleet Street still had long, boozy lunches at El Vino, the wine bar, or at Langan's, a popular restaurant owned by Michael Caine and Peter Langan in Mayfair. Langan would hurl abuse at the help and buy his guests bottles of Champagne. The editor who hired me, Michael Bateman, was an exuberant, charismatic character with a shock of flaxen hair, a raspy voice and a loud laugh. He also had a keen enthusiasm for food and wine and was a terrific cook.

I'd very much wanted to work at the *Sunday Times* and I was thrilled to get the job. It was supposed to be temporary, rewriting a guide to New York City for the Sunday color supplement. The guide had been put together by some nitwit who advised single room occupancy hotels as bargains and listed restaurants that were notorious tourist traps.

My project was a success, and I was kept on. The editor of the paper in those days was Harry Evans; the writers were nurtured, and editors were generous with their time. The atmosphere reminded me of the old *Herald Tribune*. Michael put me in charge of writing an arts page for the Lifespan section of the magazine each week and, in addition, working on a guide to the best British restaurants.

The Michelin Guide had given only four British restaurants two stars. Now Tante Claire, a fifth, had joined such established institutions as the Connaught, Le Gavroche, the Waterside Inn and the Box Tree. I took my mother to lunch at La Tante Claire, where the chef, Pierre Koffman, served a creamy, pale yellow mussel soup flavored with saffron, fresh foie gras, a fish mousse sausage with a vinaigrette that had a heady aroma of black currants and a pig's foot stuffed with morels. For dessert, *oeufs à la neige* and a *feuilletté* of pears. It was nearly fifteen years since my mother had astonished me with the oysters at Grand Central. And now I had taken her to a meal that astonished her.

⁂

AFTER I'D BEEN at the *Sunday Times* for a couple of weeks, Michael suggested we write a piece together about lunch at the Post Office Tower. You were permitted up this London landmark only by dining at the revolving Top of the Tower restaurant, which was owned by Butlins, a company famous for its holiday camps. The public gallery had been closed in 1971 after a bomb planted by the IRA exploded in the men's room of the visiting gallery. Michael wanted to see if the restaurant was still up to par. He said it had been good when it first opened.

During lunch the dining room slowly made its disorienting way from drenching sunlight into shade and round again. We ate Dover sole. It was leathery and prepared beyond recognition, stuffed with prawns and crabmeat, bread-crumbed, deep-fried and coated with a lobster sauce. *Suprême de volaille van Put* (named after the chef) was a boned chicken breast stuffed with pâté de foie gras and mushrooms. It came with a Madeira sauce, mushrooms, shallots and artichoke hearts filled with chicken liver mousse and coated with a cheese sauce—all ingredients blending into a brown wet carpet. Lunch cost as much as it would have at the Connaught.

As we ate, I dissected the components of our meal. I told Michael that it was one of the worst I'd ever had. He didn't seem to take in what I was saying.

"I'm really enjoying this!" he said as we went round and round. He didn't appear to be paying much attention to the food at all. After a while I began to have doubts about his ability as a critic. He liked everything! What was I going to do the next day when I had to sit down at a desk with him to write the piece?

He ordered another bottle of wine. By the time we got to the dessert, which I don't remember, I wasn't sure if it was the tower or my head that was spinning. Befuddled, we staggered back to the office.

The next morning we sat down to work on the article.

"We'll call it 'A Pity You Can't Eat the View,' " Michael said.

Then he began to type: "The Post Office Tower is a good place for foreigners to have their prejudices about British cooking soundly reinforced."

"Why didn't you say that yesterday?" I asked.

"We were having a lovely time."

"I know. But I thought you were enjoying the food."

"The food was awful! Why spoil our lunch by saying so?"

It was a lesson.

The truth was, even though the food was awful, I'd had a great time too.

Michael was a pioneer in food writing in England, one of the first newspaper writers to treat it as a serious subject. (He was one of the only people to score an interview with the reclusive Elizabeth David.) His pieces for the *Sunday Times Magazine* were obsessive. He campaigned against food additives and started a campaign for Real Bread. He also compiled a guide to the world's best food, to which I contributed a section on Latin America. We cooked and we ate and we drank.

In addition to working on the guide to the best restaurants in Britain, I wrote pieces on the arts. Eye patch and all, I interviewed Terence Stamp over tea at Fortnum's. He sported a nasty thin mustache because he was about to play the role of Dracula in a West End production that had black-and-white sets designed by Edward Gorey. He looked like a used-car salesman. I was wearing a pale yellow dress that set off my eye patch nicely, and at first Stamp was quite knocked off his guard. But he recovered quickly. "Dracula has lived for five hundred years," he said as he slowly stirred honey into a cup of black tea. "And the thing he really knows about is seduction. He knows *everything* about it."

Other interviews followed with actors, film stars and opera singers. But then in 1978 the *Sunday Times* went on a strike that was to last for eleven months. I was out of work again, and I missed America. I went back to New York, but I remained good friends with Michael and his wife, Heather.

The last time I saw Michael, twenty years later, he was food editor of the *Independent*. We had lunch at Pharmacy, a fashionable new restaurant in Notting Hill designed by the artist Damien Hirst. The dining room was decorated with cabinets filled with white boxes and surgical instruments; the waiters were dressed in surgical gowns designed by Prada. The silver wallpaper was made from pages of an encyclopedia of currently available drugs.

We sat down in the dining room on the second floor, in front of a wallpaper of rows of Thorazine tablets (used for schizophrenia and manic depression) and looked at the list of house cocktails. They had names such as Voltarol Retarding Agent, Russian Quaalude and Anaesthetic Compound, and the house wine was alluringly named "pH." Michael ordered a bottle of Pinot Grigio instead.

"Perhaps the idea is to make Notting Hill trendies feel at home, as if they were back in the detox clinic," he said, looking at the bartenders with their white jackets done up at the back and bar stools shaped like aspirins. "It's rather sweet."

It was rather sweet, I suppose. A Jabugo ham from near Granada sent Michael into raptures; its pink slices rimmed with a delicious pearly fat were better than any prosciutto I'd tasted. Michael was full of stories about Ferran Adrià, the mad scientist in the kitchen at El Bulli, the famous restaurant near Barcelona, where he'd been served smoked water. We had Dorset crab, char-grilled sea bass with whole cipollini braised in a red wine sauce and a salad of smoked magret with duck confit. Michael loved it all.

I never saw him again. In 2003 he was knocked down by a car on a quiet country road near his house in Norfolk. He remained in a coma until he died three years later.

PART THREE

WHEN I RETURNED TO NEW YORK early in 1979 I rang the bell of my apartment with a feeling of dread that was all too familiar. What was I going to find this time? When I'd decided to stay on in Morocco, Elizabeth had sublet my place to Ivan Schwartz, a young artist she'd met at a party. I'd had bad luck with sublets in my past travels: one tenant didn't pay the utility bills, another killed the plants, a third had failed to lock up properly so the apartment had been broken into and robbed. A young Englishwoman had smashed the big mirror in the living room with her suitcases as she left for the airport; when I arrived home the floor was scattered with shards, a timely omen of bad luck.

But today the door was opened by a smiling, handsome bearded man in his late twenties. "Welcome to your home!" said Ivan. I trailed him down the hall and turned the corner into the living room. It was festooned with paper decorations and streamers. A "Welcome Home!" sign hung over the dining table where he'd set out a vase of white tulips, a bottle of Champagne and an assortment of cheeses and breads. My cat, Bully, jumped on the table, looking for food as usual. I almost broke down. I was home, at last.

After I wrote a piece for the *New York Times* reminiscing about Easters I had spent in various parts of the world, I was offered a job as a food writer in the Living section. I finally seemed to be building some sort of career for myself. Yet William remained the reader over my shoulder. Maybe at the *Times* I'd get a chance to write about food the way I wanted to, to find my own voice.

Michael Bateman had made working at the *Sunday Times* and eating out in restaurants a delight. The newspaper was friendly, encouraging and laid-back. The *New York Times* was another story. It was as tense and competitive a place as I'd ever known, and I got off to a rough start.

Lillian Hellman was working on a cookbook. (Ned Rorem said later that Lillian's relationship with her companion and sometime coauthor Peter Feibleman was mother-son. He was the mother and she was the son.) Mimi Sheraton, a food writer and the paper's highly respected restaurant critic, was writing an article about her. Annette Grant, the Living section's sternly pretty editor, sent me upstairs to the kitchen to test the recipes. I suspected that, more than the recipes, I was being tested, all the more so since the editors and other members of the staff were coming up in the evening to inspect and sample what I had made. Hellman's recipes purported to be from her Southern girlhood. As I worked on those dishes I thought of Mary McCarthy's famous remark that everything Lillian Hellman said was a lie, including *and* and *the*.

The test kitchen was larger and much better equipped than my own. (It took me a while just to figure out how to turn on the stove.) It even had three windows. But as I looked at the recipes, I became increasingly alarmed. Finally I called Annette on the house phone.

"Don't worry," she said. "Just follow the instructions."

"To the letter?"

"To the letter."

So I cooked six pounds of tripe in a bottle of whisky.

As I sliced and chopped my way through the slithery blanket of tripe, I was reminded of my cooking classes at Sherborne when Miss Downing had made us eat our rock-hard cakes and buns. After

I had cooked the tripe, I wished I could have brought Lillian Hellman in and forced it down her throat.

Promptly at 7:00 p.m. the editors and food writers entered the kitchen like a Soviet delegation making the rounds of a factory. The "haddock to taste like shrimp" tasted like haddock. Limp, gray pieces of tripe, adrift in a sea of whisky and grease, looked like something Alcoholics Anonymous might have dreamed up to spur their members on the road to recovery. The string beans, their recipe followed to a T, were overcooked.

"You should have left the lid off," said Mimi as the group went out the door.

"*Disgusting* is not a word we allow in the Living section," Annette had said to me when I first arrived. The tripe recipe was never published.

A few days after my experience in the test kitchen, Annette called me into her office. By this time I wondered whether the *Times* didn't have a secret rite of passage for new food writers, something along the lines of procedures devised by the KGB for cracking the will of dissidents who might have slipped through their ranks. Maybe now I'd be testing William Burroughs's recipe for hogshead soup or Norman Mailer's "liverwurst to taste like foie gras."

I'd stayed at work until nine the night before trying to write something poetic about soft-shell crabs. ("They should be plump and springy to the touch with no trace of hard carapace.")

Instead of testing more recipes, however, I was asked to fill in for Mimi, who'd decided to take a leave of absence for six months. The restaurant page, said Annette, was the most widely read part of the *Times* after the theater reviews. I found that astonishing.

I'd eaten in very few of New York's best restaurants. I frequented bistros in the Village and went to One Fifth Avenue, which was three blocks from my apartment. One Fifth Avenue was owned by

George Schwarz, a radiologist at St. Vincent's, whose wife, Kiki Kogelnik, was an artist. The restaurant was in one of the city's first art deco skyscrapers and the interior was art deco, done up by the couple like the first-class dining room of the SS *Caronia*. They'd bought its chairs, tables, fittings and furnishings when the boat was scrapped. It was the place to go, the heir to Max's Kansas City. Two young Englishmen worked there—Keith McNally, who was a waiter, and his brother Brian, a bartender. It was like a downtown Elaine's. Whenever I walked in I'd see people I knew, and I felt at home. I had very little experience with restaurants in other parts of town, apart from Victor's Café, near Lincoln Center, where I'd go after the ballet for Cuban food: *ropa vieja*, fried plantains and black beans with rice.

I'd been once to Lutèce and once to La Côte Basque, years before. I hadn't been to Le Cirque, Le Cygne, La Tulipe, La Grenouille or La Caravelle. Nor had I been to any of the exotic cutting-edge restaurants like the Quilted Giraffe, Chanterelle or the River Café.

Well, as Oscar Wilde said, ignorance is like a delicate exotic fruit. Touch it and the bloom is lost.

I was given a credit card in a false name and sent out into the field. A friend gave me a disguise: a Groucho Marx plastic nose with round black glasses and bushy black eyebrows.

What more could I want? I had carte blanche to eat wherever I liked for free. Well, almost anywhere. On Friday I opened the paper and turned to the restaurant page. As a parting gesture, instead of a regular review, Mimi had written a roundup of the best restaurants in Manhattan.

In those days the *Times* didn't allow the first-person singular in restaurant reviews. Now this has all changed. I couldn't tell stories either. What was food writing if you couldn't tell stories? Just give the laundry list of what you had for dinner and a rap on the knuckles or a kiss on the cheek to the chef? The challenge was to make the reviews interesting even to people who had no intention of going to the restaurants I described. But because I was young and new to the job, I didn't even suggest trying the reviews another way. I didn't have the confidence.

I had to write up two restaurants each week. I found the responsibility nerve-racking. In London there were half a dozen widely read daily papers and they provided lively competition with one another (to add to the fun, critics even attacked their colleagues in print). But a bad review in the *New York Times* could (and often did) fold a restaurant in which someone had invested his or her life savings and put a team of immigrants out of work. On the other hand, if I praised a place, I was responsible for the hordes of people that would spill out around the block and try to get in; the owners would be forced to enlarge, losing the spirit of the place; standards would drop because the kitchen couldn't keep up; the phone would be ringing off the hook; prices would double. And so on.

I loved the theater of restaurants—and I even enjoyed the cloak-and-dagger aspect of being a reviewer, the anonymous observer taking it all down. When I made reservations I usually used the surnames of old movie stars and had my friends show up first. This worked fine until one night I arrived at a packed restaurant and couldn't remember which name I had used. "Cooper?" I stood craning my neck to see the reservations book. "Davis? Gable? Maxine Gorky?"

The person who taught me the most was the French chef Pierre Franey, who wrote a column for the paper and often used to come out with me. One night he and I were sitting in La Tulipe, a fine French restaurant in the Village that is now closed. It was on the ground floor of a townhouse. Pierre had his back to the small dining room and I was seated opposite him on a banquette. I had just been served roast chicken. He told me how his grandmother used to kill chickens when he was a boy in France. She would partially slit their throats and while they were still alive, hold them over a bucket, letting the blood drop into it. I was horrified.

"It takes a tough man to kill a chicken!" said Pierre.

Just at that moment, Frank Purdue walked in, flanked by two young blondes, and sat down on the banquette next to me.

At Le Cirque, Pierre told Sirio Maccioni that the sea bass tasted of petroleum. We had already eaten so much food that I could barely manage another mouthful, and I begged Pierre not to say anything. He might as well have told Sirio his bank had collapsed. Sirio, ashen-faced, ran to the kitchen and ordered another whole fish for us.

There are many things a chef can do on the spot once a critic has been identified. Not send out meat or fish that has been cooked halfway and then finished to order. Throw a handful of truffles or caviar onto the food. Or cook a *fritto misto* properly and not leave it sitting on a countertop.

It's common knowledge that restaurants in New York have photographs of the critics pasted on their kitchen walls. One day a friend called me to say he'd heard I had eaten in restaurant X the previous evening. "The chef was almost hysterical," he said. "The staff had spotted six other critics dining there besides you."

One night in white truffle season I was reviewing an Italian restaurant on the Upper East Side. A wizened, darkened truffle beyond its prime was produced and a few desultory flakes shaved onto my risotto. The truffle had gone off. No matter, the waiter served it anyway and I was charged accordingly.

When I came back a few nights later I happened to be seated at a slightly better table. After we'd ordered dinner, the captain suddenly looked at me as though he'd been stabbed and dashed out of the dining room. A few minutes later the maître d' appeared, all smiles, carrying the vase of flowers that had been on a sideboard in the front lobby. He set it down before us as unobtrusively as possible, moving it slowly to the center of the table much the way my cat, Bully, would slink across for a piece of food, thinking no one would notice.

Moments later, plates of risotto, "a gift from the chef," arrived and the maître d' himself appeared with a truffle the size of a tennis ball and began enthusiastically shaving it over the rice. It piled up in a white heap, like wood shavings.

I didn't see the point in writing negative reviews about new places no one had heard of. Let them close down on their own, without my help. So when I worked at the *Times* this sometimes meant visiting two restaurants in one night.

After I had condemned or praised a place, the letters would come in. A man complained that after eating at Le Plaisir, a restaurant I'd recommended, his companion had thrown up all over her boots as they waited for a taxi in the street. He'd bought them for her that very day. He enclosed the bill for the boots.

When I first started reviewing, to be sure of remembering every dish, I always brought along a tiny tape recorder and hid it in my napkin. During the meal I would talk into my lap: "Kidneys overdone but mustard sauce good." At the paper the following day, people passing my desk would be startled by the sound of laughter and tinkling glasses coming from my tape recorder as I transcribed. "So that's how you spend your evenings. Tough job!"

When I first came to New York in the mid-1960s, eating out meant a choice among steakhouses (the limpet on the bedrock of American cuisine), Jewish delicatessens, two kinds of Italian food (red and white), fancy French and "continental cuisine," the latter often served some fifty floors up where the view was infinitely more appealing than what was on the plate.

I had begun to write about food at a particularly exciting time, when New American cuisine was just getting into its stride at the end of the 1970s. Alice Waters was on the verge of becoming a household name; the top chefs were often American instead of

French. The wines would be American too; sometimes the California section of the list was twice as long as the French, and the names, such as Stag's Leap, Dry Creek, Grgich Hills, Zaca Mesa, BV and ZD, seemed to belong less in the vineyard than on the open range. The ingredients were exotic and served in novel ways. You might get a lacquer box filled with thin slices of Washington State gravlax wrapped in cucumber or a ceviche of baby Nantucket scallops served like Japanese sushi. Medallions of Wisconsin Charolais beef would arrive garnished with fiddlehead ferns and Oregon morels; New Jersey quail, a novelty for me then, was roasted rare and came with a green peppercorn sauce. I'd never heard of green peppercorns before.

Silver domes would be whisked away to reveal tiny portions marooned in the middle of oversized dinner plates (to be eaten by women with oversized shoulder pads). The sauce was no longer served on top of the food but underneath, sometimes in a yin-yang pattern, forming a pool upon which the fish or meat, cut in an unrecognizable shape, floated serenely. Dishes were garnished not with a parsley sprig but with tiny vegetables cut in ovals or julienned and tied together with a chive string, like a miniature bundle of firewood.

Robert Meyzen, the owner of La Caravelle, a classic old-school French restaurant where food was served on trolleys, didn't think much of all this. For him, it smacked of nouvelle cuisine. "Nouvelle cuisine is like women's liberation," he told me one day, drawing himself up like an antiballistic missile about to be launched. "Tomorrow everyone will have forgotten about it."

But there were more changes to come. In 1981 Odeon opened with a wild party that included just about everyone in the art world. Tables were pushed back against the walls and dancing went on through the night. Few people in those days knew where Thomas Street was, and taxis drove frantically around dark streets littered with dumpsters and cardboard boxes trying to find the restaurant, which was a former workingmen's cafeteria on a desolate block. It had large windows hung with venetian blinds, a long art deco bar, a pink and green neon clock, chrome and plastic chairs, paper tablecloths and a small frieze of the New York skyline from a 1930s Woolworth. Odeon was owned by Keith McNally and Lyn Wagenecht.

I'd known Keith since he was a waiter at One Fifth Avenue, and I'd seen Odeon when it was a wreck and under construction. So when I decided to review it, I made sure that I took along my editors from the *New York Times*. I made six visits. I didn't want to be accused of conflict of interest and, if anything, I was hypercritical. The chef was the late Patrick Clark, a young African American who had studied with Michel Guérard. Odeon was more than just a scene at the time: it was a real restaurant, and that's why it has lasted so long. It was a hangout not only for artists but also for the new breed of workers that was moving into the neighborhood: bankers and stockbrokers. Odeon set a trend and helped to open up Tribeca, a role that Keith's bistro Pastis was to play in the Meatpacking District some years later. And Odeon made restaurants so cool, it often seemed to be cooler to work in one than to be a customer there.

That year, at a French restaurant called the Palace, I had the most opulent meal I'd ever eaten. Like Odeon, it was out of the way, tucked under the Queensboro Bridge by the East River near a thrift shop and a baseball park. I went with my editor Annette, my ex-tenant Ivan and Terry Robards, the *Times* wine writer, who once wrote that when choosing French wine, just remember two names, Brian (Haut-Brion) and Margot (Margaux). I was thankful that Annette was with me, because dinner cost more than Lutèce or La Côte Basque. This was food presented as theater, but at times I remember wondering whether I was witnessing a farce.

"The people here belong in those cartoons of 'capitalism' you see in socialist newspapers," commented Ivan as we sat down on pale brocade Louis XV–style armchairs. The walls of the large, baroque dining room were hung with bad French oil paintings in expensive gilt frames. Carefully crafted displays of sugar houses and almond-paste floral bouquets were arranged on sideboards. The tables, set far apart, were laid with crystal, Bavarian china and heavily encrusted Victorian silver candlesticks dripping glass tears. Butter was served in a silver coffin.

The chef, Michel Fitoussi, was twenty-eight years old but looked about sixteen. He appeared in a chef's toque that sat down over his ears to guide guests around the kitchen after dinner. He was responsible for the massive Rodinesque sculptures of pure white lamb's fat intended to look like marble, varnished galleons made of bread and bouquets of pastry roses that accompanied the presentation of each dish.

The hors d'oeuvres listed on the menu as *émaux et camées* (literally, "enamels and cameos") arrived one by one, almost to the sound of trumpets, heralded by huge food sculptures held aloft by waiters dressed in black tie. The tentacles of a giant lamb-fat octopus embraced a large tin of American caviar from Wisconsin. A small portion of crab was carried by mammoth lamb-fat fishermen holding nets; lobster chunks were presented by a Scarlett O'Hara figure in a hoop skirt made from pink lobster shells. A four-story bird cage (sans canary) made out of thin stalks of dry pasta announced the arrival of a diminutive but unforgettable portion of angel hair in a truffle, cream and tomato sauce. Its legs in the air, a quail reclined on a dark mossy pool of sauce. The only thing missing was a lily pad.

When the bill was presented at the end of the meal, it came in an envelope, like a writ. Its perusal required the sort of smile a brave French aristocrat would have worn on the way to the guillotine. Ivan paled as he saw two months' rent on his downtown loft disappear with my signature. Annette's face was an inscrutable mask. The bill for four was more than I made in a week. I framed it and hung it on the bathroom wall.

At the end of six months, despite eating out every night and most lunchtimes, I had lost nearly ten pounds. In all that time of free food, although I tasted everything that was put before me, I don't believe I actually consumed an entire meal.

THAT SUMMER I met my future husband—a young writer, Michael Shulan—at a dinner party given by Alice Rose George, who was the picture editor of *Time* magazine. She was also one of those people who always tell you they never cook and then turn out a fabulous meal—on this occasion, blanquette de veau sprinkled with capers.

Michael was very good-looking, somber and intellectual, with a shock of black hair and large, melancholy brown eyes. He often had a cigarette dangling from his lower lip, like Jean-Paul Belmondo in *Breathless;* he read obscure Eastern European novelists and French philosophers such as Roland Barthes and Michel Foucault. He was a clear, analytical thinker and was to help me enormously with my writing. He'd grown up in Worcester, Massachusetts, and after graduating from Harvard had lived in Paris for several happy years in a nine-story walk-up in the Marais. Now he was working on a novel.

When we first met, Michael had recently moved into a loft on the second floor of a building on the corner of Chambers Street and West Broadway and was in the process of painting it. One day I went down to visit him for lunch. He opened the door wearing shiny black rubber overalls, like a diver in a wetsuit, only instead of a harpoon, he was holding a paintbrush. We ate tuna sandwiches in the pale, bare room as a thin afternoon light filtered through the windows, which were wide open because of the paint. But there was another even more pervasive smell in the room: stale garlic, onions, olive oil and searing meat.

The loft was directly above a Greek restaurant. Every day, starting at 5 a.m., fumes from the souvlaki rotisserie wafted up from the kitchen below. After a month Michael could stand it no longer. He decided to look for a place to buy downtown and in the interim, he moved into my apartment on Tenth Street.

The shelves of my small kitchen were now stacked with Mexican pots and Moroccan tajines; cast-iron pans and a wok hung on hooks at the back of the stove. I had my mother's old blender but still no food processor. There was nowhere to put it. Just the sight of all this made me laugh, especially when I thought of the photographs I'd seen of other food writers, posing for pictures in professional-looking kitchens with their combination gas and electric stoves, KitchenAid mixers and matching sets of copper pans. But the truth was, I enjoyed cooking against the odds.

For Christmas in my ridiculous kitchen I roasted a goose I bought at a Ukrainian butcher in the East Village, stuffed with prunes, apples and chestnuts. The fat made spectacular roast potatoes with crunchy skins. On New Year's Eve I made blini with caviar. I looked up *caviar* in André Launay's *Posh Food,* a book my mother had given me. "If you must give yourself the illusion that you are impressing everyone by serving caviar, then you must do it in the grand style by providing your guests with half a dozen tins of the stuff into which they can dip freely, even if they are a little bit sick afterwards."

The stuff I served was not beluga (or even sevruga, which I prefer) but orange-red salmon caviar. It was the same kind my mother used to sprinkle on top of the sour cream on her consommé madrilène, and I liked it. Besides, it was cheap. (The restaurateur Warner LeRoy once told me that when he was a boy he used to go fishing with Erich Maria Remarque in Switzerland and they used it as bait, which, as far as he was concerned, was all it was good for.) Michael and I had the salmon caviar with a pile of buckwheat pancakes, topped with melted butter and rolled over sour cream, and we drank Champagne.

I started work on a cookbook about hot and spicy food and the apartment was filled with the aroma of curries, chiles and goulash. I ordered a cord of firewood from a firm in Vermont, not realizing how much that would be; the apartment was stacked so high with logs, we had to make our way through them as though they were trenches. When the gas went out for a week, we made good use of the wood, doing all our cooking on a cast-iron pan in the fireplace.

Meanwhile, I left the *Times* (although I kept doing recipes for its regional sections and occasional features) for a job as an editor at *Vanity Fair*. The editor-in-chief, Richard Locke, had been at the *New York Times Book Review*. He was an odd choice, an intellectual, not remotely the suave man-about-town that had epitomized *Vanity Fair* in its first incarnation during the twenties and thirties. The revival, according to Condé Nast's publicity department, promised "a stylish mix of literature and art," a magazine that would "capture the sparkle and excitement of our times, our culture."

Richard had assembled an interesting, lively staff, and for close to a year, we had a great time, tossing around ideas and giving out assignments. The first issue came out in March 1983 with an impressive roster of talent. It included a new novel by Gabriel García Márquez, *Chronicle of a Death Foretold,* and articles by Calvin Trillin, Gore Vidal, Nora Ephron, Clement Greenberg and Stephen Jay Gould, among others. But the reaction in the press was swift and negative. There was an onslaught of criticism, condemning the magazine's hectic layout and its lack of stated purpose. The $10 million rebirth was labeled a disaster. After two more issues, Richard was dismissed.

One of the difficulties of working with Richard was that he kept changing his mind for no apparent reason. A story in galleys, laid out and ready to go, might be scrapped by the following morning. The editors were angered and baffled by his sudden volte-face, which seemed capricious. It was only after he'd left that we realized he had not been the one making those decisions. It was Alexander Liberman, Condé Nast's editorial director. Liberman, who had just turned seventy, sometimes seemed to drag a bit first thing in the morning, but by the end of the afternoon, he would leave the offices with a bounce in his step, energized after a day's rigorous tampering. He was nicknamed the Silver Fox, and you could almost see the chicken feathers sticking out of his mouth.

Leo Lerman fulfilled a lifelong dream when he was made editor at the age of sixty-nine, but his good fortune didn't last. Leo knew he had no power and was beholden to Liberman. He was much more in tune with the times than Richard had been, but he couldn't turn the magazine around. Over the New Year's holiday at the start of 1984, he, too, was fired. Tina Brown took over and made *Vanity Fair* into an entirely different magazine that was highly successful, focused as it was on celebrities, capturing at last "the sparkle and excitement of our times, our culture."

Shortly after Leo was fired, Diana Trilling gave a dinner party. Michael was a good friend of Diana's; she enjoyed cooking and used to invite us over regularly. She lived on the ground floor of a building in Morningside Heights, near Columbia University where her late husband, Lionel Trilling, had been a professor. Diana had a reputation as a tough, difficult critic, but she had a strong motherly side and went to a great deal of trouble with her dinners, cooking them by herself even when she was in her eighties and had very poor eyesight. She was very fond of Leo and was deeply distressed when he lost his job at *Vanity Fair*. Tonight she had also invited the composer Ned Rorem, who had known Leo for many years and was also a friend of mine. Yet the atmosphere was tense during drinks before dinner. Ned was irritated with Leo for not having published a piece of his during his tenure as editor and didn't want to let the subject drop. When Diana called us into the dining room, I was more than ready for a change of topic. She served carrot soup to start, followed by roast beef. The meat was rare and bloody, just as Michael and I liked it. But Ned and Leo complained.

Diana was furious. She stamped back to the kitchen with their plates and I followed to help. "I'll show those two," she said as she bent down and relit the broiler under the stove. She slapped the slices of beef onto a pan and shoved them under the flame with a bang that could surely have been heard back in the dining room. After a few minutes she pulled out the meat. "Not done enough."

It looked more than done enough to me. But she broiled the beef to a crisp. I set the plates before Ned and Leo, who were exchanging dagger looks across the table, and resumed my seat next to Leo. When Diana wasn't looking Leo flipped his beef onto my plate. Diana may have had poor eyesight, but she made sure that everyone finished their meat before I helped her clear away. The piece Leo had sent me was like leather.

I wanted to reciprocate Diana's invitation, but she was claustrophobic and afraid of heights (conditions with which, since losing an eye, I fully sympathized). So I was touched when at last she said she'd brave the tiny elevator to the sixth floor of my building to have dinner in my apartment. The other guest of honor was the composer Virgil Thomson, who was in his eighties. He was from Kansas City, Missouri, and had been a music critic for the *New York Herald Tribune* from 1937 to 1951. He'd also spent many years living in Paris, where he'd studied with Nadia Boulanger and had written the operas *Four Saints in Three Acts* and *The Mother of Us All* with Gertrude Stein.

I didn't want to experiment with new recipes on these two, so I made a roast leg of lamb, which I knew was one of Virgil's favorite dishes, studded with anchovies and served with flageolets. As I carried the lamb out of the kitchen, I tripped over my cat, Bully, who now weighed eighteen pounds. The roast made a pirouette in the air and landed on the coat Diana had tossed over a chair in the hallway when she came in. As Bully and I lunged for the meat, the carving knife, which lay on the platter I was holding, slid down into my thumb. I reached for a paper towel and the entire roll pulled from the holder and unraveled across the floor. I found a space for the platter, mopped up the blood, wrapped up my thumb and was trying to wash the lamb grease off the coat when Diana called from the other room, "Anything I can do to help?"

At every dinner party, usually after the main course, Virgil would fall asleep for a while and then suddenly and unexpectedly wake up. Virgil was deaf (more so to high-pitched women's voices than to men's, due in no small way I'm sure to his sexual preference for the latter). But he heard what he wanted to hear. During dinner we had a discussion about Colette. Of course, Virgil had known her well when he lived in Paris in the twenties. But he closed his eyes and his chin sank down on his chest.

While he was asleep, I said something about Colette's sad affair with "Chéri," the petulant younger lover in her novel of the same name who tortures his older mistress. "Jealousy is one emotion one never gets used to," she had written.

Virgil's eyes snapped open. " 'Chéri' was just a boring old doctor," he shouted. "I knew him well. Colette just made the whole thing up. All nonsense."

After dinner when I opened the front door to see Diana and Virgil out, the hallway was piled knee-deep with rubble. During the evening, there had been a problem with the pipes. Plumbers had pulled down the wall. We hadn't heard a thing. But the place looked like a bomb site. As Michael and I helped Virgil and Diana pick their way to the elevator, I was afraid they'd never come to dinner at my apartment again, but they did.

Roast Leg of Lamb with Anchovies

One 6-pound leg of lamb,
  bone-in

1 cup plain yogurt

2 tablespoons Dijon mustard

4 garlic cloves, mashed

2 tablespoons rosemary leaves,
  plus more for garnish

Freshly ground black pepper

1/4 cup olive oil

1 large onion, sliced

2 cans anchovy fillets packed in
  oil, drained

1/2 cup dry white wine

1 cup veal or beef stock

Prepare the lamb at least a day in advance. Trim away any loose fat and wipe the leg dry with paper towels. Combine the yogurt, mustard, garlic, rosemary, pepper and olive oil in a small bowl. Coat the lamb with the mixture and wrap it in foil. Marinate it overnight or for up to five days in the refrigerator, turning it occasionally in the marinade.

Preheat the oven to 425°F. Scrape the marinade off the lamb. Set the lamb on a rack in a roasting pan with the onion underneath, arrange the anchovies over the lamb and season it with pepper. Roast for 15 to 20 minutes, turning the lamb until browned on all sides.

Turn the heat down to 350°F and roast for 10 to 12 minutes per pound for rare, 13 to 15 minutes per pound for medium to well done.

Remove the lamb from the oven and let it rest for 20 to 30 minutes on a serving platter in a warm place on the back of the stove.

Meanwhile, make the sauce. Remove the rack from the roasting pan and pour off the fat. Add the wine and stock to the pan and bring to a boil, scraping up the cooking juices. Strain into a hot sauceboat, mashing down the onion and any bits of anchovy. Taste and correct the seasoning. Garnish the lamb with rosemary sprigs and serve with the juices.

SERVES 8 TO 10

VIRGIL LOVED TO COOK and had firm views on the subject: "When you have company, always serve a roast."

I wanted to hear what he had to say about music, but he always ruthlessly brought the subject back to food. "It's so much more interesting," he would say in his high nasal voice, going on to discuss the horrors of nouvelle cuisine, "a luxury form of Schrafft's," or how to make the best roast lamb (take off every bit of fat) or how "the unmistakable sign of a Yankee is pie for breakfast and sugar in the cornbread."

Virgil was short and round, with a bald, egg-shaped head, a mouth like a tortoise, and a body like one of those wooden Russian nesting dolls that you open to find smaller ones concealed inside. Since 1940 he'd lived in a small apartment in the Chelsea Hotel. It was cozy and Victorian, very Englishmen's club with its unpainted varnished moldings and woodwork, parquet floors and Oriental rugs. He had a baby grand piano, some fancy record equipment and paintings by his friends on the walls.

His kitchen was a former walk-in closet, even smaller than mine. The space was barely adequate for the small stove and tiny sink, although Virgil said he'd made dinner for 150 there. "My kitchen may be small but it has two entrances," he said. One of them led into the bedroom, which led into the dining room.

As he prepared dinner one Thanksgiving, he carried platters of food from the kitchen and set them out on the marble-topped dresser by his bed. We ate in a red dining room, which doubled as his office, at a long black table set with gold and white plates embossed with a T. Virgil had roasted a wild turkey that he'd wrapped in what he called its "nightshirt," layers of salt pork. When he carved the turkey I noticed he hid the oyster, which is the best part, under the carcass. After he'd passed all the plates, he took it for himself. He served wild rice and braised celery and instead of cranberry sauce (which he dismissed as "foolishness"), he'd made plums with framboise. For dessert, no pumpkin pie, but pears with Roquefort cheese.

Virgil's conversation was sprinkled with the names of his illustrious friends such as Picasso, Christian Dior, the set designer and illustrator Christian Bérard and Max Jacob, the French poet and painter, who died in a Nazi concentration camp. He was given to such comments as "I learned about seating from Lady Emerald Cunard, who was the lover of Sir Thomas Beecham. She said you should always sit eight at a table for six, six at a table for four. That way conversations are much more intimate."

He started cooking in Paris in his student days in the twenties when he lived in a small apartment that had one gas burner. The first dish he ever made was *boeuf à la mode en gelée*. He had asked the concierge for a recipe and that was what she suggested. He had no idea that he was making one of the most difficult dishes in French cooking.

Virgil maintained that America's greatest contributions to eating were hamburger and canned tomato juice. "Hamburger tastes more like beef than steak and canned tomato juice is better than the original. A great invention."

His interest in food had come from his mother, who made small cakes ("even small pies") for him in the lids of baking powder tins.

One of his most beloved dishes was Jeff Davis pie, a version of which is known in the South as chess pie. "It's not too different from what happens under pecans in pecan pie."

He said his family had made it for over a hundred years. The recipe came from his grandmother, who was a Confederate war widow when Jefferson Davis was still around. Sweet and rich, it's served in small slices along with a tart pie such as cherry, rhubarb or plum.

Virgil had no fancy gadgets. He brewed his coffee in a saucepan and strained the grounds through a sock. "If people knew about the sock, which only costs fifty cents, they wouldn't bother with those other things." He'd been making his coffee this way for sixty-five years. It was strong and black and he served it with a Hungarian apricot brandy called barack palinka.

～

Virgil Thomson's Jeff Davis Pie

Two 9-inch pie crusts
3 eggs, separated
2 tablespoons flour
1 cup light cream
2¹/₂ cups sugar
8 tablespoons (1 stick) butter, melted

Preheat the oven to 425°F. Line two 9-inch pie pans with the crusts.

Mix together the egg yolks, flour, cream, sugar and butter. Beat the egg whites until they hold stiff peaks and fold in thoroughly. Pour the mixture not more than ³/₄ inch deep into the uncooked pie crusts and bake 10 minutes at 425°F, then 30 to 40 minutes at 350°F, preferably in the center of the oven. When done, the filling should be crystalline, not gummy.

Serve at room temperature in thin slices.

SERVES ABOUT 20

THE ART DEALER JOHN BERNARD MYERS didn't have fancy gadgets either. When Michael and I first had dinner at his house in Putnam County, he was preparing a duck with a lot of theatrics, going over it with a hair dryer before he put it in the oven to make the skin come out crisp, like Peking duck. He'd picked up the idea from an Italian recipe by Marcella Hazan.

John knew everybody, and he'd cooked for them all. His guest list was a Who's Who of the arts. His gallery, which he'd opened in 1952 with Tibor de Nagy, helped introduce such painters as Helen Frankenthaler, Robert Goodnough, Jane Freilicher and Grace Hartigan. In 1970 he formed his own gallery, which showed Red Grooms, Larry Rivers and artists of the minimalist school. He also operated the Artists' Theatre, putting on plays by Frank O'Hara, John Ashbery, James Merrill and Tennessee Williams. Ned Rorem wrote music; Elaine de Kooning and Larry Rivers worked on sets.

John was generous and gossipy (sometimes maliciously so) and loved nothing more than to discover young talent. Like Virgil, he adored cooking and giving dinner parties.

What did he like to serve? "Never a roast," he said. "Steak and chops are definitely out. So are quiches, aspics, crêpes and chili con carne. People always enjoy soup, hot or cold, lots of vegetables, raw or cooked, and unusual dishes such as cassoulet, choucroûte or even Welsh rarebit."

"Some cooks have no sense of stomach," he told us as we began dinner one evening with smoked eel served with black bread and butter. "They serve roast beef followed by cake. All conversation ceases, lids start lowering, and the hostess has to rush in coffee in the hope that guests will wake up."

The duck (not considered a roast) had a greaseless skin the texture of paper, thanks to the hair dryer, and was served with potato and turnip puree. John had flavored the cavity with sage and rosemary mixed with the liver, which made for a delicious sauce. To serve it, he cut it up with a cleaver, like Peking duck. For dessert, there were baked pears sprinkled with crushed amaretti cookies.

"When I was managing editor of *View* magazine in the late forties and early fifties, I'd give a dinner every other Friday," he said. "I slowly learned that it was best not to have two stars at the table. It was a disaster when I invited Edward Albee and Tennessee. Gore

Vidal and Wystan Auden was another piece of bad judgment. But the food was good. For them I served *manzo bollito*—boiled beef—and strawberries with powdered sugar."

When Auden was his house guest for a few months John always made sure there was a bowl of cold potatoes by his bed. "When he woke up in the middle of the night Wystan liked to console himself with a cold spud. Feeding him was no problem. Two martinis before dinner, dinner no later than 7:30. Meat and two vegetables, red wine. No dessert, no coffee. He always went to bed at 9:30."

John's worst guest was Simone de Beauvoir. She came to dinner just after the war and he'd bought steaks at enormous expense. "She consumed hers without removing a Gauloise from the side of her mouth," John said. "Then she had the nerve to go back to France and write about the awful food she'd eaten in New York."

ﻉ

John Myers's Aromatic Roast Duck
(Inspired by Marcella Hazan)

1 duck (about 5^{1}/2 pounds), with the liver
6 tablespoons Kosher salt
2 teaspoons freshly ground black pepper
2 teaspoons fresh sage leaves
1 tablespoon fresh rosemary leaves

Set the duck liver aside. Boil the duck in water to cover for 7 minutes. Drain.

Preheat the oven to 450°F.

With an electric handheld hair dryer, dry the duck inside and out for 10 minutes. Combine the salt, pepper, sage and rosemary; then divide the mixture between two small bowls. Pound the raw duck liver with a mortar and pestle with the herb mixture from one of the bowls. Rub the duck cavity with the mixture. Close the opening with skewers or sew closed with cotton thread. Rub the duck skin with the spices from the second bowl.

Place the duck in a roasting pan, breast side up, and roast for 30 minutes. Lower the temperature to 375°F and turn the duck over, breast side down; roast for an additional hour.

Remove the duck from the oven and place it on a dish. Open the cavity and allow the juices to flow out. Scrape the herb-liver mixture from the cavity. To make a sauce, put the juices in a small pan, add the herb-liver mixture, and heat through.

To cut into serving pieces, use a cleaver, Chinese-style, cutting through the bone and meat. Pour the sauce over the pieces and serve. This is good with a puree of potatoes and turnips.

SERVES 4

THE CHOREOGRAPHER MERCE CUNNINGHAM and the composer John Cage were famous for showing up at fancy dinners and benefits with peanut butter sandwiches they'd brought along in a brown paper bag. John had had very bad arthritis and Yoko Ono sent him to Shizuko Yamamoto, a Japanese nutritionist who put him on a macrobiotic diet and gave him shiatsu massages. Within a week all his pains were gone. He said he hadn't taken an aspirin or medicine of any kind for the past six years. I went to Shizuko too. After her massages, all I could do was go home to bed and pass out.

Despite their macrobiotics, John and Merce were hardly ascetics. They were connoisseurs of wine, fine cooks and superb hosts. They lived in a loft hung with prints and paintings by Jasper Johns. Next to the round dinner table was an indoor Oriental garden complete with trees carefully tended by John.

One night I went to dinner there with the artist Louise Nevelson, who wore false eyelashes made of mink, a checked work shirt and a pink silk turban around her head. We began with sips of

Laphroaig, John's favorite single-malt whisky from Islay, Scotland. He served it in Japanese tea cups. Louise had brought a bunch of yellow tulips and John put them out one by one in wine bottles that he arranged in a row along the wall. To go with our whisky, we had Greek olives, crunchy string beans served with a soy and wasabi dip and thin slices of Scottish salmon served with dill with John's homemade bread. The bread had the texture of Dutch pumpernickel. I asked him for the recipe.

"When I'm about to make bread I look in the icebox and choose the things I don't want anymore," said John. "Old broccoli, carrots and so on. I puree them and make a sort of gruel, which I mix with stone-ground whole wheat flour. Then I bake it. That's all."

Merce served a 1974 Château Lascombes with a free-range chicken roasted with garlic, ginger, lemon and soy sauce in a Römertopf, a clay pot with a tight-fitting lid that sealed in the juices and was very popular at the time. The vegetables included pinto beans, kale and broccoli cooked in a bamboo steamer so that they were bright green, brown rice laced with strips of aromatic seaweed, and whole carrots and celery root baked with a dash of sesame oil. Dessert consisted of tahini crunch cookies and dates, and a tea made from a blend of Japanese green tea and roasted brown rice hulls.

John Cage's Homemade Bread

5 cups cooked vegetables puree, or gruel
5 cups stone-ground whole wheat flour
4 tablespoons minced dill
1 teaspoon salt

Combine the puree, flour, dill and salt in a large mixing bowl. Mix thoroughly. If the mixture is too liquid to knead, add more flour. If too dry, add more liquid.

Knead the mixture for 10 minutes. Turn into a bread pan. Bake in a preheated 375-degree oven for an hour and 15 minutes. Turn out onto a rack and cool.

NOTE: *John said he used virtually any leftover cooked vegetables including broccoli, kale, spinach, carrots, celery root and squash, pureed in a food processor with vegetable stock or water.*

Not long after dinner I ran into John. "That recipe for my bread," he said. "Oh dear. I think when I gave it to you, I'd had rather a lot of Laphroaig."

☙

The composer Ned Rorem and his companion, Jim Holmes, also gave lively dinner parties. I had first met Ned when I interviewed him for the *SoHo Weekly News* when I was freelancing in the mid-seventies. He was an acerbic, witty and provocative conversationalist. Since he'd given up drinking, he focused on desserts, usually huge cakes that he would boast of having bought from Carvel. One night the critic John Simon was among the guests.

Over cocktails I mentioned that I admired Robert Wilson. I'd sat through most of his twelve-hour performance of *The Life and Times of Joseph Stalin* at the Brooklyn Academy of Music, and seen *Einstein on the Beach* at the Met. Ned later wrote about John's stormy response in his diary. "So vehement is John's anti-Wilson stance that, as he speaks, he disintegrates before our eyes into a foaming red maniac clutching at the sofa's arm, then, gradually, subsides, eases into the skin of suave Mr. Simon."

Not quite. Over dinner—baked chicken in sherry, rice, carrots in brown sugar and spinach salad—I said I admired Jackson Pollock. Simon turned purple. "The only decent painting Jackson Pollock ever made was with the blood that spattered on the windshield of the car he was driving when he crashed to his death!"

At that point, guests left the table, having a sudden urge to go to the bathroom, light a cigarette or help Ned and Jim in the kitchen. When Ned returned with a *bavaroise au citron* in Grand Marnier sauce, I was foolish enough to say that I liked Mozart. This remark set John off yet again. "Mozart is shit!"

But for all his venom, I couldn't help liking John, who was a true intellectual, if a little right-wing.

~

MICHAEL HAD BOUGHT A SMALL, four-story landmarked building with two friends, and they'd each taken a floor. His was on the top, a three-flight walk-up, and it had two skylights that cast a pallid outdoor glow over the room by day. At one end, a wooden staircase led to the roof and at the other, four large windows gave onto a fire escape over the street. The loft had been a hat factory, filled with long trestle work tables and packing boxes; then it was occupied by an artist who let it fall into disrepair.

I'd never lived in a loft before, and I wasn't sure I was going to like it. It felt odd to be moving into an industrial space that had been designed not for living but for labor and machines. I loved the intimacy of Tenth Street, its fireplace and moldings, its warm colors, the dusty books gathered over a lifetime and squeezed along sagging shelves, the dead quiet of the gardens in back and nothing to disturb sleep except in winter, when the pipes and radiators clanked.

For our first dinner party on Prince Street, Michael made roast pork with apple sauce and *oeufs à la neige*. The occasion was a black-tie dinner for six.

The floor was unfinished and it sloped. Wires hung like tendrils from the pressed-tin ceiling where some of the squares, stamped with fleur-de-lis patterns, had peeled away. A grimy whitewash covered the brick walls. The back of the place looked like a detective's office in the 1930s: brown paneled rooms with frosted glass over the doors, filled with dented filing cabinets, swivel chairs and old metal desks.

Nevertheless, there were candles on our dining table, which was set with a white linen cloth bought from a thrift shop. And we were having dinner, all dressed up to celebrate, with a case of Château Simard.

The *oeufs à la neige,* floating on vanilla custard, were inspired by the ones Michael had eaten at Le Cirque where they were served in an art nouveau glass goblet veined with red and white streaks. "The legs of this goblet look like the vessels of your heart after you have eaten the *oeufs à la neige,*" Michael had said at the time, adding after a second, *"Où sont les oeufs d'antan?"*

Oeufs à la Neige

6 eggs
1¼ cups sugar
2 cups milk
1 vanilla bean
Pinch of salt

FOR THE CARAMEL

½ cup sugar

To make the crème anglaise (custard), separate the egg yolks from the whites. Reserve the whites in a separate bowl. Using a whisk, beat the yolks and ¾ cup of the sugar in a bowl until they turn pale yellow.

Meanwhile, heat the milk and vanilla bean to the boiling point.

Put the sugar and egg mixture into the upper half of a double boiler set over moderate heat. Gradually add the hot milk, stirring constantly with a wooden spoon until it coats the spoon—about 5 minutes. Do not let the custard boil or it will curdle. Strain through a fine sieve into a serving bowl and set aside.

To make the meringues, beat the egg whites with the salt until they stand in stiff peaks. Beat in the remaining $^1/_2$ cup sugar. While you are beating the whites, bring a large saucepan of water to a simmer.

Using a serving spoon, spoon out portions of the egg white in small egg shapes. Gently slide the "eggs" onto the simmering water, where they will float. You should have about 12 eggs. (If necessary, cook them in two batches.)

Simmer the eggs for $1^1/_2$ minutes. Turn them with a slotted spoon so they poach on both sides. Drain and cool on paper towels.

Float the eggs on top of the crème anglaise.

To make the caramel, combine the sugar and $^1/_4$ cup water in a small, heavy saucepan. Cook over moderate heat, stirring constantly, until the sugar is light brown. (Do not allow it to cook too fast or it may burn.) Pour the caramel over the eggs.

SERVES 6

Michael transformed the loft into a turn-of-the-century two-bedroom apartment. The wooden paneling, wooden kitchen cabinets and a wall of bookshelves were washed a pale ochre. He kept the frosted glass and put it over the new doors. On Sunday mornings, he would get up early to beat the dealers at the flea markets, returning with furniture and paintings. We had a grand piano, a refectory table that seated twelve, and a dark blue velvet sofa with matching chairs that looked very *fin de siècle* Vienna. Two immense rolls of brown paper were scrolled up over the windows as makeshift blinds, secured with string. They looked pretty, so they remained there.

The new kitchen was three times the size of the one on Tenth Street, with a large stove and a six-foot marble counter. I no longer needed to pile dishes and pans on the floor when we entertained. But the kitchen had a drawback. It was open, and I was not a particularly neat cook.

Dean & Deluca had expanded from a small neighborhood cheese shop into a fancy food emporium on the opposite side of Prince Street. (Later the store moved to even larger premises on Broadway.) Its tiled floor and hanging feathered game reminded me of Harrods Food Hall, where the prices were equally prohibitive. The store was always crowded; the new residents of rapidly gentrifying SoHo and the tourists who poured in on weekends had the money to explore this overpriced world of aged balsamic vinegars, boutique extra-virgin olive oils, sun-dried tomatoes, caperberries, exotic mushrooms and artisanal cheeses.

A year after we had moved in, Michael and I were married in the loft by a woman lawyer in the presence of about a hundred and fifty friends. Since there was no elevator, guests paused on the threshold after they'd climbed the stairs, gasping for breath.

When I was growing up I'd subscribed to the sentimental belief that I'd have a church wedding as my parents had done. After the ceremony, the long white bridal dress would be wrapped in tissue paper and packed away in a trunk for my daughter to look at years later (like my mother's, which, alas, had ended its days in shreds in the dressing-up box). No wide-eyed twenty-three-year-old as my mother had been on her wedding day, I wore a turquoise silk suit designed by a friend, with a turquoise pillbox hat and a small matching piece of veil. The jacket had padded shoulders, a cinched waist and a straight skirt. The turquoise I'd picked out was not a good color, and I felt that I looked more like a flight attendant than a bride. Instead of an organist we had a pianist, and after we were pronounced husband and wife, Michael smashed a glass on the floor under his foot in the Jewish tradition. As for the food—

catered hors d'oeuvres since it was an evening party—I remember not a thing.

⁂

WHEN WE FIRST MOVED INTO THE LOFT, Prince Street was quiet, free of traffic lights and of peddlers selling everything from movie scripts and baby clothes to military medals and handmade jewelry. At night, however, the street intruded on our lives with a vengeance. Con Ed dug up the road and put a heavy metal plate over the hole they'd made. Every time a car drove over it, there were two loud thuds, like hammer blows. Idling delivery vans roused us in the small hours of the morning when they parked in front of Dean & Deluca (which had yet to move to Broadway) and the adjacent health food store. Then the early-bird brigade of garbage trucks arrived.

In the evening, punctually at 6 p.m., a burst of tap dancing signaled the first class in the studio across the street, and the floor above would flash with a photographer's strobe lights. All night long, lights blazed on the third floor of the building on the corner of Greene Street. It housed a sweatshop crammed with illegal Chinese immigrants who worked on sewing machines until dawn. For several weeks a homeless young black man who wore a Mohawk lived in a white laundry cart he parked outside our front door. Inside the cart he had an old mattress and a white mushroom-shaped Eero Saarinen table set with broken chairs. At night he made his cart even cozier by lighting candles inside. He put out a sign that read, "Moving South. Donations Accepted."

In March, Michael and I went south. Early one morning we were lying in bed in Barbados, listening to the water lap on the beach, when the telephone rang. Arthur Carter, publisher of *The Nation,* for whom I was a theater critic, was on the line. He said he was starting up a weekly newspaper, centered on the city, that would have a strong voice in local politics. He wanted the paper to be controversial and intended to hire writers of widely differing opinions. Was I interested? I could write whatever I wanted, including restaurant reviews, and I'd be the features editor.

I thought, why not? I'd left *Vanity Fair* after Leo Lerman was fired, and freelancing didn't bring in much money. *The Nation* paid its contributors, as Calvin Trillin once noted, in the "high two figures."

Carter, a former investment banker, had amassed a fortune and didn't mind the prospect of losing a couple of million dollars a year. But this venture sounded eccentric, to say the least. He planned to model the paper's layout on the *New York Times,* publish it on pink paper, like the *Financial Times,* and name it after a British newspaper, the *Observer.* His lawyer, John Sicher, who had edited another of Carter's papers, the *Litchfield County Times* in Connecticut, was to be the editor. In the beginning, the paper would be free, slipped under the doors of residents with the zip code 10021, the richest district of New York.

The *New York Observer*'s offices were also in the 10021 district, in a red brick mansion Carter owned on 64th Street between Madison and Park Avenues. Each morning, instead of taking an elevator to a colorless cubicle as I'd done at jobs in the past, I climbed a sweeping marble staircase to the master bedroom on the third floor of the townhouse. This was my office. It had a working fireplace, wall-to-wall carpeting and large windows hung with heavy beige brocade curtains. I sat in a leather armchair behind an enormous wooden desk that within days was piled high with unsolicited manuscripts, almost all of which would turn out to be useless. I'd only been there a few weeks when I discovered I was pregnant.

Some months later, on the night of May 2, I was at home in New York, lying in bed watching a video of *My Beautiful Laundrette,* when my water broke. I blamed it on the film.

The next morning I dialed my editor at the *Observer,* Suzanne

Mantell, to tell her that I had to go into the hospital and would be late with the week's restaurant review. "Why don't you write the review before you go in?" said Suzanne. "You're not going to feel much like it later."

I was furious but then I realized she was right. I sat down at the table and began to cry. My literary masterpiece for that week was a roundup of restaurants for Mother's Day. There would be truffled ravioli and soft-shell crabs at the now defunct Sign of the Dove, duck breast with huckleberries at La Gauloise (also gone) and an all-you-can-eat buffet at Gotham Bar and Grill.

At nine o'clock that night I gave birth to my son, Alexander. When they brought him to me, a tiny, fragile creature wrapped in a white cotton blanket, I knew, as every mother does at that moment, that my life had changed forever.

Six months later I was wheeling Alexander down the street when an elderly woman stopped me. "What a lovely baby! How old?"

I told her.

She beamed. "Mine's fifty!"

&

FROM THE BEGINNING, Michael and I would take Alexander to restaurants with us in his carry cot. It was fine when he was small, just sleeping or gurgling away to himself, and we often went to a friendly Italian restaurant on Lafayette Street called La Donna Rosa. A friend of ours used to go there all the time too with her baby daughter, who was just a few months younger than Alexander. One afternoon, as she was having a late lunch, the baby began to cry. Moments later, a large man in a loud striped suit appeared at the table. He was holding a bottle of brandy, a glass and a cork. "Compliments of the gentleman across the room," he announced in a husky voice.

He dipped the cork in the brandy and waved it under the baby's nose. The baby stopped crying immediately.

"The gentleman would like to meet you."

She followed him to the back of the dining room where a group of men were seated around a table. She recognized the gentleman at once. He was John Gotti. She thanked him and fled.

When Alexander reached the age of two—a stage my mother once described as like having a permanently drunk house guest—we started a habit of going to Chinatown on weekends. It was a pleasant walk from Prince Street, and I liked to explore the food shops and stalls along Mulberry and Mott Streets and look for bargains on Canal Street. Alexander had reached that time of a child's life when meals no longer draw peacefully to a close; they disintegrate. We would find ourselves beating a swift retreat from a restaurant after having to part with the sort of tip a mobster might leave when the boys had gotten a little out of hand.

In Chinatown things were more relaxed. So from the time Alexander was old enough to bang on a glass with a chopstick, we ate dim sum on Sundays. The advantages were manifold. First, the noise level in most Chinatown restaurants at that hour was enough to drown out any tantrum. Being jostled in line while waiting for a table didn't faze Alexander. He was used to worse in nursery school. Entertainment was provided in the form of fish, frogs, turtles, shrimp or eels floating around in various degrees of sluggishness in tanks at the door. And he always appreciated the cuisine, less because of its gastronomic subtleties than because the food, when sprinkled with soy sauce, contained a good deal of salt, which in a child's pantheon of desirable tastes is second only to sugar. He loved wontons, most of all in soup.

After lunch we would go to my favorite Italian coffeehouse, Caffè Roma, on the corner of Broome and Mulberry Streets in Little Italy. We always ordered the same thing. He had a cup of hot chocolate and a plate of tricolor cake, made from layers of red, pink and chocolate sponge under a rim of dark chocolate icing, cut in small rectangles. I would have an espresso and a plate of chewy cookies made of almond paste and topped with pignoli. The bill always came in higher than our dim sum lunch.

We kept up these excursions for more than fifteen years.

ele

Wonton Soup

$1/2$ pound boneless lean pork, ground

1 tablespoon soy sauce

1 tablespoon oyster sauce

1 tablespoon sesame oil

1 tablespoon Chinese rice wine or dry sherry

$1/2$ teaspoon sugar

1 tablespoon fresh ginger, grated

1 scallion, white part only, minced

1 teaspoon cornstarch

Freshly ground white pepper to taste

24 wonton skins

$4^1/2$ to 5 cups homemade chicken stock

2 scallions, sliced

Put the filling ingredients in a bowl and mix well. Place a wonton skin in front of you. Cover the remaining wonton skins with a damp towel to keep them from drying out.

Moisten all four edges of the wonton skin with water. Place a teaspoon of filling in the center. Fold the wonton wrapper in half, making a triangle, and squeeze down firmly on the ends to seal it. Use your thumbs to push down on the edges of the filling to center it. Fold the wonton wrapper one more time: push the wings up and hold them in place between your thumb and index finger. Wet the corners with your fingers. Bring the two ends together, so that they overlap, and press to seal. They should look like a tortellini. Repeat with the remaining wontons. They can be frozen at this point if you wish to cook them later.

When ready to serve the soup, bring the chicken stock to a boil and add the wontons. Cook them for 1 to 2 minutes, or until the edges are somewhat shriveled and translucent around the filling. Return to a boil and add the sliced scallions. Off the heat, stir in a few extra drops of sesame oil. Ladle into soup bowls, allowing 6 wontons per person.

SERVES 4

IT WAS TEN O'CLOCK in the morning one fall day in 1997 when I was ushered through vast mirrored doors into the gilt and wood-paneled lounge of the Oak Room at the Meridien Hotel on Piccadilly. I was in London to interview Marco Pierre White, the first British chef to get three Michelin stars. I was jet-lagged and already on my second cup of coffee when he arrived, looking as though he'd just rolled out of bed after a hard night. A tall, burly man with unkempt dark curly hair, a paunch and a day-old beard, he was dressed in a white T-shirt, crumpled black pants and a brown felt hat. He could not have looked more out of place in this prim setting of Louis XVI furniture, crystal chandeliers and large oil paintings in the style of early Picasso. I felt I ought to be asking him questions about grunge music, not food.

Much has been written on the subject of White—how he was raised on a council estate in Leeds, worked his way through some of the best restaurant kitchens and opened Harvey's on Wandsworth Common where, within a year, at the age of twenty-six, he received his first Michelin star. Now, twelve years later, he owned seven of London's most famous and historic restaurants, with more on the way. The only place he was actually cooking was the Oak Room, which was the most expensive restaurant in Britain.

White was a genius at publicity. With his good looks and infamous rages, he'd already established a reputation as the enfant terrible of British cuisine. He'd been photographed naked next to a pig carcass. He'd charged customers for autographs and had even begun issuing contracts to people who booked tables for six or more at the Criterion, his restaurant on Piccadilly Circus. They were required to fax back a legally binding document that specified arrival and departure time, plus the exact size of the party. Any breach of the agreement resulted in a no-show fee on their credit card. When I told this to my father, he was apoplectic.

White's cooking was French, but he boasted that he'd been to France only once, just for a day. "I don't see the point of going abroad." He went to Paris not to explore great restaurants for ideas, but to cook lunch for Sir Rocco Forte, his future partner, at Longchamps in Paris. "All I ate was a *pain au chocolat* at La Coupole."

I made the mistake of asking White whether he thought the Michelin Guide was biased in favor of French cooking. "It's a French guide!" he exclaimed indignantly, raising his voice. "Michelin did more for gastronomy in Britain than any other organization. They don't criticize, do they? They don't make sarcastic comments. They don't destroy people's businesses, do they, with facetious comments? They created a standard, didn't they? There was something for chefs to work for. Twenty years ago chefs were second-class citizens, weren't they? I came from a working-class family. I came from the poor side of town. I was very young when I got my stars."

A few days later I took my parents and Philippa to the Oak Room for dinner. As we had cocktails in the overdecorated lounge, my father looked at his watch. "It's 8:05 and we haven't been shown to our table yet. What was it you said about a contract?"

The Oak Room used to be the hotel ballroom (more wood paneling and gilt). The place was very stiff, not exactly the spot you would choose for an intimate dinner. I had expected to see sheiks with their entourages, or tables of Japanese tourists, but on this night the other customers, apart from a smattering of businessmen, were tweedy English couples who looked as though they'd come up from the country for a day's shopping and an extremely expensive night out.

When Philippa sat down she got a splinter in her foot under the table. Then she asked the waiter if there was pork on the menu (such as a nice piece of roast pork with crackling, the dish she makes at home). "We have pigs' cheeks," he replied.

The family meal was not off to a good start. But the food was brilliant, beginning with a tiny scallop in a pool of black ink sauce, topped with a miniature fried squid with curled tentacles that looked like a spider, and ending with soufflé Rothschild. "I hope there's a bag of gold at the bottom," said my father. "We're going to need it for the bill."

Just two years later, at the end of 1999, White made his last meal in the Oak Room. He announced he was moving away from haute cuisine and handed back his Michelin stars. "The future of dining out is all about affordable glamour."

During the next seven years, White's empire of "affordable glamour" was to expand to include more than half a dozen restaurants and bistros and a chain of pizzerias called Frankie's, making him one of the richest men in England. He said that people were getting tired of the sort of formal, old-fashioned temples of gastronomy that the Michelin Guide liked so much and instead wanted to go somewhere more fun and entertaining.

In January 2001, the mantle was passed to Gordon Ramsay when three Michelin stars were awarded to his restaurant in Chelsea. He thought Marco had sold out: "He's gone Planet Hollywood." They no longer spoke.

When I met Ramsay for breakfast at the chef's table in Claridge's kitchen, he was poised to take over restaurants that had been bastions of English traditional dining at three of London's most famous old hotels—Claridge's, the Connaught and the Savoy. I'd eaten at all of them when I was at the *Sunday Times*. At the Connaught they still offered savories such as welsh rarebit, deviled sardines and crôque monsieur at the end of the meal. Now all this was about to change.

Like a true Scotsman, Ramsay had a bowl of porridge for breakfast (but without a splash of whisky). The booth, which looked onto the kitchen, could be booked for dinner so customers could watch the cooks in action. It was a hot ticket, because many people had seen the infamous BBC documentary *Boiling Point*, in which hidden cameras showed Ramsay hurling abuse at his kitchen staff: the best publicity he could have wished for. There was also another, more unsettling feature: a hidden camera trained on the tables in the dining room so the kitchen could see when the customers had finished their food. "Nothing strange about that," said Ramsay. "Daniel has one in New York." And so do many other top restaurants nowadays.

Ramsay, as just about everyone knows thanks to his television shows, is six feet two, with a bashed-in face like a boxer's, deeply etched with lines, a mop of short blond hair bleached at the tips, large hands and brawny arms. He also has a sense of humor. I liked him immediately; there was something winning about his pent-up restless energy and his rapid-fire, urgent way of speaking, peppered, of course, with four-letter words. Like Marco's story, his has taken on mythic proportions: the ex-footballer whose life changed after he took a job in a hotel restaurant where the food was like my lunch with Michael Bateman at the Post Office Tower. "The vegetables were done in butter and put on a hot plate for three hours," said Ramsay. "New potatoes were sprinkled with granules of Bovril to color them while they roasted in the oven. Ghastly! The food was reheated for evening service. The beef was gray."

Marco hired Ramsay at Harvey's because the latter had "quick fingers." Ramsay held them out like a soldier displaying an old war wound. They were covered with horizontal white scars. "Those are from opening scallops. What I learned at Harvey's is that once you cut your fingers there"—he drew his finger across his knuckles— "they keep reopening. So you stick them in salt. By the end of service, the wound will have dried."

Of course, I was impressed.

After our breakfast interview he invited me to spend time in the kitchen during the dinner hour at his three-star restaurant in Chelsea.

That evening I was shown into a small, silent, L-shaped room filled with young people in white caps and striped butcher's aprons. There were nineteen, including two women, in the brigade, which was headed by a Yorkshireman, Mark Askew. Only one was French. "It's rare to have French because they fucking don't like to work weekends," said Ramsay.

Some of the cooks were arranging tiny chanterelles, spirals of tagliatelle and thin slices of foie gras on various large plates set with purple paper mats printed with the restaurant's logo. Others spooned thick, dark stock from a saucepan around rosy slices of lamb and floated fillets of sea bass on a cream sauce dotted with caviar. They stuck translucent slices of dried apple into crème brûlée and placed small cones filled with mousse on tiny glass pallets. They looked like a brigade of soldiers but instead of answering "Sir!" to an order, they responded with "Oui!" even though most of them were British. I was astonished to see that they tasted every ingredient in a dish before it went out. (To cleanse their palates, they were supplied with a choice of Evian or Badoit; tap water would interfere.)

I was starving. Ramsay gave me a taste of a jellied chicken consommé laced with foie gras mousse and slivers of *poulet de Bresse*. "We're fed up with snobby, so we don't call it gelée; we call it chilled," he said.

It was the middle of dinner and the pace was fast and intense. "Service! Pick up!" he shouted at a waiter who had come through the door. "Hey, guys! *Aujourd'hui*, OK?"

A customer sent back the spring lamb. It was milk-fed and the flesh was so pale he thought it was overcooked. Ramsay went out to the dining room to explain. "Food that's left on the plate goes straight back in the kitchen by law and we taste it," he said upon his return. "Any waiter caught dropping a plate off with uneaten food on it is sacked on the spot."

Out front the scene was in stark contrast to the drama back-stage. The room, decorated with a frosted-glass screen of pirouet-ting dancers, was dark and tranquil, candles flickering on the tables, which were set along suede banquettes.

Back in the kitchen, a cook brought over a soufflé. It was creamy beige in color and puffed more than a couple of inches above the rim of the dish. "We always make three at a time and taste one be-fore we send the others out. Ah! It's perfect, bulging at the sides. I know already that it's *mollet* in the center—just undercooked." We dipped in our spoons.

Askew brought us a fillet of bass with tapenade inserted into slits in the skin, served on a plate dotted with tomato puree. "That's not ketchup," Ramsay said, unnecessarily. "Robuchon used ketchup! I nearly died when I saw that. So did Michel Roux at Le Gavroche, in a marinade. And After Eight mints in their fucking chocolate par-fait!"

Ramsay was planning more restaurants, from Tokyo to Dubai. But the place he really had his sights on was New York. When he fi-nally opened there at the end of 2006, the critics began gunning for him from the first week.

He was accused of cooking by numbers. Of being flawless, yes, but boring. Of course, there were plenty of reasons to go after a hy-perextended celebrity chef such as Ramsay. He now had an empire of a dozen restaurants, with more on the way, and he wanted to add another notch to his belt. Was he in the kitchen? Well, he was on two of my four visits. Suppose Marco Pierre White had opened a restaurant in New York. Would he have fared any better?

A year later, Ramsay got two stars from the Michelin Guide.

Gordon Ramsay's Pan-Fried Fillets of Red Mullet with Saffron, Fennel Puree and Pink Grapefruit Vinaigrette

If possible, have the fishmonger fillet the red mullet for you.
It will save you time.

FOR THE FENNEL PUREE

1 fennel bulb
1 1/2 tablespoons butter
Sea salt to taste

Freshly ground black pepper
2 sprigs thyme
1/4 cup heavy cream

FOR THE VINAIGRETTE

1 orange
1 lime
1 blood orange
1 pink grapefruit
2 tablespoons diced fennel
1 tablespoon pear or white wine
   vinegar

2 tablespoons extra-virgin olive
   oil
1 teaspoon chopped fresh
   chervil
1 teaspoon chopped fresh dill
Sea salt and freshly ground
   black pepper

FOR THE RED MULLET

8 red mullet, boned and
   cleaned, heads
   removed

Sea salt and freshly ground
   black pepper
1 teaspoon saffron threads
1–2 tablespoons olive oil

Dice the fennel bulb into evenly sized pieces. Set aside 2 table-spoons for blanching.

Melt the butter in a small, heavy saucepan and add the remaining fennel. Season with salt and pepper and cook slowly until tender, 20 to 25 minutes. After 10 minutes, add the thyme sprigs. If necessary, put a trivet under the saucepan so the fennel doesn't burn.

Once the fennel is completely soft, remove the thyme sprigs. Add the cream and warm through. Blend the fennel in a food processor until smooth. Return the puree to the saucepan and warm over very low heat.

Make the vinaigrette. Bring a small pot of salted water to the boil and blanch the 2 tablespoons diced fennel until tender (approximately 1 to 2 minutes). Drain.

Peel the citrus fruits and cut out the segments, removing the pith. Cut the segments into small dice. Place the diced fruit in a pan and add the diced fennel, vinegar, olive oil and herbs. Warm the mixture gently and adjust seasoning to taste.

Season the red mullet fillets with salt and pepper. Crumble the saffron and sprinkle it onto the fillets. Sauté them in olive oil in a large, warm pan for approximately 1 to 2 minutes skin-side down, 30 seconds on the other side. If you need to do this in two batches, keep the cooked fish warm in a low oven.

Spoon four mounds of the fennel puree in the middle of four warm plates and spoon the vinaigrette around them. Place the fish fillets on top of the puree.

SERVES 4

NOTE: *This is adapted from a dish served at Gordon Ramsay at The London in the London NYC Hotel.*

ﻋﻠﻰ

IN SEPTEMBER 2001, shortly after I returned from London, the World Trade Center was attacked. Every New Yorker, of course, has stories about that day.

From their classroom window at Grace Church School, the children in Alexander's eighth-grade class had seen the second plane hit the South Tower. When Michael and I heard the news, we walked straight over to his school. Anxious parents gathered in the lobby. One of the fathers had a radio and said, "They've attacked Washington."

"This is not a movie," Michael kept repeating. But it seemed like one. When we stepped outside the school onto Fourth Avenue, hundreds of people, many of them covered in dust, were walking uptown in silence, like zombies. There was a sweet, sickly smell in the air. We bought the last available face masks for sale in a drugstore and Michael went downtown to see what he could do to help. I walked back to the loft with Alexander and his school friend Giovanni, who lived in the Bronx and couldn't get home. As we crossed LaGuardia Place, we saw another downtown building in the distance crumble to the ground. "It's not a movie," I said to myself.

Later, I walked over to St. Vincent's Hospital on Seventh Avenue and 11th Street to see if I could give blood. The line stretched around the block. I thought, in the meantime, I'd stock up on food at the A&P, which was one of the few stores in the neighborhood that hadn't closed.

I stood in line for two hours. As we waited, a middle-aged woman elbowed her way past me to the shelves and picked up a small can of tomatoes.

"These are diced," she said loudly to no one in particular. "I want sliced ones."

An Irishman with a small ginger mustache and a beer belly, dressed in a tight white T-shirt and baggy jeans, reached up and handed her a different can. She looked at it and waved it away. "Those've got chiles."

I pointed her toward another brand. She shook her head. "Diced."

"I don't believe this!" He threw up his hands. "They're blowing up the city, and she wants sliced tomatoes!"

Everyone laughed. But I had a certain sympathy for her. Perhaps insisting on the sliced tomatoes was a way of making the other events disappear. Sliced tomatoes, and all's well with the world.

When I came out of the supermarket, the line for St. Vincent's was gone. There was no need for blood.

I didn't feel like eating. I certainly didn't feel like writing. I had nothing to say. Like many New Yorkers, I just wanted to stay home. Restaurants seemed irrelevant.

Yet the people who owned restaurants downtown were struggling to keep their businesses going. Most places closed and their chefs and cooks went to work feeding the firefighters and workers at Ground Zero. In the weeks that followed, SoHo seemed eerily to have returned to the way it was in the 1960s. The streets were barren, restaurants and stores were boarded up, and after dark, a funereal silence replaced the late-night traffic from the bars and clubs. But the *New York Observer* hadn't stopped printing, and the editor, Peter Kaplan, expected to see restaurant reviews.

The store in the building on Prince Street was empty and Michael got together with three friends, Alice Rose George, Gilles Peress and Charles Traub, and turned it into a gallery showing photographs of the attack. The exhibition, called "Here Is New York," remained up for a year and went on to travel around the world. Anyone, professional or amateur, could submit pictures. They were printed in an identical format, pinned on wires and sold for $100 each, all the proceeds (totaling over $850,000) going to the Children's Aid Society.

A month after the attack, I walked down to Montrachet, Drew Nieporent's restaurant on West Broadway near White Street. Many of the streets were as desolate as they'd been when the restaurant first opened in 1985. Yet the sky where the Twin Towers once stood was lit up by an eerie glow, as though a spaceship had just landed there. I was surprised to see that business at Montrachet was brisk, although there weren't the usual tables of young professionals in striped shirts and dark suits. Most of the customers looked as though they had wandered in from the neighborhood. I wondered how many of the missing office workers had been at the World Trade Center on September 11.

After dinner I stepped out in the street and looked again at the awful glow above Ground Zero. But when I turned around to walk uptown, there was the Empire State Building. It was all lit up, red, white and blue. You'd have thought everything was perfectly normal and that nearly three thousand people hadn't just died less than half a mile away.

ᕦℓᕤ

A FEW MONTHS LATER, I flew back to England. This time I had no plans to take my parents out to dinner at the latest restaurants in London. They had moved to Marlborough, a small town in Wiltshire, and my father was dying.

All I could do for him was cook. It was as if by cooking I thought I could save his life. He was upstairs in bed, watching the sunlight play over a cluster of small vases I had arranged on the chest of drawers by the window. I'd brought the clay ones back from Mexico and Morocco. The white glass one was from Tiffany's, an eightieth birthday present for my mother. When he felt better, perhaps he'd paint one of the still lifes he called his "Morandi's."

"What would you like for dinner this evening?" I asked. "Dover sole? Rack of lamb? Cumberland sausages? Shepherd's pie?"

His face brightened at the last suggestion. "Shepherd's pie! Why not? That would be nice."

My father loved good food, but he was never a cook. He liked to make kippers (boneless and boil-in-a-bag) for Sunday lunch, sardines on toast and lamb chops. He'd drive all the way to Richmond for a particular brand of Portuguese sardines just because they were boneless, like the kippers. He mashed the sardines with mustard and lemon juice, spread them on toast topped with a slice of tomato, and browned them under the grill. His method for cooking lamb chops was foolproof. When the smoke alarm went off, they were ready. They came out perfect every time—if you like your chops well done.

Downstairs, my mother was on the sofa with the *Times* cross-word puzzle and a magnifying glass. "Isn't there a *w* in *nerve-racked?*"

"No. Yes. I can't remember. Is there?"

"*Nerve-wracked* doesn't fit."

"He wants shepherd's pie for dinner," I said. "I haven't made one in years."

"You're going to make it?" She was astonished. "We always buy ours."

There was a time when it would never have crossed her mind to buy ready-made food. But her enthusiasm for the kitchen was long gone. Now my mother found it an effort just to steam a packet of frozen peas.

I biked to town, past council houses with their community gardens battened down for winter, past red brick mansions with mullioned windows, gravel drives, croquet lawns and names like Meadowlands, Beechcroft and Long Acre. Dogs raced, barking, along high fences backed by bushes so thick you could get only tantalizing glimpses of the large gardens and tall trees behind them. I bounced unsteadily over the cobblestones through a narrow arch-way dating from the 1600s where a shoe shop's window display—black thigh-high boots with multicolored bows up the back—looked right at home in its Elizabethan setting. I crossed the High Street, which is so wide that the cars are parked in the middle as well as on the sides, and locked up my bike on a railing outside Waitrose.

"No need to do that, my dear," said an elderly woman in a long tweed coat. "This is Marlborough."

You'd never have guessed it from the contents of Waitrose su-permarket: Indian take-out, blood orange juice, obscure Asian fruits and vegetables, fresh sardines, sea scallops in their shells with their roe, organic pork and sausages from Prince Charles's es-tates, chanterelles, pheasant, sushi, fresh Japanese noodles. When I was growing up, there wasn't a shop like this anywhere in Britain; not even Harrods Food Hall, with its gold-lettered green vans that delivered exotic foodstuffs to gentry around the country, came close. In Waitrose, farmers clad in muddy green Wellington boots and padded jackets, red-faced men in blue-checked shirts and tweeds, and women in jodhpurs, smelling of horses, stood patiently in line, their carts full of things that five years ago they never knew existed.

Food for fun. Food for love. Food for keeping death at bay.

It was over three decades since I'd made a shepherd's pie. I walked over to the frozen foods section and looked up the ingredients on the back of the packet of Waitrose's "perfectly balanced shepherd's pie." I had expected to find a list of chemicals, but instead it was made with "lamb gravy (49%) and mashed potatoes." The "lamb gravy" consisted of "lean minced lamb (45%), water, tomatoes (15%), vegetables (10%), carrots, onions, maize starch, tomato puree, wheat flour, salt, garlic puree, malt extract, white pepper, Worcestershire sauce, bay leaf. Average 22% lamb in product as sold."

Carrots? Tomatoes? I didn't remember those in a shepherd's pie.

I took out my cell phone and called Philippa, who was in London. She'd looked after our father for several weeks in her flat while his hip had been operated on earlier in the summer. "You're not going to like this," she said, "but in the cupboard there's a jar of ground gravy granules. I use about a cup."

"Gravy granules!"

"It's nursery food. That's what he likes."

Of course. Memories of childhood. But I doubt his mother cooked with gravy granules. I remembered Gordon Ramsay's scornful recollection of the hotel kitchen where he'd been made to sprinkle the stuff on roast potatoes to make them brown in the oven. "Ghastly!"

I sautéed the onions and garlic in olive oil and added a great deal more than 22 percent ground lamb. After the meat had browned, I poured off most of the fat (not all of it; my father used to say the fat was the best part). I stirred in some chopped rosemary, thyme and parsley, along with a spoonful of tomato paste and a glass of white wine. Not your usual shepherd's pie. Was I straying too far? Then I looked at the jar of Oxo gravy granules. Oh, well. Sorry, Gordon. I sprinkled in a teaspoonful.

Put cooked lamb in Pyrex dish. Spoon mashed potatoes on top. Bake in oven for 20 minutes.

I let the mixture cook until I heard the perky opening bars of a familiar theme music on the radio.

The Archers.

I have a Pavlov's dog response to that music.

The Archers = dinner.

The Archers first hit the airwaves of the BBC on New Year's Day, 1951. This saga of the daily life, domestic quarrels and love affairs of a West Country village called Ambridge comes on for fifteen minutes, six days a week, to be repeated the following afternoon in case you missed it. The series, with its gripping tales of calves getting their heads caught between the slats of fences, troubles at the vicar's garden party, or a young farmhand learning new modern milking techniques, has galvanized Britain from the day it aired. I first heard *The Archers* when I was seven, at my grandparents' house in Sherborne. They never missed an episode if they could help it. Nor did anyone else. After the seven o'clock news, the jaunty theme music would strike up, bringing households around the country to a halt. In the breakfast room at Penrhyn, Ganga would pour out a round of whisky and settle back in his chair by the coal stove, putting his feet up on a footstool. Before the final strains of *The Archers'* theme music faded away at the end of the show, my grandmother would race to get the food ready. Now, in Marlborough, it was my turn.

Take the pie out of the oven. Dot with butter. Run fork lines over the top. Sprinkle with a little sweet Hungarian paprika. Brown under grill.

Nursery food. It's what he likes.

"I don't want wine with dinner," said my father. "I'll have a glass of sherry and soda with ice if you don't mind. It's supposed to increase the appetite."

Sherry with ice! Sounds like an American habit!

My father was a member of the Wine Society and every month a new selection would appear: two cases of frugal "Everyday Reds" that cast the net far and wide, and included bottles from Chile, Australia and South Africa. For dinner parties, he ordered the more expensive burgundies and Bordeaux from France. One year he'd made his own wine from a kit and labeled the bottles "Château Hodgson *mise en bouteille en famille.*" Like Monty Python's famous Château Chunder, "a fine Australian table wine," it was "guaranteed to open up the sluices at both ends."

Château Hodgson was stored in the wine racks under the stairs and brought out only as a last resort when guests stayed too long and drank too much. My father never stinted on wine. He wasn't the sort of host who uncorks the last bottle with the main course.

Now, my father had lost his taste for wine entirely. He barely sipped his sherry and soda. My mother and I drank a bottle and a half of Everyday Red.

The shepherd's pie emerged from the oven browned and sizzling at the edges, just like my grandmother's, which she used to make with the leftovers from a roast. I spooned out a minuscule portion for my father and dotted the plate with a few peas and broad beans.

"It looks like nouvelle cuisine!" He took a taste and then sank back onto the pillows, staring at the ceiling.

After dinner, I wrapped the remains in foil and put them in the freezer for my father to try another day.

⁂

FOOD KEEPS DEATH AT BAY. As long as he eats, there is hope. So I cook every day.

When I arrived at the beginning of the week, my father was eating just nouvelle cuisine–sized pieces, and we had joked about it. Now he is finishing small helpings. We are making progress: tonight, smoked haddock, braised celery, peas, mashed potatoes and raspberries with crème fraîche.

He's getting better. So the next day, to hell with the expense, we have Dover sole meunière, peas, cauliflower with capers and new potatoes with chives. The sole is tossed in a little flour and sautéed in butter until lightly browned.

But my father stays in bed. He's listening to a concert on the radio. "I love the noise of Shostakovich," he says, "and I love the bits of poetry, too."

Later I go back to fetch his tray. It's untouched. The music rages.

Downstairs, my mother is still at the dinner table. "I'm sorry you have to do all that cooking."

There is a big wide hole inside me, and I keep on cooking to fill it.

The next day I make osso buco. He doesn't want any. He wants a boiled egg. He has a special gadget that pricks a tiny hole in the egg. I mustn't forget to use it to prevent the egg from bursting in the water.

During the night, he thinks he sees a nun kneeling in the corner of the bedroom. He walks over to her and falls, injuring his hip. So Dr. Glover wants him to go into Prospect Hospice, only for a week, so they can adjust his pain medication. My father is shaken by this suggestion.

"Don't worry," says the doctor, sensing his distress. "It isn't simply a place you go to die. Many more people come out than don't."

My father gets up and slowly makes his way into his study. He is shrunken under his dark blue flannel dressing gown. He doesn't bother with slippers and his bare feet look white and vulnerable. He picks out a small gold box that, when opened, neatly unfolds into a white enameled palette and a tray of water colors. We pack that and some sketchbooks.

Prospect Hospice is in Wroughton, a village that lost its beauty when it became a suburb of Swindon. The one-story red brick building is brand-new and doesn't feel like a hospital; it's not noisy and hectic and has no smell of antiseptic and disinfectants.

My father is wheeled into a large, airy room where four beds are hung with filmy white curtains. The curtains remain closed around one of the beds, and from behind them we can hear hoarse, rattling gasps, as though someone is suffocating. People of all ages are coming and going through the curtains with tense, drawn faces. When I come in the next morning, the curtains are drawn back and the bed is empty, neatly made up and ready for the next patient.

The picture windows of the hospice room, which my father shares with two other men in their eighties, look out onto a terrace decorated with a sundial, beyond which is swampy land teeming with bullrushes, and open fields. In the evening, the sunlight sweeps across the landscape under low clouds and the bullrushes are gold in the reflection.

All three men fought in the Second World War, sent off when they weren't much more than boys to do their bit for King and Country. They talk about the war as if it happened yesterday. At home, my father had rarely discussed the matter except to say, "We were buggered about a bit."

A woman dressed in a neat gray suit comes into the room and stops at his bedside. She's from a religious order. My father doesn't like the church, except as a subject to draw or paint.

"We had a chaplain here yesterday," he says, trying to get rid of her.

"Did you have a little chat?"

"A little chap? Yes, he was very small."

I HAVE BROUGHT my father some new earphones for his radio. He doesn't want to miss *The Archers*. That evening he listens as well to an interview with John Mortimer, who wrote *Rumpole of the Bailey*.

Mortimer says he'd asked one of his daughters what she wanted to be when she grew up.

"I don't know," she replied, "but I know what I don't want to be."

"What?"

"A member of the public."

The other daughter Mortimer thinks will be a writer. They are in the bath together and she says, "Daddy, I don't love you."

He says, "Oh, does that make you sad?"

She says, "No, I find it interesting."

"Definitely going to be a writer."

I have brought my father his favorite apples—Cox's orange pippins—and bananas, satsumas and figs.

Before long there's a smell of rotting bananas by his bed and fruit flies on the figs. By the end of the week I have taken all the fruit away.

"Would you like anything?"

"Death, please."

"Well," says my sister when she comes to visit him, "at least you won't have to do Christmas."

My father laughs. He hates Christmas even more than he hates the church.

We sit by his bed for hours.

"Sometimes I sits and thinks," my father used to say, "and sometimes I just sits."

I step out into the rain and walk down to the bus stop in the dark. The road shines like ink, the huddled houses across the street have their lights on and televisions are flickering in the small front rooms. You have to keep a lookout for the bus because if the driver doesn't see you he'll keep right on going, and then you have to call a taxi, which runs you twelve pounds.

I stand in the street and start waving when the red-and-cream-colored Wilts & Dorset bus rounds the corner, all steamed up inside, its handful of passengers creating a fug in their damp clothes.

I feel like a bird in the rain, head bent, its feathers sticking up and clumped together.

My father has decided he's ready to go. We've brought him the telephone and everyone has said goodbye. Is this how you do it? Call round and say goodbye on the telephone? Goodbye to Cousin Anne Field (a retired brigadier who was head of the women's army). Goodbye to Celia, his older sister. Goodbye to his nephew Humphrey Hodgson and goodbye to Bernard North, the friend with whom he used to go out to paint. Nice knowing you. Look after yourself. Enjoy the rest of your life. Goodbye to my mother, who comes for a last visit, bewildered and confused.

"Are you in any discomfort?" I take hold of his hand.

"I've been lying here for years."

"You've been a wonderful father," says Philippa.

"I just want to rock off."

I squeeze his hand.

"The trouble is you never know the point of departure," he says. "Just let go."

"I have let go. The trouble is it won't bloody come on."

We put on a tape of Elgar's *Enigma Variations,* hoping he'll go out on a wave of that music he loves. The strains of Nimrod swell up and the tears keep running down his cheeks, but he doesn't go.

Die! Please die!

AT 3 A.M. THAT NIGHT my father stopped breathing and died.

The next morning he lay in a bare empty room they call the chapel. He was as white as a marble knight on a tomb in a cathedral, dead white; his hands were cold; his nails were already going black; his lips were white.

Wake up!

"Wakey, wakey, rise and shine
The morning's fine

The sun will burn your eyes out!"

I'm ten years old and he's getting me up for school.

I turned my back on him and looked out the window, hoping he would call me. When I was a child we used to play a party game called Grandmother's Footsteps. You kept moving until "grandmother" called and then you froze. If you moved, you were "out." I stood completely still.

The rain was streaming down the window and dripping off the bushes outside. "Help!" I whispered. "Someone help me! Bring him back!"

When I returned to the house in Marlborough, a delivery man had left a box of plants at the back door. Inside the box was a tamarisk tree, aquilegia in little plastic pots and daffodil bulbs. All ordered by my father and ready to be planted for the spring he wasn't going to see.

That night at seven o'clock I put on *The Archers* and sat down to listen with my mother. "Ooh pet!" said one of the characters, an old lady talking to her daughter. "I went out to get the laundry and the soot was coming out the chimney and I thought, your father'd fix it! Then, pet, I remembered he was dead."

When the theme music came on at the end of the program I went to the kitchen to get the dinner from the oven. I opened the freezer to look for some peas and there, sitting on top of a week's supply of food he'd never eat, was the shepherd's pie I had made for my father.

A Shepherd's Pie for My Father

1 medium onion, chopped
1 garlic clove, minced
2 tablespoons olive oil
1 pound ground lamb
1 tablespoon chopped fresh
  rosemary
1 tablespoon chopped fresh
  thyme
2 tablespoons chopped Italian
  parsley

1 teaspoon tomato paste
1 cup dry white wine
1 teaspoon Oxo gravy granules
  (optional)
Mashed potatoes (about 4
  cups)
1 teaspoon butter
1/2 teaspoon sweet Hungarian
  paprika

Preheat the oven to 350°F.

Sauté the onion and garlic in olive oil in a large skillet until tender, then add the lamb. After the meat has browned, pour off most of the fat.

While the meat is cooking, preheat the broiler. Add the rosemary, thyme and parsley to the lamb, along with the tomato paste and wine. Sprinkle in the gravy granules. Cook, stirring, for about 10 minutes.

Put the lamb mixture in a baking dish. Spoon the mashed potatoes on top and dot with butter. Run fork lines over the top and sprinkle with paprika. Bake for 20 minutes.

Just before serving, remove from the oven and brown under the broiler.

SERVES 4

Life's a bit like a sardine tin, isn't it? There's always that little bit in the corner that you can't get out.

—ALAN BENNETT AS THE VICAR IN *BEYOND THE FRINGE*

FOOD FOR SYMPATHY. Food for love. Food for keeping death at bay.

My parents are dead now. My mother died a year and a half after my father. I'm alone in their house in Marlborough. I look through the cupboards and drawers in the kitchen and the dining room. Silver grape scissors! The silver, handed down from two generations, is wrapped in graying plastic bags. Silver salt cellars, pepper grinders and silver mustard dishes inlaid with blue glass bowls. Silver cigarette cases, silver containers for cigarettes, silver napkin rings engraved with our initials. Who would use those now? The silver Victorian candelabra, the Georgian candlesticks and the silver candle snuffer shaped like a miniature paper hat. Silver sugar bowl, tea set, a cut-glass fruit bowl with a silver rim and silver serving spoons. A fish slice. A silver cake knife. A silver container for the bread board.

Who's going to polish all that? In England there was no Hannah, of course, as there had been in Berlin, so before a dinner party the silver was spread on the dining room table and my mother would spend the afternoon polishing it. (My parents kept on entertaining for years after they'd returned home for good, only their guests included my friends and Philippa's: rock musicians, actors and writers, as well as diplomats. Everyone loved those raucous evenings.)

The place mats: Buckingham Palace, the Tower of London and Tower Bridge, the Houses of Parliament. Bone-handled knives and forks, kept in wooden display trays also under a graying plastic wrap. Wedgwood cups and saucers, Royal Doulton china; booklets in my mother's desk drawer for ordering replacements if they chipped or broke.

Wine decanters. Sherry glasses. Always a glass of dry sherry before lunch with the one o'clock news. It wasn't the sherry that raised my father's blood pressure. It was the news.

In the kitchen, *batterie de cuisine* ready for battle. CorningWare dishes, bought because they were cheap, made of a type of glass that burned when you used it on top of the stove. Orange Le Creuset casseroles lined with white enamel from Elizabeth David's shop in London. Always used with a piece of foil under the lid ever since my mother had read that the orange had a dangerous chemical in it and should not go near food. Plastic bags. To save money, my mother used to rinse them out and hang them up to dry on a clothesline.

The "pinger" for timing the cooking down to the last second. The scale for weighing pasta. Bottles of red and green pasta sauces. "Premasticated and predigested," my father would say aloud, looking at the contents listed on the back of a jar.

A container of dried-up cheese grated by my mother. "He always likes a lot of Parmesan and he doesn't like to grate it himself."

My father's needle contraption to make a hole in an egg before it was boiled so it wouldn't burst in the water. It was a small yellow plastic trough with a sharp spike on a spring in the center. If you pressed down on it unwittingly while rooting in the drawer, the spike drove itself into your finger.

The dark blue enameled pan never to be washed, used for omelettes. The expensive stainless steel skillet that gave my mother a stomachache the first time she used it and burned the bacon.

"Now look what's happened! The pan is wrecked. And we can't afford another one."

But after a short soaking, the charred bits had wiped off without leaving a trace. The pan is still in perfect condition, unblemished, forty years later.

Mouli kitchen scissors for chopping herbs, a pestle and mortar for making pesto sauce the right way, not in the blender. A skewer for testing meat, a meat thermometer for inserting into the center of a roast.

Under the stairs are racks of wine and bottles of whisky, sherry, vodka and gin. Remember the ads for White Horse whisky? "You can take a white horse anywhere." And remember that rare species, a suitable boyfriend, a "white horse."

When Granny was old she couldn't hold her whisky like she used to. My parents made hers half-strength. They poured Cutty Sark for themselves because it was pale, and White Horse with lots of water for her. She never knew, because the drinks were the same color. It was my father's idea.

There were also my contributions to the kitchen: the tajine, which had gathered dust after a few dishes. Clay pots from Mexico too had gathered dust after a while; just as well, since it turned out they were painted with a lead-based glaze.

On the wall, a row of knives. All of them still razor-sharp. The carving knife with the bone handle and a thin, worn-down blade.

I see my father standing at the end of the dinner table sharpening that carving knife. ("All joints on the table shall be carved," he'd say to us when we were children. "Elbows off!") We are having roast leg of lamb, well done, the way he likes it. He cuts the meat into thin brown slices that he puts on one of the heated green Wedgwood plates piled in front of him and passes it down the table. There is a crispy bit at the end of the lamb, which he cuts in half and shares with Philippa. We hand around the red wine gravy, the mint sauce, roast potatoes and steamed broad beans.

"Start while it's hot."

We start. By the time my father has finished carving, we're ready for more. "You'll just have to wait."

But he gets up anyway and continues to slice the meat. The rest of us fall silent.

"Nought but munching sounds were heard," he says as he sits back down and picks up his knife and fork. "Delicious fat!" he says after a mouthful. "It's the best part."

Tonight, I take some food from the freezer and put it in the microwave. English fare: cod with chips and broad beans. No sense in letting it all go to waste. I sit down with a glass of my father's Wine Society "Everyday Red" and plug in a video my sister had made for my father from some of his 8mm films. The elephant races, the Montagnard, the Vietnamese officials in their white linen suits.

What happened to them all? I remember when Lyndon Johnson invaded Vietnam in 1965, we'd been in New York, and my father had woken me up early in the morning to tell me about it. "This is monstrous! Johnson's a bloody fool!"

All through my childhood I had never known the true nature of my father's job. But in New York, when I was a guide at the United Nations, I was old enough to be told. Every day he used to drive me to work, parking his car in the garage under the UN building. One morning as we swung onto the East River Drive he had something to say to me. I was immediately filled with a sense of foreboding. Was he going to announce that my parents were about to divorce?

What he had to say instead came as a complete shock. He was not, as I had always thought, a member of the Foreign Office. He worked for MI6, the British Secret Intelligence Service.

My father a spy! I was horrified. No wonder my mother used to say she felt "wrong." Now I did too. Our life may have been a sham in one respect because we had No Money and lived like millionaires. But I'd believed at least that my father was a diplomat.

In Vietnam, those mysterious trips to the north had been to see, among other things, how much the Viet Cong had infiltrated the villages of the Montagnard.

Now he told me all the Russians who worked in the United Nations building were spies. Even the guides. That was why he had chosen this moment to break the news.

He asked me if I would like to join "the Firm," as it was called.

"No!" I replied vehemently.

"Good," he said. "I didn't think you would, but they asked me to find out if you'd be interested."

I often wonder what he would have done if I had said yes.

Then he added, "I'm a busted flush anyway."

Of course, after my father told me he was a spy, nothing changed—on the surface. I adored my father. I loved him as much as I always had, and I never let on how distressed I really was. Philippa had a better response. She saw our father with new eyes: James Bond.

But, in truth, I was devastated. I'd been proud to have a diplomat for a father. But I hated the notion of a spy. Of course I was naïve. But now I understood that it was no coincidence that most of the places where we'd lived had erupted shortly after our departure.

Indeed, some pretty illustrious figures had been spies. Among them Graham Greene, Noël Coward and Somerset Maugham, who'd written, "The work of an agent in the Intelligence Department is on the whole monotonous. A lot of it is uncommonly useless."

In fact, my father probably spent most of his time behind a desk.

But the other, deadlier aspect of my father's job was one I couldn't even bear to think about. George Blake, whom I'd liked so much when I was fourteen in Berlin and unaware that he was a KGB mole, had turned over dozens of agents to the Russians. (He boasted in his memoir *No Other Choice* that they'd numbered four hundred, but he'd made sure nothing bad would happen to them.) One of those men could have been my father. Maybe he was next on the list. Was Blake the one who exposed my father's identity to the Soviets, making him a "busted flush"? I never did find out how his cover was blown. Or in what capacity he worked before or after being exposed.

In 1966 Blake escaped from Wormwood Scrubs and went via East Berlin to Moscow, leaving his wife and three children behind. He said afterward in an interview, "To betray, you have at first to belong. I never belonged." He is eighty-five and, as of this day, still living in Moscow.

I have always wondered what it was that motivated my father. He wasn't a political zealot. When "the rather nice louche" man came to see him in Beirut after the misunderstanding over the uniforms and offered him the job in MI6, why did my father agree? My father always accepted authority and did what he was told without question. Such as the time when he was a small boy and his bicycle was stolen and his parents had said too bad, but there we are, you're not getting another one. Did he shout and yell because it was so unfair? Most certainly not! That was the way life was, after all. As he wrote to me in school, quoting the Bible, of all things, "It is hard for you to kick against the pricks . . ."

So he just got on with it.

But not long after he left the United Nations, my father had had enough of MI6. "I never liked it much anyway," he said one day. He retired early with the rank of counsellor (one notch below ambassador, my mother pointed out). He took a job at British Petroleum, taking care of security for their pipelines and oil rigs.

Then the unthinkable happened. Glasnost. The Communist Soviet Union and not, as Engels had predicted, the bourgeois capitalist state, "withered away." The Cold War that my father had secretly fought for twenty years was over.

At sixty he became a painter, full time. "It's what I should have been doing all along."

The figures in his paintings are always alone. They look like strangers in their settings, and even a little sinister. A figure in a raincoat, collar up against the wind, strides past a boarded-up pub.

A man strolls alone by the Thames, not looking at the river, but down at the ground. In another picture, a man is seated on an empty bench in a park, staring at the trees as if he thinks they're going to fall on him. Inside an empty church, a dark silhouette, visible from behind, is hunched over in one of the pews. Those men are my father.

In Marlborough, after dinner, I put on Elgar's *Nimrod* very loud. It is the first time I've heard it since Philippa and I had played it for my father in the hospice, and watched helplessly as the tears had trickled down the sides of his face. I'd thought they'd never stop, an unending stream of grief not so much at the prospect of death but because his life was about to be over and he still had so much left that he wanted to do.

I go upstairs to my parents' bedroom. The small vases on the chest of drawers by the window are just as they'd been on my father's last day here. I think again of his "Morandi's" and how I'd hoped he'd do another painting. I think of the shepherd's pie he was too ill to eat a few days before he left for the hospital, and how he liked to cook lamb chops that set off the smoke alarm when they were done.

In London, when Alexander was seven, I had introduced my parents to Japanese food. When first I suggested the restaurant Nobu my father voiced a concern that eating Japanese food was not quite patriotic, given their treatment of British prisoners of war. He also asked if we would have to sit on the floor.

On the day we went to Nobu he waited for us outside the house with mounting impatience, pacing back and forth by the car, looking at his watch, the way he'd been doing for years. He had a pathological horror of lateness, with the result that we were always early for appointments and often had to drive around for a while before announcing our arrival somewhere. Over the years he would infuriate my mother by going downstairs while she was still getting dressed and waiting outside in the street by the car, leaving the front door of the house wide open.

Fifteen minutes early, along with Philippa, we drew up to the Metropolitan Hotel, an unprepossessing modern building sandwiched between the Hilton Hotel and the Four Seasons in Mayfair. A scattering of young men, dressed in black like gangster bodyguards in a French thriller, solemnly opened the car doors. We walked up a flight of marble stairs into the restaurant, where we were greeted with a chorus of *"Irashaimasei!"* a Japanese greeting energetically delivered by an exotic-looking international staff, also dressed in black. As we sat in the long, stark, minimalist, all-white dining room, which had a low sixties-style ceiling, polished wood and illuminated glass, we investigated a bowl of salty edamame beans, slipping off the green pods and eating the beans like popcorn.

As I took notes in a pad I hid under my napkin I thought, ironically, this aspect of my job is not so different from the one my father had. When I review restaurants I'm on a covert mission. I have an assumed name. I don't want to be identified. I eavesdrop on other people's conversations. I whisper into a tape recorder. I try to melt into the background, unobserved. Like a spy!

Nobu's food was unlike anything my parents, in all their travels, had ever tasted. Black cod was flaky and moist under a salty brown miso glaze. "New style" sashimi, salmon and shrimp, had been seared for a second and topped with garlic, sesame seeds and olive oil. Lobster on a raft of asparagus sported a gold-sprinkled *shiso* leaf like a sail. A tempura of sweet oysters was topped with slivers of truffle and daikon radish; wild mushrooms were surrounded by dark leafy greens on a sizzling platter.

"It looks like something from *Journey to the Center of the Earth,"* said Alexander. He'd been thoughtfully provided with a pair of chopsticks secured with a rubber band around a wad of paper and was trying to resist the temptation to stick them up his nose like his heroes Calvin and Hobbes.

But the dish that provoked the most enthusiasm was the yellowtail sashimi. Each piece of fish was topped with a paper-thin slice of jalapeño chile and a cilantro leaf. So simple. We liked its mellow, citrusy taste so much my father ordered another round.

"As Granny would say, you could give it to anyone."

ele

Yellowtail with Jalapeño Nobu

YUZU SOY SAUCE

1/2 cup yuzu juice
1/4 cup soy sauce

4 yellowtail fillets, 3 1/2 ounces each
1 teaspoon finely grated garlic
Cilantro (coriander) leaves
2 jalapeños, sliced into thin rounds

Combine the yuzu juice and soy sauce.

Using a very sharp knife, slice the yellowtail as thinly as possible, about 1/8 inch thick.

Arrange the yellowtail slices in a circle on each plate. Top each slice with a dab of garlic, a cilantro leaf and a jalapeño round. Pour the sauce around the fish and serve.

NOTE: *Yuzu juice is available at Asian markets and online.*

SERVES 4

~~

TWO YEARS LATER, in 2004, the grief over my father's death had abated, replaced by an underlying sadness that's an inevitable part of growing older. Life goes on, and so do frivolous pastimes, like having meals in restaurants with friends. One night I was dining on the Lower East Side at Schiller's Liquor Bar when Keith McNally, who was the owner of this hot, amusing and excruciatingly loud restaurant that had opened in the late summer, brought over the chef, Jeremiah Tower, for a glass of Champagne. I'd long admired Jeremiah, who revolutionized American food with his California cuisine at Chez Panisse before most of these people were born. As we observed the youthful crowd pouring through the door, he suddenly said, "You know the restaurant I'd most like to go to in New York? La Grenouille."

I was astonished. La Grenouille was one of the last remaining grand old bastions of French haute cuisine in New York. It had opened in 1962, the year of the Cuban missile crisis. The rich, powerful and fashionable, from Richard Nixon to Gloria Swanson, had flocked to this opulent, flower-bedecked restaurant, vying for a table in the front room where they could see and be seen as they dined on such delicacies as frogs' legs and Grand Marnier soufflé.

Jeremiah and I made a date for lunch at La Grenouille the following week. The first person I recognized when I walked in was Arthur Schlesinger. He had probably been there on opening day.

Jeremiah was perched at the bar, nursing a glass of Champagne. "I do think $18.50 for a glass of Pol Roger is a bit naughty." It was also a bit naughty for him to have ordered it since I was paying. It cost nearly half the price of the prix fixe lunch.

We settled ourselves at a table near the front door and surveyed the scene. The room, with its scarlet banquettes, mirrors, gold brocade–covered walls and pink boudoir lamps, still sparkled. Owner Charles Masson's flower arrangements were as magnificent as ever: huge sprays of quince blossoms and, on each table, vases of roses. Barbara Cartland would have been right at home here, as was the dowager at the opposite table, who wore a white turban and was bedecked with so many pearls and diamonds I was surprised she could hold her head up.

"She's with her jeweler from Cartier across the street," whispered Jeremiah, who recognized him. Scores of waiters and captains in black tie were posted around the room, professionals of a certain age who were not moonlighting actors and who didn't tell you their names or refer to themselves as "servers."

The kitchen was run at the time by a British chef, Ian Scollay, who'd revisited some of the classics and added a few new things of his own, but mostly La Grenouille was producing the sort of traditional haute cuisine that had existed in the time of Escoffier. "This is how people once lived!" said Jeremiah, and promptly ordered a bottle of Chassagne Montrachet.

We had a chicken liver sausage and a coarse chunky terrine followed by Dover sole, brought over for our perusal by the captain and expertly boned, served with a pungent mustard sauce. Roast chicken "grand-mère" was surrounded by pearl onions, smoked bacon, roast potatoes and artichokes. "It looks like an illustration for a cookbook," said Jeremiah.

For dessert we had a soufflé that was perfumed with rosewater. The captain wheeled round the dessert trolley, which was laden with *oeufs à la neige,* chocolate mousse and fruits tarts and cakes.

We chose a walnut tart that tasted as though it had been made just hours before.

It was a wonderful lunch. "And no music," said Jeremiah. "What a relief."

A few days later I came back for dinner. At a nearby table, a woman who must have easily been in her nineties, in a long black evening dress, was dining alone. When she got up to leave I saw that she was blind. The maître d' rushed over and grabbed her hands. She beamed. "Cha cha cha!"

He took up the refrain. "One, two, cha cha cha . . ." They cha cha'd out of the restaurant, and he helped her into her car, which was waiting outside.

I asked him about her as I was leaving. She was indeed in her nineties. "She comes in two or three times a week," he said. "And every time we go out, 'One, two, cha cha cha!'"

Before long, La Grenouille and Le Périgord would be the only old-timers left.

But now we had an important new restaurant. Thomas Keller opened Per Se in Time Warner's new building on Columbus Circle.

Eating at Per Se has little to do with dining in the normal sense of the word. It is more like an audience participation show, scripted and directed by the chef. Instead of serving three or four courses, Keller's menu is broken up into a series of small tastes. As one dazzling dish after another emerges from the kitchen, you can't talk or think about anything else but what is on the plate set before you, beginning with the chef's signature salmon tartare, served like a scoop of ice cream in a miniature cone. The dishes are presented like exhibits in a jewelry shop, the curved white plates painted with a minimalist splash of sauce—vermilion piquillo peppers decorating a purple-skinned square inch of red mullet, or a dab of orange to set off a turbot cheek.

When Michael and I went there for dinner, the meal lasted the same length of time as a performance of Wagner's *Siegfried*. It was six o'clock when we sat down, and we staggered to our feet shortly after eleven.

About three hours into the meal I felt like one of those charity thermometers with a red line of "mercury" that rises inch by inch as money is raised. The tiny, impeccable dishes, three or four mouthfuls apiece, were starting to add up.

Meanwhile, across Central Park the buildings were glowing pink-white in the reflection of the sunset. Below, a neon ring around Columbus Circle lit up the skateboarders twirling around inside. After we'd had a crispy croquette of sweetbread, a sliver of lamb tongue with sweet corn, a scrambled pheasant's egg topped with a truffle coulis, and many other dishes too numerous to name, a waiter brought a whole roast chicken to the table. I was stunned. My red thermometer had reached the top. But summer truffles had been placed under the skin of this fabulous bird, of which we got a couple of heavenly perfumed inches of meat. After a cheese course came a crescendo of desserts, among them a "Snickers bar" made with milk chocolate, salted caramel and peanuts.

I was a girl again, in my school uniform, standing outside the sweetshop by Sherborne Abbey, mouth and hands covered with chocolate.

The meal at Per Se was the most groundbreaking I'd had until, in the spring of 2007, I went to Alinea, a Chicago restaurant opened by a Keller protégé, thirty-two-year-old Grant Achatz. Achatz had been Thomas Keller's sous-chef at the French Laundry, but his food sounded nothing at all like the classically based new American cooking of his former boss and mentor. His inspiration was the radical new cuisine pioneered by the molecular gastronomist Ferran Adrià at El Bulli in Spain. Achatz had spent several days in Adrià's kitchen, and upon his return entered into the spirit by creating a shrimp cocktail that you spritzed into your mouth, a "virtual" pizza made from edible paper, and bubbles of mozzarella that had tomato trapped inside them.

Alexander was now a student at the University of Chicago. I decided to pay him a visit and test his mettle with Alinea's marathon twenty-four-course, five-hour dinner known as the "Grand Tour." The restaurant is in a small gray townhouse in Lincoln Park, a quiet residential neighborhood in the northern part of the city. On our way in we caught a glimpse of the kitchen, where we could see a team of young cooks with close-cropped hair and spotless whites hunched over two lines of steel tables. They looked like chemists in a science lab.

A host led us upstairs into a hushed, brightly lit dining room and seated us at a polished mahogany table that was the size of a senior partner's office desk in a law firm. It was bare but for two beige napkins folded in perfect, neat rectangles. A waiter silently put a silver bar that looked like a pen holder on the table and stuck a sprig of rosemary into it. That was our place setting.

Alexander darted me a look worthy of Raskolnikov.

Moments later another waiter appeared with a tray bearing a miniature pedestal made of white porcelain. Instead of a Greek bust, it held a golden ball decked with pearls of smoked steelhead roe. "Our liquid croquette," he said. "Raise it to your lips, throw it straight back, and eat it in one mouthful!"

We obeyed, and at once an astonishing succession of tastes and textures—among them sour cream, cucumber, radish, lime, candied endive—flew by, like a landscape seen from a racing train.

We were guided through dinner by a staff of reverential waiters dressed in black suits from Ermenegildo Zegna who acted like tutors, explaining each course and instructing us how to eat it. Everything about the meal was designed to catch the diner off balance, from the hot potato and truffle served on a pin over a bowl of chilled soup, to the skate laid out like a lizard's spinal column, with brown butter, lemon and capers that were powdered and heaped on the plate like doll-sized sand dunes. The food was served on sticks and pins and metal racks, on forks balanced over bowls and on plates that acted like canvases, displaying magnificent, brightly colored works of edible art, and even on a white linen pillow that deflated under the plate, filling the air with a scent of lavender so powerful the people at the next table looked up in astonishment.

"This reminds me of Jacques Tati," whispered Alexander.

At last the waiter took the rosemary out of the silver bar, which became a rest for chopsticks. He brought over a stainless steel stand containing a hot terra-cotta brick upon which sat three cubes of lamb, and proceeded to poke the rosemary into a hole in the hot brick, releasing its potent scent. You could feel the heat rising as you picked up the lamb pieces, which were rare and juicy, the best lamb we'd ever eaten.

Our last dessert in the Grand Tour arrived on a gadget that looked like the prongs of a miniature upside-down umbrella. "It's called 'the Squid,'" explained the waiter. "It serves a function of keeping fried food from getting soggy."

Nestled inside the prongs was a caramel-coated Meyer lemon in a tempura batter, speared on a cinnamon stick.

On our way back to the hotel I asked Alexander what he thought. "Would you rather have gone out for a steak?"

"Certainly not," he replied. "But I felt I was eating on Mars."

Normally, food brings with it associations and memories, recollections of childhood, a sense of place. But this was something entirely new. After that meal, I wondered what Alexander would be eating in restaurants thirty years from now. Was this the cuisine of the future? Food that feeds not just the body but the mind (and requires a team of instructors telling you how to eat it)? Will the properly equipped kitchen in a top restaurant boast an induction cooker, a laser torch, a dehydrator, an immersion circulator for poaching *sous vide,* and an "anti griddle" to freeze food within seconds? And what kind of utensils will we be using? Will the dishes of today seem as old-fashioned as those I had on the ship when I was twelve: the chaud-froid of shrimp, veal Marsala and truffled chicken quenelles?

Now when I read those menus from the *Victoria,* I remember the shy, awkward, skinny, too-tall girl I was, traveling from one country to another, determined to hold on to the memory of every experience by pasting it into an album. Half a century later, I'm still on that ship.

ACKNOWLEDGMENTS

This book has been long in the making. My husband, Michael Shulan, tirelessly read the the manuscript in its various stages and made suggestions. I am also deeply indebted to Joyce Johnson, Guy Lesser and Maggie Simmons for their close readings. Hilton Als, Alice Rose George, Jennifer Josephy, John Rockwell and Ivan Schwartz all contributed thoughts and ideas. And I thank W. S. Merwin for telling me so many years ago that I should write down my stories.

I'm extremely grateful to my editor and publisher, Nan A. Talese, my agent, Robert Levine, and Steve Rubin, Doubleday president and publisher, for their help and encouragement and seeing the book through.

I have not invented characters but I have changed a few names. Some of what I remember from my early childhood was amplified by stories my parents used to tell and by recollections shared with my sister, Philippa.

Parts of this book have appeared, in different forms, in the *New York Observer*, the *New York Times, Vanity Fair, Condé Nast Traveler* and *O, The Oprah Magazine*.

BIBLIOGRAPHY

Blake, George. *No Other Choice: An Autobiography*. New York: Simon & Schuster, 1990.

Child, Julia, Louisette Bertholle, and Simone Beck. *Mastering the Art of French Cooking*. Volume One. New York: Knopf, 1961.

Child, Julia, Louisette Bertholle, and Simone Beck. *Mastering the Art of French Cooking*. Volume Two. New York: Knopf, 1970.

Clay Large, David. *Berlin*. New York: Basic Books, 2000.

David, Elizabeth. *A Book of Mediterranean Food*. London: John Lehmann, 1950.

———. *French Country Cooking*. London: John Lehmann, 1951.

———. *Italian Food*. London: MacDonald, 1954.

———. *French Provincial Cooking*. London: Michael Joseph, 1960.

Fest, Joachim. *Speer: The Final Verdict*. New York: Harcourt, 1999.

Launay, André. *Posh Food*. New York: Penguin, 1967.

Soltner, André and Seymour Britchky. *The Lutèce Cookbook*. New York: Knopf, 1995.

INDEX

NOTE: Page numbers in **bold type** indicate recipes. There is also a separate list of recipes beginning on page 333.

grandparents. *See* author's
grandparents; Ganga; Granny

Granny (author's grandmother), 8, 13,
26–27, 34, 72, 110–17, 284, 294
author's correspondence with,
185
as cook, 26, 27–32, 78–81, 110,
114–17
death of, 192
and Irish politics, 110–12, 113
marriage, 112–13
in New York, 132
recipes, **28–30, 80–81, 115–17**
as student, 112
as teacher, 26, 78–79, 83, 111
See also author's grandparents

Grant, Annette, 236, 237, 243, 244
Greene, Graham, 296
Gregorio (San Cristóbal workman),
184–85
Grenouille, La, 301–3
Gruen, John, 173
Guest, Roy, 223, 224
Guevara, Che, 125

ham, 159, 180, 231
Hamilton, Carolyn, 105, 107
Hannah (Berlin cleaning lady),
95–96
Harvey's, 271, 274
Hawsley, Wilfred (pseudonym),
47–48, 55, 56–57, 64, 65, 76

Hazan, Marcella, 255, 257

health
author's meningitis, 85–86, 117–18
eye tumor, 197–98, 214, 217–27

Hellman, Lillian, 236–37
Hemenway, Robert, 170
"Here Is New York" exhibit, 280
Hess, Rudolf, 101–2
Hillary, Edmund, 36, 38
Hirst, Damien, 230
Hitler, Adolf, 87, 90, 101, 102
Hitler's bunker, Berlin, 90
Hodgson, Humphrey (author's
cousin), 289
Hodgson, Lyla (author's mother),
7–9, 10–11, 13, 18
and author's health problems, 85,
86, 222
in Beirut, 22–23
as cook, 127–30, 247
on crossing to Sweden, 39–40
death of, 292
in Egypt, 13–14, 18, 20
in Germany, 87–88, 89, 94, 97–99,
102, 104
in London, 222, 228
in Marlborough, 282, 285, 289,
290
marriage, 9, 10–11, 97–98, 141–42
in New York, 126–30, 140–42,
143–44
recipes, **46–47, 128, 129–30**
school days, 72, 73, 75

RECIPE INDEX